CHINA'S RED MASTERS

CHINA'S RED MASTERS

POLITICAL BIOGRAPHIES OF THE CHINESE COMMUNIST LEADERS

ROBERT S. ELEGANT

GREENWOOD PRESS, PUBLISHERS
WESTPORT, CONNECTICUT

The author wishes to express his appreciation to *The Reporter* for permission to reprint that portion of Chapter 8, "Confucius to Shelley to Marx," which originally appeared in that magazine.

Acknowledgment is made to the following publishers for permission to quote from their copyrighted works:
William Heinemann Ltd. (Great Britain): *Journey to Red China* by Robert Payne.
Institute of Pacific Relations: *The Struggle for North China* by George E. Taylor.
W. W. Norton & Co.: *A Son of China* by Sheng-Cheng.

When, with all the strength of your country of ten thousand chariots, you attacked another country of ten thousand chariots, and the people brought baskets of rice and vessels of congee, to meet Your Majesty's host, was there any other reason for this but that they hoped to escape out of fire and water? If you make the water more deep and the fire more fierce, they will just in like manner make another revolution.

THE MENCIUS

以萬乘之國伐萬乘之國簞食壺漿以
迎王師豈有他哉避水火也如水益深
如火益熱亦運而已矣　　　孟子

CONTENTS

CHINA'S RED MASTERS

1. AN EMPIRE FALLS

On the morning of April 24, 1949, the insistent beat of chanting voices swelled up in the squares of downtown Nanking and rolled through the narrow side streets to awaken her citizens. On the campus of Nanking University students sang as they danced the *yang-kor,* the *carmagnole* of the Chinese Communist revolution. They were soon joined by workers and clerks waving poster portraits of Mao Tse-tung, and banners painted with red characters proclaiming: "We Welcome the People's Liberation Army!" By the time the sun began to kindle the cold dawn, they had all been caught up in a giant snake-dance which kicked and shouted its way across the city. As morning spread over Nanking, more and more persons joined in the turbulent *yang-kor,* a folk-dance which had been performed only at rice transplanting time until it was taken over by Communist organizers. Since then its sinuous conga-like patterns and strident chants had served, as they were serving now, to awaken latent reformist enthusiasm in both peasants and professors.

The dancers paused for five minutes, standing with ears cocked and apprehensive grins on their faces. Reassured by their leaders, they flung themselves into the dance with mounting vigor. From the north, farmboys dressed in the quilted winter uniform of the People's Liberation Army began to march into Nanking by squads and platoons. When they reached the center of the city, they stationed themselves at

11

streetcorners to await the entrance of the Communist army. Shopkeepers and householders, opening doors and windows, were harried by calls for hot water, but in each case the soldiers punctiliously offered a few notes in return. They had been instructed to take nothing from the people without payment. After their money had been waved aside, the young soldiers turned to inspect the city as they chewed on their breakfast rolls. They were still dazed by the ease with which they had taken Nanking. The Nationalists had simply packed what they could and fled on the preceding day, leaving the city without a government for almost sixteen hours.

The demonstrators aroused no special interest among the "liberators," whose advent they hailed. Although there were more participants, this *yang-kor* was essentially no different from those which had been whipped up to welcome the Red troops in other towns in the path of their southward sweep. But the conquerors nudged each other gleefully as they took in the broad prospects and Western-style buildings of the city of Nanking. Even imperial Peiping had been less striking than this southern capital of China, whose very existence was a symbol of the past glory of the Kuomintang, which had restored it from a provincial market town to the administrative center of the nation. To the east of the city, in Chung-shan Park, stood the massive marble mausoleum of Dr. Sun Yat-sen, founder of the Kuomintang, whose principles both sides in the civil war claimed as their own. Downriver lay Shanghai and the sea.

The soldiers who wore the red star had reason enough for rejoicing. Nanking had fallen without a fight, and with it the hopes of the Kuomintang, which would thenceforth be a government without a capital and, soon enough, without a country. As Nanking awakened to the spring morning, its Nationalist defenders were scattered over the countryside, streaming like bewildered ants in the direction of Shanghai, where the mayor had erected a board fence to keep the Communists out. Chiang Kai-shek, who had built Nanking as his own

12

monument even more than Dr. Sun's, was sulking in Chekiang to the south, while another general sat in the shaky chair reserved for the president of Nationalist China. Subordinate generals were examining their consciences and preparing either to flee or to come to terms with the Communists. Before the Red armies stretched a chain of triumphal entrances, marked by the dancing of the *yang-kor* and the flaunting of banners. Before the Kuomintang lay a series of scurrying retreats which would bring them to their St. Helena, the island of Formosa. Mao Tse-tung, who had lost his guerrilla capital at Yenan in the Shensi hills two years earlier, had grasped victory after a twenty-two year struggle.

It had been an intensely personal kind of war, like a family feud, punctuated by reconciliations and recurrent outrages—and underlaid by a persistent bitterness. The Kuomintang and the Communists hated each other as only intimates can. For twenty-two years, through the period of the United Front against Japan, through wartime differences which could not be patched up by General Patrick Hurley's intercession, nor by General George Marshall's last reconciliation mission, they had remained constant in their ultimate aims—for each the extermination of the other. Since 1927, two small bands of determined men—one desiring to retain what it held, the other inspired by Messianic certainty of its mission of salvation—had contended for power in China. The battle was met on every plane of existence, the economic, the political, the military, and the ideological. And the side which was weaker, in all aspects but the ideological, won final victory, driving the Kuomintang from the Chinese land.

When the Kuomintang skyrocket sputtered out with the loss of Nanking, the Nationalist regime was still greatly superior to the Communists in military power. It held most of the important cities of China; it was recognized by all foreign powers as China's legal government; it was receiving vast quantities of material assistance from the United States; and it had sizeable gold reserves. The Communists had none of these assets, yet they won the remaining battles out of hand.

Communist armies pouring out of Manchuria and the Northwest had spread across China with a rapidity which made their victory look easy. It seemed as if the Communists had hurled no decisive blows against the structure of Kuomintang rule, when it fell to pieces like the one-horse shay.

One wonders whether Mao Tse-tung and Chu Teh merely marked time for twenty years and moved in at the opportune moment. Or were they laying mines whose explosion precipitated the Kuomintang's collapse? It is hard to understand how a refugee government, beset by foreign and domestic enemies, could endure for twenty years, and then seize power in the space of two. The central questions raised by the Communists' success may be simply stated: How could a handful of resolute fugitives bend the inarticulated power of the Chinese masses to their will? And what was the source of their resolution?

The riddles posed by the third Chinese revolution of the twentieth century are not to be easily solved. But one course of investigation is clearly indicated, precisely because the revolution was made by a small band of sworn brothers allied against the world. The mainstreams of the Chinese Communist revolution run clear in the lives of the Communist leaders.

*   *   *

Interpreting history by analyzing the careers of leading figures is a delightfully facile method. But often deep-running historical movements are slighted because of too much concern with General A's taste in neckties or the manner in which Premier B's wife died. However, in China, where every aspect of existence has been undergoing readjustment in response to one major stimulus, a preference for green neckties, or none at all, may be quite significant. Chiang Kai-shek and Mao Tse-tung display the two aspects of China's schizophrenic response to the events of the past hundred years. Chiang's absolute confidence in modern military methods is bolstered by a two-thousand-year-old view of social relationships, while Mao Tse-tung's ultra-modern scientific analysis of society is put forward by a man who spends his leisure time writing poetry in a classical idiom which is a distillation of all that is anathema to him.

Two zealots stand at the head of the contending parties, each convinced that he alone is acting in the interest of the Chinese people. Chiang is moved by infinite confidence in his ability to play the role he has assigned to himself: the great man, who will preserve traditional Chinese civilization through his mastery of the technics of the West. He was stubborn and opinionated from the beginning, and his scope of understanding became ever narrower until he degenerated into the self-willed despot excoriated by most neutral observers, Chinese and foreign alike. He was finally constrained to reject any objective interpretation of events, and often those events themselves, which conflicted with his conception of himself as a Machiavellian Prince endowed with traditional Confucian virtue and wisdom.

Mao Tse-tung stood firm in his conviction of the absolute validity of the Marxist diagnosis of the ills of Chinese society —and the unshakable correctness of the Lenino-Stalinist prognosis. Unlike Chiang, he felt no need to believe that he was the man of destiny; it was sufficient for him to *know* that he moved with destiny. Yet his zealotry was more firmly grounded than Chiang's, for it enabled Mao to stand up to the total failure of ten years of grueling underground work, and to endure two decades longer as the leader of a fugitive regime under constant physical attack by a powerful enemy. Mao's will was always stronger, because it was supported by a body of formulated doctrine, while Chiang relied upon the reassurances of his own intuition in times of crisis.

Although Mao Tse-tung himself may be a stronger individual than Chiang Kai-shek, the forces under his direction were, until very recently, incomparably weaker than those commanded by Chiang. The question recurs: How could the Communists overrun China with the feeble forces at their disposal? The answer lies in the essential nature of the Chinese Communist movement, which must be sought in its historical springs.

*   *   *

On November 2, 1839, the British gunboats *Volage* and *Hyacinth* stationed themselves at Chuenpi off Hong Kong, where they could command all channels leading to the port of Canton. The British High Commissioner in China, tired of unreasonable interference with trade, and smarting under the financial loss inflicted by Chinese confiscation of a shipload of opium, had decided to show his strength. On the morning of November 3, British lookouts spied twenty-nine war-junks moving downstream with silken banners flat against the breeze. On board, drums pounded and cymbals clashed as the junks halted to exchange notes with the gunboats. Failing to gain satisfaction, the junks resumed their course and the British warships opened fire.

The engagement was neither protracted nor particularly bloody. The English ships were almost untouched and the Chinese withdrew after four junks had been sunk. But it was the most decisive battle in two thousand years of Chinese history. The European world had served notice that China must open her gates to their goods, their consuls, and their God. The Opium War, which grew out of the incident at Chuenpi, was ended by the Treaty of Nanking on August 29, 1842. Hong Kong was ceded to Britain, a foreign-administered customs system was established, and the right to appoint consuls was granted. Subsequent treaties enlarged the scope of Chinese concessions to the West, and subsequent wars with Great Britain and other Western powers resulted in the signing of new treaties and the extraction of new concessions.

Fifty years earlier, George III had sent Lord Macartney to Peking to arrange for an exchange of ambassadors between

16

himself and Ch'ien Lung, the reigning Emperor. Ch'ien Lung, aghast at British impertinence, replied:

"Our dynasty's majestic virtue has penetrated unto every country under Heaven, and Kings of all nations have offered their costly tribute by land and sea. As your Ambassador can see for himself, we possess all things. I set no value on objects strange or ingenious, and have no use for your country's manufactures. This then is my answer to your request to appoint a representative at my Court, a request contrary to our dynastic usage, which would only result in inconvenience to yourself. I have expounded my wishes in detail and have commanded your tribute envoys to leave in peace on their homeward journey. It behooves you, O King, to respect my sentiments and to display even greater loyalty and submission in the future, so that, by perpetual submission to our Throne, you may secure peace and prosperity for your country thereafter."

The Chinese wanted no truck with them, but the British thirsted for the vast profits they believed could be earned in trade with China. The Chinese Empire, whose fundamental tenet of existence was its superiority to all other nations, could not enter into international relations on a basis of equality, but the British felt they had to trade. Two worlds met, one young and brazen, the other old and complacent. Linguistic, temperamental, and economic gaps were so wide that there could be little communication across them. When the British launched the Opium War in 1839, they had completely failed to understand the nature of Chinese society. Only a miracle of enlightenment could have made the British aware that they were destroying China.

The Chinese were, however, beginning to recognize the threat posed by European material power. Secure in their conviction of moral superiority, they examined the bloody extremity of Western civilization which had been presented to their gaze—and shuddered. Recovering from their disgust, they concluded that the barbarians could be dealt with quite simply. Europe might enforce her will upon China because she possessed cannon and was in command of modern military technics. To drive the barbarians off, Chinese officials concluded, China had only to acquire the technical knowledge necessary to construct and use the new weapons. It would be simple for the Empire to build a ring of iron around itself and go about its accustomed business in safety.

It seemed quite easy—and proved impossible. Along with cannon, Europe brought to China a flock of new ideas which shook her more deeply than the roar of broadsides off the Taku forts, or the tramping of the allied armies marching on Peking in 1900. The Taiping Rebellion of 1848 to 1865, which Communist historians have characterized as peasant risings, was in part stimulated by these new ideas. Hung Hsiu-ch'üan, the Taiping "Emperor," described himself as the younger brother of Jesus, come to earth to see God's will done.

That annoying institution, the periodical press, was planted in China by missionaries seeking to spread the Gospel. Chinese with special interests soon realized that they had in their hands another Western technic which could be employed by Chinese as well. A swarm of "mosquito journals" was hatched. The function of each such paper was simply to propagate its publisher's opinions. The concept of a press dedicated to public service was a late arrival; aside from a few outstanding exceptions, there has never been a free and responsible press in China. Through the press, and through the circulation of Western books in translation, a hundred hair-thin channels were opened for the introduction of Western ideas and mores into China.

Their chief effects were simple, and fatal to the Chinese monarchy. Chinese learned that China was not the center of the human world, and that a Western biologist named Darwin had deprived the human animal of his special status by tracing his origins to the same protoplasmic slime which had bred all life on earth. The next step was obvious: an ignoble beginning presaged an ignoble end. The two squat pillars of the well-bruited Chinese serenity were badly shaken.

The Chinese had never pondered deeply on the origins of mankind, any more than he had doubted the continuation of imperial rule. Dynasties might come and go, but the Empire would endure forever. So it was with the human race. Before he learned of Darwin's work, the educated Chinese had been secure in his knowledge that both humanity and the Empire would continue further into the future than he could possibly imagine. This certainty of human survival had provided all the eternity he needed, serving him in the same way the formal concept of "God" served the European.

It was unfortunate that China's rulers should have been subjected to these traumatic revelations in the middle of the nineteenth century. The Empire's condition was not good. Quite independently of the demands of the West, whose effects were limited to the inhabitants of the coastal fringe, the vast interior of the country was undergoing one of its recurrent periods of economic dislocation.

China had risen to a peak of prosperity during the life of the Emperor K'ang Hsi, who reigned from 1662 to 1723. The Manchu rulers had taken advantage of the abundance of all things to decree a series of tax reductions. In 1722, K'ang Hsi abolished the head tax which had been levied annually on every subject of the Empire. Within a hundred years China's population had increased threefold.

Soaring population brought with it traditional evils: land became concentrated in the hands of a few; most farmers were working plots too small to support their families; great numbers of landless men drifted into banditry and begging. So it had been in the third century A.D. just before the collapse of the Han dynasty, and so it was in the nineteenth century just before the collapse of the Ch'ing dynasty. History's traditional therapy had been a period of revolutionary disorder, which served the dual purpose of reducing the population and bringing into power a new dynasty which would redistribute the land. The incursion of the West, with its debilitating effect on the power of the Manchu dynasty, may have hastened its collapse, but China's fundamental economic crisis was independent of the coming of British opium and cannon.

If the Empire had been strong and its people prosperous, it would have been better able to withstand the physical and psychological impact of the West. But the structure against which England threw her weight in the Opium Wars was already weakened by internal rot. Within, the people gazed in fear at the sagging beams, while without, Europe, unable to find a door, battered at the walls. A few devoted officials within the edifice hurried from wall to wall trying to patch up cracks as they appeared, but their efforts were hindered by the clutching hands of those who protested that the repairs were defacing the structure. And some groups began to pound away at the walls from inside, declaring that the entire structure must come down to make way for a new one.

The leaders of present-day Chinese Communism were born into this atmosphere of desperation in the twenty-five years which preceded the toppling of the Ch'ing dynasty in 1911. Constant frustration, uncertainty as to the future, and the casting aside of traditional moral values gave rise to a new type of Chinese. The intellectual of 1820 had more in common with his ancestor of 820 than with his great-grandson living in 1920. He of 1820 was a staid and rather smug young man, assuring himself of good grades in the civil service examinations and a successful career in official life by intense study of the Confucian classics. Confucian doctrine provided him with pat solutions to all the social, spiritual, and intellectual problems that he would encounter in a lifetime. His great-grandson was a neurotic seeker after lost truths, suffering from acute mental indigestion brought on by his attempt to get down at one gulp a platterful of contradictory concepts which had been several centuries brewing in the West. He was not to be found sitting home with *The Analects* or *The*

Mencius open before him. You would look for him in the middle of a street demonstration or among a group engaged in joint study of Karl Marx or Tolstoy. Because he was a displaced person, emotionally and intellectually, he was inclined to radical extremism.

An entire social group suffered from a mass inferiority complex—a general *Asiatic* neurosis. The bile of inadequacy and the dust of frustration seasoned their every mouthful. They were estranged from their parents, who, living out their lives amid the debris of shattered principles, could not understand the new forces which drove their sons. And the sons, still uncertain of what they believed or wanted, could find no soil for their roots. In the port-cities where they congregated, young intellectuals were constantly reminded that it was no longer a glory but a burden to be a Chinese. A hundred small indignities drove home the realization that it was most unpleasant to be an *Asiatic* with a great past and no foreseeable future. In defense some expounded an adolescent racism, which boasted that the yellow race was the true super-race and reached back as far as the Mongol conquests for confirmation. Others sought consolation in the pastel world of pure art or looked for strength in the world-wide solidarity of the oppressed.

This *Asiatic* neurosis, stimulated by the constant pain of being a Chinese, was aggravated by a communal guilt feeling. Under the tenets of Confucianism, the official ideology up to 1912, the educated man stood *in loco parentis* to the people. The intellectual of 1920, though straining at the bonds of Confucianism, had not yet broken them. The miserable condition of the people was a constant reproach to him, a reminder that he had failed in his stewardship. He consoled himself by declaring that he was striving to obtain the material advantages of Western civilization for the people. But he saw that they enjoyed few of those advantages after eighty years of commerce with that civilization, while they had been deprived of the security formerly provided by a static society which placed the highest value on well-adjusted social relationships. It seemed that China had fallen between two stools.

It was not only the destructive thrust of the West into the fabric of Chinese civilization which dismayed young Chinese. China's statesmen had displayed only ineptitude in their efforts to deal with the European powers, and malicious obstructionism on the part of men whose interests were threatened by the new policies had checkmated even their feeble attempts. The first move to reform the structure of government had been made in 1898, as a result of China's humiliating defeat at the hands of Japan in 1895. A group of reformers under the leadership of the Cantonese political philosopher K'ang Yu-wei had secured the young Emperor's approval of a string of mild reforms. For a hundred summer days, edicts poured out of the palace at Peking like grain from the thresher. Armies were reorganized, schools and a university established, railroads laid down, and a free press guaranteed—by decree. Unfortunately, the Chinese Emperor did not possess the transcendent power of Gilbert and Sullivan's Mikado; the order and its execution were not synonymous. Few concrete reforms had been effected when in September, 1898, the Empress Dowager, with the assistance of General Yüan Shih-k'ai, once more seized power to countermand most of the reform edicts.

The Empress Dowager's plan for resisting the barbarians was radically different from that advanced by the reformers. She would not condescend to adopt Western technics. Instead she encouraged the development of a semi-official militia, whose purpose was the expulsion of the foreigner. She chose as her instrument a political society known to the West as the Boxers. In 1900, the Boxers, with the tacit support of the Court, began a campaign to frighten foreigners out of China. The eruption of anti-foreign demonstrations and massacres culminated in the siege of the legation quarter of Peking, which was lifted by a hastily organized European army. The victorious powers seized upon the Boxers' excesses as a pretext for extracting fresh concessions from a shaken China. The Empress Dowager returned from her refuge in the Summer Palace at Sian to sign a series of decrees punishing the "insurgents" and granting indemnities and new privileges to the Western nations.

Journalist Liang Ch'i-ch'ao took up his pen. He had been forced to flee to Japan, where he lived until 1907, for his minor role in the Reform Movement of 1898. The Japanese permitted him to publish journals which advocated constitutional monarchy and the modernization of China's fundamental institution. Since the Empress Dowager had set a price of 100,000 *taels* on his head and had prohibited the circulation of his writings, the problem of distribution was acute. However, the International Settlement at Shanghai provided an ideal clearing-house for reform propaganda. Liang Ch'i-ch'ao's writings entered China there and were smuggled from Shanghai into the interior, where they found an eager audience among students. The universities were deluged with publications.

But the rigorously logical arguments of Liang Ch'i-ch'ao were not the spark which could set China on fire. Although Liang provided the moral and intellectual basis for reform, it was left to the revolutionaries led by Sun Yat-sen to set the emotional fires with the incidents they sponsored and the inflammatory publications they circulated. Sun Yat-sen, a Cantonese educated in Hong Kong and Honolulu, was a new Chinese. Despairing of the Manchu dynasty as an instrument for strengthening China, he had called for the establishment of a republic before the turn of the century. He had founded the Raise China Society in 1894 and the Revolutionary Unity Association *(T'ung-meng Hui)* in 1905. While Sun raised money and sympathy abroad, his followers in China stage-managed risings and demonstrations, and those in Japan poured a stream of revolutionary journals into the mother country. Dr. Sun's efforts won wide adherence to the cause of democratic socialism.

The traditionalist Court at Peking, goaded by Chinese and foreign assaults, finally gave ground. A series of edicts which began in 1903 outdid the reformers of 1898. The army was reorganized, the civil service examination system was abolished, and legislative bodies were convened in the provinces. But it was too late for reform. In 1911, the rug was pulled from under the Manchus by a T'ung-meng Hui revolt, which began in October in Hankow and had spread to fifteen provinces by December. The Manchu Emperor was forced to abdicate, and the Chinese Republic was proclaimed on January 1, 1912. / The Revolution had succeeded.

Sun Yat-sen was called home from abroad to assume the presidency of the new republic. After a few days he resigned to make way for Yüan Shih-k'ai because he believed that Yüan, who was trusted by the conservatives, had the broad popular support needed for the task of making the Republic work. Yüan, who had betrayed the reformers in 1898 and the Emperor in 1911, was soon moved to betray the Republic by his colossal ambition and egotism. He played with the foreign powers, the royalists and provincial war-lords in his efforts to make himself first dictator and then emperor. His death in 1916 capped the failure of a coup which would have set him on the throne.

China was sucked into a political whirlpool. Every strutting general set himself up as a bush league emperor, and fed his anemic ego on blood and gold. There would be no point in describing the shifting alliances of war-lords which fought their battles up and down the nation, for the only consistent factor in them was greed for loot. The Revolution, designed to strengthen China against the West, had made her more vulnerable. The Republic had deprived the Chinese of the slight measure of security they had enjoyed under the Empire.

Young Chinese, sickened by ubiquitous self-seeking and corruption, turned toward scholarship and the arts, and away from government service, which had been the traditional road of ambition. Education, they declaimed, was the panacea for

China's ills. Only when Science and Democracy had been spread by popular education could China participate as an equal in world affairs.

Ch'en Tu-hsiu founded the *New Youth* magazine in Shanghai in 1915 to awaken youth to its mission. When he was made dean of the College of Letters at Peking University in 1917, Ch'en moved the magazine to that city. Just before the move to Peking, the issue of January, 1917, carried Hu Shih's article "Some Tentative Proposals for the Reform of Chinese Literature." Hu called for abandonment of the obscurantist literary style which required years of intense study of its readers and writers. He further urged authors to employ an idiom closer to the spoken language. In the February issue of the *New Youth,* Ch'en Tu-hsiu took up Hu's proposals and expanded them in an article which proclaimed "A Revolution in Chinese Literature." Despite the vehement opposition of old-style scholars, literate China took up the Hu-Ch'en proposals and enacted them into reality. By 1922, an author who wanted to be read was compelled to write in the vernacular.

Chinese peasants in revolt, unlike their Russian counterparts, had rarely burnt books. But they had had reason to do so. The complex classical idiom could be mastered only by men with years of leisure to devote to its pursuit. Since proficiency in letters was a prerequisite for obtaining official position under the Empire, a small group had long enjoyed a monopoly on power. Even under the Republic most roads were closed to the common people, for inability to write the classical language was equivalent to illiteracy and barred advancement. The literary revolution knocked down some bars. (Though artistic and scholarly writing was almost entirely in the vernacular style after 1920, the Kuomintang insisted that government documents be couched in a semi-classical style.)

Success in remaking the tools of literature and scholarship increased the self-confidence of Chinese intellectuals. They ached to try their muscles in the political ring, and in 1919 the chance came. On May 4, students in Peking rioted to

25

protest the government's acquiescence in the award of Shantung Province to Japan under the Versailles Treaty. In a week of rioting, the insurgent students roused public opinion to a pitch which made it impossible for the government to sign the treaty.

The May Fourth Incident marked the first time in modern Chinese history that public opinion dictated government policy. Chinese historians have called it the turning point in China's twentieth-century history. They maintain that Chinese politics and thought from that time to the present have radiated from May 4, 1919.

At that moment, the situation seemed little changed by the week of bloodshed. War-lords still ruled the people of China, sacrificing thousands to their ambition and caprice. Dr. Sun Yat-sen was just managing to hang on to the city of Canton in the southeast corner of China. Foreign nations, skillfully playing the old balance-of-power game with the numerous Chinese factions, could take such action as suited their advantage. And all the while, the people suffered and died. The Revolution had foundered.

In July, 1921, the first session of the Chinese Communist Party met secretly in the French Concession of Shanghai. Ch'en Tu-hsiu was elected secretary-general to command the mission of salvaging the Revolution.

26

2. A VILLAIN AND A HERO: CH'EN TU-HSIU AND CH'U CH'IU-PAI

The Chinese Communist creed, like all socially effective mythologies, provides believers with a duad of demigods. The spirits of darkness and light are represented in the hagiology by two dead men who served successively as secretary-general of the Communist Party of China—Ch'en Tu-hsiu and C'hü Ch'iu-pai. Ch'ü is extolled as chief of the honored dead sacrificed in the revolutionary struggle, while Ch'en's name is never mentioned without the word "traitor" appended. But it was Ch'en Tu-hsiu who created the Party and guided its early years, while Ch'ü Ch'iu-pai, who succeeded Ch'en, served only a short time before he was removed. Even after Ch'en Tu-hsiu's resignation from office, his name was carried on the Party rolls for a time. But his espousal of Trotskyism provoked immediate expulsion, and insured that his memory would be execrated by the devout Stalinists of the Chinese Communist Party.

Both Ch'en Tu-hsiu and Ch'ü Ch'iu-pai were primarily interested in letters, and both came to politics obliquely by way of their cultural interests. Ch'ü was Ch'en's successor in linguistic research as well as in the Party; Ch'en stood for the simplification of the written language and Ch'ü advocated romanization. Today the plain style, championed by Ch'en Tu-hsiu, is universally employed, while not even the Communists have carried on Ch'ü Ch'iu-pai's experiments with an orthography easier to learn than the traditional Chinese characters.

Spiritually, Ch'ü Ch'iu-pai was Ch'en Tu-hsiu's stepchild. Although the forces which Ch'en helped release as a revolutionist against the Manchu dynasty, an opponent of Yüan Shih-k'ai, an editor of the *New Youth,* and factotum of the Chinese Marxist movement shaped both Ch'ü's career and his character, the two were so different temperamentally that years of enforced intimacy revealed no real affinity between them. Ch'en, the belligerent idealist, broke with the Party of his own accord, while Ch'ü was realistically adept at shaping his convictions to his needs.

Ch'en Tu-hsiu made a glowing reputation because he remembered childhood resentment in later life. For centuries before his birth in 1879, Chinese boys of good family had been irked by the brain-sapping course of classical study which qualified them for service as government officials. But Ch'en Tu-hsiu, grown up, did more than complain. In 1917, his ardent sponsorship of a "Revolution in Chinese Literature" blasted the hard fabric of traditional Chinese culture, which had been a foundation of the Chinese political system. The shock waves of that explosion reached every corner of China, clearing the way for the bourgeois revolution of 1927 and the Communist revolution of 1949.

*   *   *

Tu-hsiu's* father died soon after the boy was born, leaving unfulfilled the promise of a brilliant official career. A holder of the first degree, the elder Ch'en had been a minor official. Tu-hsiu's mother was determined that he should fill the role

---

* I owe most of the material on Ch'en Tu-hsiu in this chapter to a comprehensive monograph by Julie Lien-ying How, entitled *The Development of Ch'en Tu-hsiu's Thought, 1915-1938,* which is projected for publication in autumn, 1951.

his father's death had vacated. At the age of six, Tu-hsiu dutifully began to memorize the classics under his grandfather's tutelage. The old man was a harsh tutor; rewards for excellence were rare, but an unsatisfactory recitation was invariably followed by caning. Ch'en Tu-hsiu later recalled: "When my grandfather beat me and I didn't cry, he would fly into a rage and declare that I had the makings of a first class robber. . . ."

The old man complained that the boy, who could perform brilliantly when he wished to, was flouting authority by brazenly resisting the acquisition of knowledge. Young Tu-hsiu, in turn, protested against the rigid discipline and the intellectual barrenness of classical studies. He was later to ascribe his violent distaste for the classical style of literary composition to his grandfather's dogmatic pedagogy.

Despite the clashes between grandfather and grandson, life was pleasant in the Ch'en household in the town of Huaining, Anhwei Province. The family land-holdings and commercial enterprises yielded an income large enough to keep Tu-hsiu, his mother, his older brother, and two older sisters in considerable comfort, and there was enough left over for opium to feed his grandmother's addiction. And Tu-hsiu, to satisfy his mother's ambition, submitted himself to his grandfather's will and spent long hours over his paper-bound books.

When Tu-hsiu was nine, his grandfather died, but the boy's studies continued, at first under a series of tutors, all of whom he detested impartially, and later under his older brother. In 1898, when he was seventeen, Ch'en Tu-hsiu took the district or *Hsiu-ts'ai* examination. It was the first step toward a government post.

When the lists were published, his mother, elated to find that he had passed first in the county, insisted that he take the examination for the next degree at Nanking, the provincial capital, the following year. Tu-hsiu gave in to his mother's ambition and sat down to his books once more. But he had begun to doubt that the examination system was producing the kind of civil servant the Empire needed. Just three years earlier, China had capitulated to Japan's Western-style army and navy. The force which had broken Chinese resistance was recruited by conscription, a method effective because Japan had adopted a system of compulsory education to train her men in Western technics. But China continued to prepare her young men for government service by requiring of them intimate familiarity with the two-thousand-year-old writings of the Confucian school.

In 1899, Ch'en Tu-hsiu journeyed to Nanking to take the examinations for the degree of *Chü-jen*. He was not happy about the purpose of his trip, but he was not so blasé as to remain uninfected by his mother's enthusiasm. Despite his own misgivings, sitting for the second degree had been a great event in the life of the Chinese scholar for nearly two thousand years. Few holders of the *Hsiu-ts'ai* or bachelor's degree attained the second degree, which carried with it appointment to office. And if he, Tu-hsiu, made a first again, he might even be called to Peking to receive the congratulations and favor of the Court, even before he took the last degree. So his mother said.

Upon his arrival at the examination halls, Ch'en found reality a monochrome reflection of the bunting dream. Within a dusty enclosure he saw row upon row of small ridge-roofs, each one covering a number of cells. (In lay-out, shape, and size the examination cells differed little from the lockers at any expensive American beach club. But they were not so large as cabanas.) He knew that he would be locked into a hot cell for several days, while he was writing his exams. Food and water would be passed in by proctors, who were charged to watch the candidates as closely as they would condemned prisoners. (A thousand years before, an emperor had decreed that manner of administering examinations to the intellectual flower of the nation.)

His full grown distaste for the classics reacting with his disgust at the manner in which the examinations were conducted, Ch'en Tu-hsiu came to hate the entire classical tradition. He left the examination ground to read the works of K'ang Yu-wei and Liang Ch'i-ch'ao, two of the reformers whose efforts had been frustrated by the intervention of the Empress Dowager in the preceding year. K'ang Yu-wei, a Confucian scholar, had sought to find in Confucius authority for adjusting the machinery of government to the realities of international politics. Liang, a journalist, propagandized for the adoption of Western technical skills in order to strengthen the nation.

Envisioning a noble career under the guidance of Liang Ch'i-ch'ao, Ch'en threw up his classical studies for good. He wished to master Western learning. Since both Britain and Japan had enforced their will on China through sea-power, he considered marine engineering an attractive branch of the New Learning, which could also help strengthen China. Escaping through a mist of maternal tears, Tu-hsiu left the ancestral home for Chekiang Province, where the Truth-seeking Academy (Ch'iu-shih Shu-yüan) offered courses in naval architecture.

To appease his mother, he accepted the bride chosen for him by the family. She was to give him two sons, and be left behind when she proved politically dilatory.

At the Truth-seeking Academy, Ch'en began to study English and French, in addition to his technical courses. In 1900, at the age of twenty-one, he went to Tokyo to enroll in the Higher Normal School, which encouraged Chinese students. Ch'en had found his career; he was to be a teacher until his death.

While pursuing his studies at Normal School and later at Waseda, Japan's great private university, Ch'en found his fellow students inflamed with radicalism. Impatient of reformers who wished to preserve the Manchu dynasty, most of his classmates joined the revolutionary societies which had found refuge in Japan. Ch'en was already a convert to social democracy, but he could not associate himself with any of the revolutionary groups, for he was repelled by their crude chauvinism. He felt that Sun Yat-sen's slogan, "Exalt the Chinese race, destroy the Manchu race!" was an expression of a narrow racism which could not benefit the Chinese people. Ch'en Tu-hsiu remained aloof from the active revolutionaries, and in 1907 left Japan for France.

The atmosphere of pre-1914 France was the most congenial he had known. In the nation which had first proclaimed the magic slogan *Liberté, Egalité, Fraternité!* he permitted himself to follow his literary predilections in forgetfulness of China's need. French literature became a minor passion, and the French "a godlike race of men" for him. His Francophilia was strong in politics too, for he saw in French parliamentarianism qualities which might be adapted to serve China's needs. He was to continue to worship the French spirit until the "betrayal at Versailles" made him set his face against all things Western, and turn to the Eurasian colossus for guidance.

When Ch'en returned to China in 1910, he was absolutely convinced that there could be no compromise between the senile Orient and the vigorous Occident. Orientals, he wrote, must cast every vestige of decaying Orientalism from them, lest they be destroyed. There could be no "blending of the best of each culture." Rather must the East adopt all Western institutions, substituting them for all Eastern institutions. The Orient, he continued, emphasizes formal values, the Occident practical values. Because of these antithetical standards the West encourages material progress and the East is a civilization of conservators rather than innovators.

Since the essence of Orientalism is the maintenance of the status quo, the retention of any Eastern institutions would effectively prevent the utilization of Western material knowledge. Those qualities of Western civilization which must be transplanted to the East, Ch'en Tu-hsiu summed up, are its dynamic science, its respect for the individual, and the concept of the equality of all citizens before the law. If those

Ch'en Tu-hsiu, first secretary-general of the Chinese Communist Party. The Party today honors his cultural achievements, but has denounced the man as a Trotskyite "traitor."

Ch'ü Ch'iu-pai, who succeeded Ch'en as secretary-general. Ch'ü was executed by Chiang Kai-shek in 1935, eight years before Ch'en's death.

TRIANGLE

Chairman Mao Tse-tung and Commander-in-Chief Chu Teh review troops of the "People's Liberation Army" from American-made jeeps captured from the Nationalists.

Dead-eye Liu — General Liu Po-ch'eng, chairman of the Southwest Administrative Area and commander of the Second Field Army. His troops have occupied Tibet.

qualities were honored in the Orient, there would have occurred a moral revolution and an automatic political readjustment.

With his visions of a new morality, Ch'en Tu-hsiu returned to China in 1910 to press for its creation. The times were favorable to radical ideas. Although Ch'en did not participate in the T'ung-meng Hui because of his repugnance for Sun Yat-sen's racist doctrines, he was nevertheless a revolutionist, who called for the replacement of the reigning dynasty by a democratic political system. In 1911 he became secretary to Po Wen-wei, governor of Anhwei Province, a more important post than the high school principalship he had accepted immediately after his return from France. After the Revolution of 1911, Po Wen-wei, as military governor of Anhwei, named Ch'en commissioner of education in the provincial government.

At the age of thirty-two, after a long period of preparation, Ch'en Tu-hsiu was ready to embark upon his true vocation of educator. He felt that it was time he settled down. There were four persons dependent on his earnings, for his wife had already given him two sons. At home in Huai-ning, old Mrs. Ch'en was happy that her stray petrel had found a perch—and would no more be sending for money from places with strange names. She shook her head over the foolishness he believed in, but was delighted that he had found an official post. And really this "republicanism" need not be taken too seriously, for the Emperor still lived in the Forbidden City in Peking, and the chief officer of state was the great viceroy Yüan Shih-k'ai. It was true that the Emperor was in retirement, and Yüan did bear the strange title of "President," but the Emperor had never really ruled, and a title did not matter so much as the man who bore it and exercised supreme authority.

President Yüan Shih-k'ai in Peking would have agreed completely with Mrs. Ch'en had they sat down to discuss politics. He saw the so-called Republic as an interregnum, which would be succeeded by a new dynasty under the Yüan family. As soon as he assumed office in February, 1912, Yüan Shih-k'ai began to plot to that end. The Constitution made the president subordinate to Parliament, a situation which he found intolerable. In the spring and summer of 1913, Yüan negotiated a loan from a consortium of foreign bankers. Parliament, opposing the granting of railway concessions as collateral, refused to endorse the loan, but Yüan went ahead on his own. That summer Sun Yat-sen gave the signal for revolt against Yüan's usurpation. This "Second Revolution" was suppressed in short order by Yüan's armies, and the dictator, dismissing Parliament, settled himself more comfortably in the seat of power.

Mrs. Ch'en's reaction to these events has not been recorded. She probably approved of Yüan's assumption of power, though she hardly knew what kind of creature this "Parliament" was. But her son Tu-hsiu was horrified by Yüan's crypto-dynasticism. Though not of the Kuomintang, he supported the Second Revolution, writing and speaking against Yüan Shih-k'ai throughout 1913. When the counter-revolution triumphed, Ch'en was forced to flee alone to Japan to escape imprisonment.

This time the family gave him up; no more money would be forthcoming for this unnatural son, who was constantly in opposition to authority and his mother's wishes. For two and a half years Ch'en lived the life of an impoverished scholar in the Japanese capital, earning just enough by writing and teaching to keep himself this side of death. A friend who visited him there reported that he would often find Ch'en reading in his undershirt, while a damp shirt hung on a line above the bed. He had just one shirt, which he washed himself to prevent its thin threads from being torn by rough handling.

In the summer of 1915, with Yüan's power on the wane, Ch'en felt that he might safely return to the mainland. He exchanged complete for semi-exile, settling in the French Concession of Shanghai. In September, 1915, he entered upon the course which was to lead him to a peculiar eminence as the grand impresario of Chinese culture for the next decade. With the assistance of friends, whom he charmed into compliance, he established *Hsin Ch'ing-nien,* subtitled *La Jeunesse.* It seemed at first to be just another one of the journals which bright young men, temporarily barred from politics, were putting out to give themselves the illusion of activity.

The *New Youth* proved quite different, for Ch'en Tu-hsiu had at last come into harmony with the times. His public wished him to be more, rather than less, radical. His intransigent, questing spirit was the spirit of the age. His ready solutions to social problems, his advocacy of a thorough overhauling of morality, education, and economics provided the answers the bewildered "new youth" sought. Popular response to his articles startled Ch'en himself only slightly less than it did his backers. There was a run on each issue as it appeared, and a strong market developed for back-numbers as teachers and parents tried to find out what the youngsters were so excited about. The first issue, reprinted and reprinted again, sold more than two hundred thousand copies in all.

Ch'en proclaimed that Messrs. *Sai-yin-ssu* and *Teh-mo-k'o-la-hsi*—Science and Democracy—could be the saviors of China. But first the bonds of feudal Confucianism must be stricken from their wrists to free them for activity. The old must be totally destroyed before the new could be erected. And so on through many issues, exhorting, pleading, threatening, extolling, scolding, and condemning, with the didactic note always dominant. Ch'en, the teacher, wrestled with the youth of China for their souls. Young intellectuals were entranced by the prophet who promised to make a revolution in politics by first remaking morality and culture.

*   *   *

China fell into anarchy after Yüan Shih-k'ai's defeat, which was brought about in large measure by the opposition of the press. The dignity of Parliament and the presidency were baubles with which a succession of militarists adorned themselves. In disgust, the best minds of the nation turned from politics to seek cultural careers. One scholar wrote: "In my humble opinion, politics is in such confusion that I am at a loss to know what to talk about. Ideal schemes will have to be buried for future generations to unearth. . . . As to fundamental salvation, I believe its beginning must be sought in the promotion of a new literature. In short, we must endeavor to bring Chinese thought into direct contact with the thought of the world, thereby to accelerate its radical awakening. . . . The method seems to consist in using simple and simplified language for the wide dissemination of ideas among the people."

To that task Ch'en Tu-hsiu was to give his labor for the next five years. The pedagogue rose to the personal challenge implicit in the slogan calling for "A new literature as a tool of education!" Science and democracy could best be taught to the people in their own language, and not in the ultra-refined jargon which scholarly convention demanded of serious writers. Moreover, the other enemy, the Confucian tradition, depended upon the literary language for its survival. Ch'en still remembered the welts his grandfather's willow wand had raised on his palms. The literary language, he concluded, was the aspect of Chinese civilization which must be destroyed first to allow of the adoption of Western institutions.

While Ch'en Tu-hsiu was coming to his decision, another Chinese, half the globe away from China, was concerned with the same problem. While studying agriculture at Cornell University, young Hu Shih had been pained by the low state of Chinese literature. Perhaps, he mused, if authors wrote in a style close to the spoken language, there might be a rebirth of Chinese literature comparable to the Renaissance which occurred in Europe when her writers began to use the vernacular. Hu Shih toyed with the idea for a time and then put it reluctantly away, for his friends laughed when he spoke of it.

But rowing on Lake Cayuga one afternoon with a Chinese girl, he spoke of his dream again. She was sympathetic, but unimpressed, challenging him to back his theory by writing a poem in the spoken language.

That poem—a poor effort—was the beginning of the New Literature Movement. Hu Shih soon sold himself on the merits of his idea, and in the January, 1917, issue of the *New Youth* appeared an article from his pen entitled "Some Tentative Suggestions for the Reform of Chinese Literature." Hu timidly suggested that the time had come to consider the possibility of utilizing the vernacular as a model for literary style. (Previously only plays and novels, considered rather vulgar by the literati, had been couched in a style comprehensible to the ear.) The energetic Ch'en Tu-hsiu agreed, and Hu found himself borne to fame on the waves of Ch'en's enthusiasm. In the February issue of the *New Youth,* Ch'en published an article under his own by-line entitled "On the Revolution in Chinese Literature." A reformer with an idea had been taken over by a revolutionist with a mission.

Ch'en wrote: "A movement for a literary revolution pioneered by my friend Hu Shih is now in progress. I am willing to brave the enmity of all the pedantic scholars of the nation and aid in hoisting the great banner of the revolutionary literary army. On the face of this banner shall be written in large characters the three great principles of the revolutionary army: 1) To destroy the painted, powdered and obsequious literature of the aristocratic few, and to create the plain, simple and expressive literature of the many; 2) to destroy the stereotyped and monotonous literature of classicism, and to create the fresh and sincere literature of realism; and 3) to destroy the pedantic, unintelligible and obscurantist literature of the hermit and recluse, and to create the plain-speaking and popular literature of the masses."

Thus the proclamation; its tone more political than aesthetic; its intent pedagogical rather than critical. Discontented writers and teachers were to take up Ch'en's proposals and enact them into reality through practice. In 1920, the Ministry of Education at Peking decreed that primary-school texts should be written in *pai-hua*—plain language. Ch'en Tu-hsiu continued to publish articles clarifying his position, but the campaign had been won in the first battle. Ch'en was enshrined as co-leader with Hu Shih of the Chinese Renascence, and the *New Youth* was followed as the bellwether of the New Literature Movement. Later, young intellectuals were to grow impatient with the hectoring tone of Ch'en's articles, as did Kuo Mo-jo and Chang Tze-p'ing.* But for the moment, Ch'en Tu-hsiu was supreme, beyond criticism.

For once, recognition did not lag behind accomplishment. Ts'ai Yüan-p'ei, the old liberal writer and journalist who was president of Peking University, made Ch'en Tu-hsiu dean of the College of Letters. Peking University, nicknamed Pei-ta, was one of the few institutions created during the abortive Hundred Days Reform of 1898 that had not been destroyed by the Empress Dowager's counter-reformation. Having its origins in a reaction against traditional Chinese culture, it endured as a center of experimental thought, and was recognized, even by undergraduates of other universities, as the foremost institution of learning in China. Ch'en's appointment as dean gave the seal of academic respectability and high scholarly purpose to his linguistic experiments.

His faculty included some names which later became great. Hu Shih, newly returned from America to be professor of philosophy, was later to be appointed Chinese ambassador to Washington. Li Ta-chao, professor of economics and librarian of the university, was to become joint chief with Ch'en Tu-hsiu of the Communist Party and die in a war-lord's garrote. And Chou Tso-jen, though living all his life in the shadow of his brother Lu Hsün's superlative achievement,† was to be recognized as a great stylist in modern Chinese literature. These men, acknowledging Ch'en as their leader in fact as

---

* See Chapter 8. † See Chapter 6.

well as title, associated themselves with the *New Youth* to raise its fame higher.

But Ch'en found that political responsibility was a co-tenant in the bower of cultural prestige. He was expected to be a minor prophet on political affairs, and with no false show of reluctance, he took on the job. With Li Ta-chao, he founded the *Weekly Critic* as a political organ, in an effort to preserve the cultural emphasis of the *New Youth*—a policy to which he did not long adhere. He had already written: "I do not believe that politics can do everything, and I believe that it can create unmitigated evil in society," but still he urged upon his disciples active participation in politics in the interest of economic progress. As for himself, while opposed to the party system, he still desired constitutional democracy as a safeguard for the rights of the individual. On economic theory he was vague.

While not yet sure what he wanted, Ch'en Tu-hsiu knew what he did not want. Under his direction, the College of Letters at Pei-ta became an incubator for revolutionists. The students, in their dormitories built on a compound like a monkish cloister, would be up until two or three in the morning arguing aesthetics or foreign policy. "Lights out" was at midnight. Or they might come pelting into sanctuary behind the college walls after participating in a public demonstration, with the city police hot after them. Ch'en was never a parlor pink, content to talk away any inclination to act, and his students took their color from him. Theory demanded direct action, but sometimes action would anticipate theory.

* * *

Certain Chinese statesmen thought the first World War offered an opportunity to consolidate China's position in the family of nations. In 1917, China entered the War on the Allied side, hoping that her status as an ally would assure protection of her interests at the peace conference. Although China's contribution to the Allied war-effort was limited to a few labor battalions, she was seated at the conference table. But her representatives were powerless to prevent cession to Japan of Germany's former interests in Shantung Province. Nevertheless, the Peking government, recognized abroad as the legal government of China, proposed to sign the Versailles Treaty, acquiescing in the alienation of Chinese territory.

This was too much for the students. Incited by their teachers, Pei-ta students rushed through the narrow alleys of Peking into the squares and public places. Ignited by Chinese oratory—as inflammatory as any in the world—they moved toward action. Someone started the word going: the minister of communications—known as the chief of the "pro-Japanese clique"—was entertaining the Chinese minister to Japan.

The mobs had found a purpose; they converged on the house. The door was battered down, and panting students poured into the banquet room beside the formal garden to find the company at their wine. With fists and cudgels they beat the "traitors," while the rest of the company escaped through the back door. A detachment of police arrived and seized seven students, whom they promptly declared the ringleaders. The student mob barricaded themselves in the Law School at Peking University, while the police laid siege to the building. The riot began on May 4, 1919.

Ts'ai Yüan-p'ei, president of Pei-ta, succeeded in making the university's peace with the authorities after some days. But Ch'en, and other professors whom the authorities held responsible for inciting the students, were reduced in rank and soon forced to resign. Not content with this punishment, the war-lord government threw Ch'en Tu-hsiu into prison for eighty-three days "for distributing pamphlets."

Despite Ch'en's humiliation, the students won. Inflamed public opinion made it impossible for the Peking regime to sign the Treaty of Versailles, and China concluded a separate peace treaty with Germany. This victory was the first of the wave-like effects of the May Fourth Incident. Public opinion, awakened by the students, had forbidden the government to sign, and the government had not signed. The public realized its power, and from this realization flowed whatever democracy prevailed in China between the wars. The May Fourth Incident widened into the May Fourth Movement as full reports spread to the provinces. Mao Tse-tung in Hunan and even little Lin Piao in Hupei, were caught up in a movement to re-examine all traditional values—aesthetic, political, and moral.

When he was released from prison in the fall of 1919, Ch'en, who had written at the beginning of the year that Communism was not suitable for China, once more affirmed his political faith. In an article called "Build the Foundation for Popular Rule," he wrote: "No country has yet practiced social and economic democracy, but democracy is comparatively better developed in England and the United States than in other countries." His disgust with France, which he held largely responsible for the terms of the Versailles Treaty, led him to omit the country he had previously described as "the creator of culture, the light of the world, opposing German militarism in the fight for freedom."

He was disillusioned, to a lesser degree, with all the nations of the West, and with the principles of government they professed. As early as June, 1919, he had rejected constitutionalism, parliamentarianism, and representative government. In its place he offered an amorphous utopianism of his own creation. "We must," he wrote, "break down the barriers between the governors and the governed," so that the people, participating directly in government, will become both the rulers and the ruled. He proposed to establish governmental organs whose "total membership" would include all adults subject to their direction. Administration would be carried out by officers chosen from among the members for short fixed terms. Organs elected on a geographical basis would be supplemented by corporate bodies drawn from various industries. Unlike the old Chinese guilds, Ch'en's corporations would include all persons in the industry, exceeding in scope even the

41

modern American industrial union, since they would take in management as well as labor.

Ch'en's proposals for "direct participation" in government were an expedient designed to fill a lacuna in his political thinking. He had abandoned Western-style democracy and had not yet embraced Communism. But his conversion to Marxism did not wait long after his renunciation of representative democracy. By the end of the year 1919, Ch'en Tu-hsiu, already half-convinced, had turned from the West to the Soviet Union. He would soon be a passionate Marxist.

' Ch'en seems to have turned to Marxism, which offered a showcase full of ready-made instruments, because his own "corporatism" carried no method of implementation. The "scientific" cant, which is the intellectual heart of Communism, was also a strong attraction to the "pro-scientific" Ch'en. By the spring of 1920, his conversion was complete. After that time he would no longer be concerned with political theorizing, but with action in the cause of Communism. As a good Marxist he affirmed that politics, embracing all spheres of human activity, was the only proper pursuit of man.

Taking his own words as his text, Ch'en became hyperactive in the organizing and propaganda work required of a practicing Communist, although he was not formally a member of any party owing allegiance to the Communist International, since none existed in China at the time. After his release from prison in Peking, he went to Shanghai, where the French Concession offered some protection from police interference. In May, 1920, Gregory Voitinsky, secretary-general of the Far Eastern Bureau of the Comintern, arrived in, Shanghai with his wife and a Chinese aide. He had been referred to Ch'en by Li Ta-chao in Peking. At Ch'en's home, 716 Avenue Joffre, they met to plan the strategy of the Chinese Communist movement.

Three men—Ch'en, Voitinsky and Voitinsky's Moscow-trained Chinese aide—mapped out an ambitious program.

42

The Russian wanted Chinese Communism to enter the political war on all fronts. He advised the formation of a Communist Party and the organization of labor unions, study clubs, publications, and schools. But Ch'en Tu-hsiu, conscious of the paucity of his resources, counseled moderation. Putting a tentative toe into the muddy waters, he agreed to sponsor an organization to be known as the Chinese Socialist Youth Group. Toward the end of August, 1920, an organizational meeting was held in the dingy office of the *New Youth* at 2 Avenue Joffre. The chief figures were Ch'en Tu-hsiu, Gregory Voitinsky, Chang T'ai-lei, who later headed the Canton Commune, and Tai Chi-t'ao and Shao Li-tze, both of whom later were to go over to the Kuomintang.

In the fall, the Socialist Youth Group began to expand, stimulated by a contribution from the Comintern, via Voitinsky, of $5,000 gold a month. Ch'en Tu-hsiu founded a branch in Canton, and other branches were soon set up in Peking, Hankow, Changsha, Tsinan and other important cities. Abroad, notably in Tokyo and Paris, Chinese students organized overseas branches. In Shanghai, a Foreign Language School trained students who proposed to study abroad. Russian was the chief subject.

Ch'en Tu-hsiu himself was almost too busy to devote any time to his creation. He had been called to Canton to become minister of education in the government of General Ch'en Chün-ming, an associate of Sun Yat-sen's, and would not pass up the chance to practice his pet theories. Despite his own declaration that he had put aside all other pursuits to devote himself wholly to politics, Ch'en's heart was still in teaching. In his political activities he was pedagogue first and revolutionist second. Like some of the greatest Western statesmen, Ch'en Tu-hsiu based his conduct on the unspoken conviction that politics was an extension of education. This despite his adherence to the Marxist dogma which holds that education is an extension of politics.

As minister of education for Canton Province, he attempted

to imbue his students with his own respect for *sai-yin-ssu,* and to train them in the scientific method. But he was prevented from seeing the experiment through, for in the summer of 1921 he broke with his sponsor in Canton and returned to Shanghai to tend the revolutionary stew which he and Gregory Voitinsky had put on the fire a year earlier.

The pot was boiling furiously. During Ch'en's absence from Shanghai, the comrades had set up the General Labor Secretariat of China to organize workmen for the revolution. That was the first step away from the previous concentration upon intellectuals, a step in a direction approved by the Comintern, which held that the proletariat must be the basis of the Chinese revolution. Through its organ, the *Labor Weekly,* and through the efforts of T'an P'ing-shan, a Canton longshoreman's son who was later to be the Red chief in the south, the Labor Secretariat began to extend its influence among railroad workers and merchant seamen.

Voitinsky and Maring, a later arrival from Moscow, were pressing for further commitment in the shape of a formal Communist Party of China. Although Ch'en Tu-hsiu was still absent in Canton, the inaugural session of the National Congress of the Communist Party of China was convened on July 1, 1921 in the French Concession of Shanghai. The eleven delegates who sat down to draw up a platform for the new party represented approximately fifty persons.

Among those representatives were: Chang Kuo-t'ao, who was to remain one of the leading figures in the Party for a decade; Li Ta, now one of the chief theoretical writers of the Party; Liu Jen-ching, who would later follow Ch'en's Trotskyite "deviationist" course; and Tung Pi-wu, now a vice-premier of the Central Government of the People's Republic of China and one of the grand old men of the Party.*

A junior delegate was a heavy, earnest young man from Hunan, named Mao Tse-tung, whose preoccupation with

---

* See Chapter 5.

peasant organization was considered a trifle peculiar, since the Comintern itself had declared that the base of the Chinese revolution would be the industrial proletariat of the cities.

The other delegates followed the orthodox line. They announced that they represented both the laboring and the farming proletariat, but displayed greater concern for the city workers. They noted that China's bourgeois revolution must precede the Socialist revolution, and cautioned the Party to alertness against the time when native capitalists became enemies instead of uneasy allies.

At this First Congress, the absent Ch'en Tu-hsiu was named chairman of the Central Executive Committee, Chang Kuo-t'ao was placed at the head of the Organization Bureau, and Li Ta was assigned to direct propaganda. The Central Committee was charged with the primary mission of establishing a perfect liaison with the Communist International.

In China itself, the Party undertook the transformation of Shanghai University into a "training school for revolutionary cadres." Ch'en Tu-hsiu became dean of the College of Letters, finally free to test his pedagogical theories without interference from opposing politicos. He assembled a faculty which included Mao Tün, later a major novelist, and young Ch'ü Ch'iu-pai, Ch'en's successor in the Party, who had returned from Moscow to head the Sociology Department.

*   *   *

Though the Party had hardly begun, Ch'en Tu-hsiu's star had already reached its zenith before the year 1921. His leadership of the New Literature Movement and the May Fourth Movement were to be his greatest achievements, while the Party he fathered was to grow toward power under the guidance of other men.

The seeds of the disputes which were to split the granite of the Party were put into the earth in 1922. Ch'en emerged from a second prison term—a silver star to wear on the service ribbon of his previous imprisonment—into the middle of a great debate on the question of joining the Kuomintang in its struggle to unify China and put down imperialism.

A Communist Party conference, held at West Lake in Hangchow in August, 1922, favored joining the Nationalists. Sun Yat-sen, isolated by Ch'en Chün-ming's defection, was inclined to view the plan favorably, though he rejected a Comintern proposal for immediate alliance. Ch'en Tu-hsiu, writing in the *Guide (Hsiang-tao)*, also approached the problem, but in a most delicate manner. He attempted to distinguish between those bourgeois elements with whom the Communists might make common cause, and those who were the unrelenting enemies of the proletariat. In the same publication he discussed a recurrent issue—the most appropriate popular base for the Communist revolution. The peasants, he felt, were too diffused to provide a satisfactory foundation, while the self-conscious industrial proletariat were sufficiently concentrated and sufficiently sensitive to Communist appeals to be used. (Mao Tse-tung, working in the countryside, disagreed, and was to break sharply with Ch'en on that issue the following year.) But, continued Ch'en, we Communists cannot achieve our aims while China is held in colonial subjugation by the forces of Western imperialism. We must, therefore, make common cause with Sun Yat-sen's Kuomintang, which also seeks to unify China by expelling the imperialists.

Into this atmosphere came another man from Moscow, Joffe, special Soviet emissary to the nations of the Far East. He and Sun Yat-sen held a series of discussions climaxed by the Sun-Joffe Declaration of January 1923, which announced that neither man considered China suited to Communism and pledged the Soviet Union's assistance to the Chinese Nationalist revolution. Fifty-three members of the Kuomintang and the Communist Party had already met on November 4, 1922, to draw up plans for the reorganization of the Kuomintang. Ch'en was among the delegates to this conference. A year later came the Kuomintang's decision to accept those mem-

46

bers of the Communist Party who made individual application for membership.

In the beginning, the collaboration was eminently harmonious. Chou En-lai and Lin Tsu-han headed the Communist section of the faculty at Chiang Kai-shek's pet Whampoa Military Academy, and Li Ta-chao was elected co-chairman with Dr. Sun of the Kuomintang Congress, meeting in Shanghai in January, 1924. Ch'en Tu-hsiu became a member of the Central Executive Committee of the Kuomintang, and Communist T'an P'ing-shan chairman of the Kuomintang's Organization Bureau.' It was only later that the right wing of the Kuomintang, egos swollen with a string of military successes, decided that they could do without the assistance of the Reds. But the end of the unnatural alliance was due in equal measure to the activities of the Communists, who insisted upon organizing workers in their own interest, despite their formal adherence to the program of the Kuomintang. By 1927 it had become clear that the partners were incompatible. ·

Though tossed by these political storms, Ch'en Tu-hsiu did not jettison his intellectual interests. Indeed, his position as secretary-general of the Communist Party required him to act as the advocate of Marxism before the tribunal of the intellectuals who made public opinion. In late 1923, the Chinese intellectual world was entranced by a grand polemic, growing out of a dispute between the "Scientists" and the "Humanists." All values were cast into the ring to be mauled, fought over, and finally demolished or accepted. Ch'en, proclaiming himself a Scientist, displayed the Communist wares. He announced that the choice before China might be simply stated: either anarchy or enlightened dictatorship. He and his followers, he continued, preferred the second alternative, the rule of self-conscious leaders who had been trained to analyse "objective conditions." Morality was meaningless, since the only criterion of an action's moral validity was the object it sought.

47

The Kremlin's intelligence section must have been pleased; their man in China was displaying a gratifying orthodoxy in his opinions. But there was consternation in Moscow when further reports began to come in. Ch'en Tu-hsiu was hedging on the promise of the eventual classless society—the pot of gold at the end of the Marxist rainbow. He wrote that he looked forward to the time when the state should have decayed. That was good enough for Moscow, but Ch'en went on to say that the classless society, like all other human institutions, would itself decay, to be succeeded by new epochs. He concluded, completely out of bounds, with the statement that no system created by man could be permanent.

Later there were other difficulties, and more pressing ones. Michael Borodin, the Kuomintang's Soviet adviser, was influential in the councils of the Communist Party, but he and Ch'en could not agree in their assessment of the Kuomintang. Ch'en later reported that his cooperation with the Nationalists had not been freely given, but was rather forced by Borodin's insistence that such was the will of the Comintern. Ch'en reported that he had constantly fought concessions to the Kuomintang, while Borodin had urged them. The Party was later to charge that Ch'en Tu-hsiu had followed a policy of "right opportunism," of boot-licking the Kuomintang in defiance of Comintern orders.

But in the year 1925 these disputes within the inner circle of the Communist Party were merely a portent; the actual work of revolution was progressing, in cooperation with the Kuomintang. A resolution passed by the Central Committee of the Comintern in that year advised the Chinese Communist Party "to fight with the right wing of the Kuomintang, organize the left and unite with them, and to criticise the center. We must form a revolutionary union with the Kuomintang of the proletariat, farmers, coolies, and all oppressed elements. . . ."

This policy Ch'en Tu-hsiu followed. In late 1925, the port of Hong Kong was completely tied up by a strike of merchant seamen, which was at least half political in character. In May, 1925, the All-China Labor Federation was established by a conference in Canton. The new organization was a branch of the Red Trade Union International. Leninism, in concert with the policies of Sun Yat-sen, was declared "China's salvation." Membership in the Communist Party grew from 1,500 on January 1 to 3,000 by May 30, 1925.

But the Kuomintang was becoming wary of its allies. A conference of the right wing, held in November, 1925, in the Western Hills near Peking, expressed alarm at the success of Communist agitation among workers and coolies. Cadets of the Whampoa Academy were also becoming too sympathetic to Communism. The anti-Communist campaign which was to erupt the following year was planned in the Western Hills.

In March, 1926, a coup within the Kuomintang placed Chiang Kai-shek in command of the city of Canton. Communists and members of the left wing were slain and their organizations dispersed, while Wang Ching-wei, the heir of Sun Yat-sen and leader of the moderate left, was forced to flee. Ch'en Tu-hsiu urged withdrawal from the entente, but was overruled by the Comintern bloc in the Central Committee, on the order of Borodin. In May, 1926, the Kuomintang's Central Executive Committee passed resolutions depriving the Reds of responsible offices in the Nationalist Party and severely limiting their representation on party organs. Again Ch'en called for the break and again he was overruled. In June, 1926, the Fifth Congress of the Communist Party expressed its desire to continue cooperation with the Kuomintang. On the fourth of June, Ch'en Tu-hsiu composed an open letter to Chiang Kai-shek, affirming the loyalty of the Chinese Communist Party to the national revolution and denying any intention of sabotaging the joint effort. He was later to claim that this letter had been written to the order of the Comintern and not as an expression of his real views.

Once again success postponed the final split. On July 9, 1926, Chiang Kai-shek's armies marched north from Canton on the first leg of the Northern Expedition, which was to destroy the power of the war-lords. By September they had taken Hankow, the Detroit of China, and by December a Provisional Government had been established in that city. The left wing of the Kuomintang and the Communists dominated the Hankow Government. The Hankow General Labor Union was a mainstay of the Provisional Government and the center of Communist agitation in central China. Ch'en Tu-hsiu himself went to Shanghai to join Chou En-lai in organizing fighting labor unions there.

In Shanghai the break-up came. Chiang Kai-shek, supported by a cabal of bankers and gang leaders, turned on the union activists, who had seized the city against his coming. His armies marched in to disarm the workers and massacre them. Ch'en and Chou En-lai fled to Hankow, where the left-wing government was still opposed to Chiang Kai-shek. Only seven days earlier, Ch'en and Hankow's chief, Wang Ching-wei, had jointly proclaimed the unity of the Kuomintang left wing and the Communists in the face of Chiang's ambition. But the moderates soon found reason to distrust the Communists. On May 21, 1926, General T'ang Sheng-chih was ordered by the Hankow Government to move against the Communist-sponsored peasant unions in the Changsha area. Exceeding his orders, General T'ang bloodied himself in the infamous Hunan Peasant Massacres, driving new adherents into the Red camp.

Once the break-up had started, the end came fast, for the Central Committee of the Comintern, sitting in Moscow, took a hand in the confusion. A secret telegram was despatched to Borodin in Hankow ordering the Reds to ignore the orders of the Provisional Government when they conflicted with their own aims. Another Comintern representative, the Indian Roy, showed the telegram to Wang Ching-wei, who decided in a rage to cast out the Communists. Later the Comintern ordered Communists to leave the Government, but remain in the Kuomintang, and on June 30, Agriculture Minister T'an

50

P'ing-shan, a Communist, asked for a "leave of absence." A further order, dated July 4, 1927, called on the Communists to continue to cooperate with the "national revolutionary bourgeoisie" as long as such cooperation did not interfere with the independent task of arming the peasants. The same order requested that the Party be purified of "opportunistic elements."

On July 15, 1927, the Central Committee of the Kuomintang clarified the issue. Kuomintang members were told that they might not continue to be members of the Communist Party. On July 19, the Army expelled its Communists.

Ch'en Tu-hsiu resigned from his Party offices, declaring: "The Comintern wishes us to carry out our own policy on the one hand, and forbids us to leave the Kuomintang on the other. I see no way out, and cannot continue my duties." The Party did not accept Ch'en's resignation, preferring to dismiss him in the Emergency Meeting held at Kiukiang on August 7, a week after the Nanchang Rising.* That meeting, under the direction of Mao Tse-tung and C'hü Ch'iu-pai, castigated Ch'en Tu-hsiu for "right opportunism," convicted him of violating and ignoring the Comintern's orders, and blamed his errors for the total failure of Communist tactics. Ch'en, gone to Shanghai for his health, could not reply to the charges, nor might he have done so had he been present.

*　　*　　*

In Ch'en's place, the August Seventh Emergency Meeting elected Ch'ü Ch'iu-pai secretary-general of the Party. Ch'ü's chief qualification was his unquestionable loyalty to Moscow. Ch'en Tu-hsiu had been a skittish servant at best, executing the Comintern's orders under compulsion. Ch'ü Ch'iu-pai, who had entered the Party in the Holy City itself, would be more obedient. Ch'en had visited Moscow to attend a con-

---

* See Chapter 3.

ference in 1922, but Ch'ü, living among the Russians for several years, had received his revolutionary indoctrination at their hands.

Moreover, Ch'ü's background was more acceptable to the Party, with its inverted snobbishness. Ch'en had been distrusted because he, an intellectual, was the son of wealthy landholders. Ch'ü's father had been an impoverished school teacher. And Ch'ü was a younger man—only eighteen at the time of the Russian Revolution—too young to have been infected by the cancerous "bourgeois attitude" which had eaten away Ch'en's usefulness to the cause.

But Ch'ü Ch'iu-pai was hardly a proletarian. When he was born in the town of Ch'ang-chou in Kiangsu Province in the year 1899, his father still possessed an adequate library and a collection of valuable paintings and seals. Ch'iu-pai's mother, it is reported, was an educated woman who wrote passable classical poetry to relieve herself of the strain of raising a large family on a tiny income.

On their own testimony, most eminent Chinese seem to have been borne by poetry-writing mothers. Though the Westerner is startled by the picture of a nation whose educated women are all poised on the edge of the perfect poetic image, there is little reason to doubt the tradition. The composition of classical Chinese poetry requires less inspiration than training in its rigid conventions. It is not difficult to write good poetry in classical Chinese—and next to impossible to write great poetry. But this tradition, too, is passing with the passing of the classical language, and the generation of Chinese now rising to eminence will be more likely to recall that their mothers played good jazz piano—an accomplishment requiring about the same degree of technical skill as writing passable classical verse.

Of Ch'iu-pai's father we know little, except that he was thoroughly irresponsible. When social psychologists can once more pursue their researches in China, they may well look into the significance of the dominant role played by the female parent in the recollections of prominent Chinese. In most cases the father is a sinister or a feckless individual, whose threat to the children's happiness and well-being is parried by the mother's devoted cleverness. Ch'iu-pai's father was a shadowy figure, who contributed little to the boy's development beyond the initial act of procreation.

· Despite the emphasis on the poverty of the Ch'ü family which marks all accounts, it is reported that Ch'iu-pai was sent to school. A Chinese family with pretensions to scholarship would give up all material advantages before surrendering its social status by failing to educate its children. The boy was trained by his father in the traditional manner before he was ready to enter school. But once he began to attend classes, his education was conducted in a more modern manner. The principal of the higher primary school which Ch'iu-pai attended was a sympathizer with the anti-Manchu revolution. He instituted a program of military training for the youngsters in his charge, and indoctrinated them with the teachings of Dr. Sun Yat-sen. According to his Communist biographer, it was at higher-primary school that Ch'iu-pai received his elementary "education in national revolutionary thought."

Each night he would come home to the ramshackle Family Temple, which had been the Ch'ü's dwelling since they had been forced to sell their home. They lived there on the sufferance of the community, which was bound by custom to provide for the indigent scholar and his family. But the assistance was not liberal; the children were in a worse position than the preacher's family in a poor American town. And when the elder Ch'ü began to sell his paintings and books, the end was plainly in sight. Soon afterwards they began to trade their extra clothing for rice.

Before this stage was reached, Ch'iu-pai had been graduated with distinction from primary school, and had begun to go to middle school. As is so often the case with bright poor children, he set out to demonstrate to his wealthier classmates that their money was not a token of real superiority. It was always a happy day when the son of fat Mr. Li, the wine-merchant, was placed in the middle of the class, and he, the son of a lean scholar, at the head. Others might arrive in silk robes, carrying carved ivory brush-cases, but he surpassed them all when the marks were posted.

After graduation from middle school, the grinning figure of poverty barred the road he would travel. Ch'iu-pai wanted to continue on to a university, preferably Pei-ta, but there were others nearer home. Instead, he was forced to take a post teaching primary school in a village about three miles away. Since his father, in his nonchalant fashion, had stopped contributing to the suport of the family, Ch'iu-pai had to send the greater part of his meager salary to his mother to help feed the younger children.

One warm day, while listening to the resentful drone of his rustic pupils, Ch'iu-pai was called from class. His mother, the note said, was very ill, and he was to leave at once. When he reached the Family Temple, he found his mother lying dead on a pallet. Strewn beside her were a few matchsticks; she had committed suicide by eating their heads.

Even in his grief—his mother had been the one sure place in the world for him—Ch'iu-pai felt released. He would thereafter follow his own ambition unhindered. Late in 1916, he set out for the Hankow area, where his father's sister, the wife of a rich landholder, was living. Life had become simple, for he need only win her assistance to go on with his studies. But his uncle refused to aid him in any manner, and suggested that his speedy departure would be most agreeable. So, like all penniless students, he set out for Peking. He was fortunate beyond the common lot in having a cousin living there. But he was to be disappointed again.

In his own words: "After my mother's suicide and the break-up of our family, I drifted up to Peking. I planned, first to enter Peking University to study Chinese literature, and later to pass my days as a teacher. I was completely without the highflown desire 'to govern the nation justly, and bring peace to all under heaven.' I felt that I, a bookworm with a strong inclination toward the literary art, could not devote my energies to becoming an official and amassing wealth. I lived in the house of my cousin, Ch'ün-pai, after my arrival in Peking, for I hoped that he would be able to help me with the tuition at Peking University. But he could give me no assistance, and urged me to take the examination for government clerk. I failed the examination and . . . therefore decided to enter the free Russian Language School established by the Foreign Office, which was looking toward expansion of its activities. Thus, in the summer of 1917, I began my study of the Russian language, all unaware of the Russian Revolution, which was taking place at that very moment, and without any knowledge of the importance of Russian literature. I thought merely that such studies would provide me with an agreeable way of filling my rice-bowl.

"In 1918 I began to read widely in current magazines, and began to make advances in my thinking. As a result I revised my view of life. However, because of my temperament, I did not arrive at true revolutionary thought, but merely at a 'rationalization of pessimism.' Therefore, when a few friends and myself organised the *New Society Magazine,* I felt an affinity for the Tolstoyan Anarchists. Basically, I was of no account politically. Although I took part in political activities for an extremely short time during the period of the May Fourth Movement, I was so deeply engaged in reading the famous writers of Russian literature, thumbing my dictionary all the while, that I had hardly a moment to spare from my studies. And so, completely heedless of the various kinds of political 'isms,' I remained ignorant of modern ideologies.

"In the first stage of the May Fourth Movement, I was elected one of the representatives of the Russian Language School, and since none of my fellow students particularly desired to be 'cadremen,' I gradually became the 'political leader' of the school and organised the students for political activity. It happened that Li Ta-chao, Chang Sung-nien and some others were in the process of organising the Marxist Study Club, and I entered the club because I had become interested in social thought, and particularly in recent Socialist ideals, through reading a few chapters of the Russian work *Woman and Society*. This was about the end of the year 1919.

"In 1920 the character of the student movement changed completely, as a process of dispersion took place. Student associations lacked enthusiasm, and I went back to my reading. And then there came an opportunity to go to Russia. The *Peking Morning Post* wanted to send a correspondent to Moscow, and I was suggested. Since I wished to see the 'New Nation,' and especially because I hoped to use the opportunity to perfect myself in the Russian language, the offer was an occasion for joy. I immediately left for Russia. That was August of 1920.

"For the first several months I lived on black bread and little else, so that my empty stomach growled at me. But afterwards the Russian Civil War came to an end, and conditions improved as the New Economic Policy was put into effect. For several months I employed a private tutor to assist me in my study of the Russian language, Russian history, and the history of Russian literature. At the same time, I sent dispatches to the *Morning Post,* paying especial attention to the news of the Russian Communist Party, and studying its literature. I also looked into the concrete accomplishments of the Russian Revolution. At the time my own sentiments did not go beyond sympathy with the Communist Party, and a measure of understanding. If I did not think of entering the Communist Party, even less did I dream that I would become one of the founders of the Chinese Communist Party.

"But at the time, no one could be found in Moscow, besides myself, who could translate from Russian. I was therefore appointed translator and assistant professor in the Chinese Section of the Far Eastern University, which was established in the autumn of 1921. In connection with my duties, I launched into an intensive study of theoretical Marxist literature. On the other hand, I was drawn away from my studies in pure literature as time went by. After a very short time (the fall of 1922), Ch'en Tu-hsiu arrived in Moscow as the representative of the Chinese Communist Party. (By then I had already entered the Party under Chang T'ai-lei's sponsorship.) I was assigned as Ch'en Tu-hsiu's interpreter, and when he left for China, I put in a request and was permitted to return to Peking with him. When Yü Yu-jen, Teng Chunghsia, and others established Shanghai University, I travelled to Shanghai in the summer of 1923, and was asked to become dean of the faculty and chairman of the Department of Sociology."

Ch'ü modestly omits to say that the stories he filed as correspondent for the *Peking Morning Post* provided the only information available to Chinese on the progress of the Russian revolution. His dispatches were later collected under the titles *A Journey Through the New Russia* and *A History of the New Russian Revolution*. Although they were suppressed by government order, these accounts, circulated surreptitiously, played a large part in shaping the Chinese attitude toward the experiment. Nor were his literary aspirations completely frustrated, though he was always sheepish about them, since they seemed frivolous in an Iron Bolshevik. Ch'ü continued to write short stories, and became widely known for his revolutionary poetry in the peasants' own language. He was respected for his dicta on the function of literature in revolution, for he was primarily a scholar rather than a leader in political action. His elevation to the top Party post was an error which was speedily corrected, since he was secretary-general for only one year, from 1927 to 1928.

During his brief career as mentor-in-chief of the Party, Ch'ü remained true to Moscow's desires, or what he imagined Moscow wanted. Immediately after his return to China, he had been violently opposed to cooperation with the bourgeois Kuomintang, but as soon as it became clear that the Comintern thought collaboration best, he reversed his field, and from

1925 to 1927 there was no more ardent advocate of close relations with the Kuomintang. As an editor of the *New Youth* and editor-in-chief of the Party organ, the *Vanguard*, Ch'ü beat the drum for unification. He sat on the Executive Committee of the Shanghai branch of the Kuomintang, and was in all ways a model Kuomintang member until Moscow issued the order to withdraw.

' In short, it was the Russian connection which accounted for the brief eminence that Ch'ü Ch'iu-pai enjoyed, for he himself was not a practical politician of any stature. Ch'ü's importance diminished as the Chinese Communist Party began to make its own way under the leadership of Mao Tse-tung, who worked out his program first and won Russian approval later.' In 1928, Ch'ü was sent to Russia as delegate to the Comintern, which at the moment was not of paramount importance in the affairs of the Chinese Soviet, tucked away in mountainous Kiangsi Province. Upon his return to China, he was made chairman of the Department of Education in the Kiangsi Soviet. It was an important post, but one of the second rank.

As a writer and elder statesman of the Party, he enjoyed great prestige, but there is significance in his elevation to the status of elder statesman at the age of thirty-three. The leaders of the Party were learning to govern through practical experience, spurning the intellectual pastime of evolving theories to meet situations which might never occur. In such circumstances, Ch'ü was not of great service, and in 1934 he was judged to be of little value to the Party. His chronic tuberculosis was used as the pretext for leaving him in the area about to be abandoned by the Red forces. He was given a title, "Chief of Affairs for the Southeast Area," but there were few affairs to manage. Sporadic raids by partisan bands were the chief Communist activity, and General Ch'en Yi was left behind to manage that part of the business.

In April, 1935, while travelling in Wu-p'ing County, Fukien Province, Ch'ü Ch'iu-pai was arrested by troops of

58

the 14th Battalion of Chiang Kai-shek's Special Service Force. In prison at nearby Ch'ang-ting, Ch'ü could not avoid comparing his fate with Ch'en Tu-hsiu's. The older man had also been seized by the Kuomintang, three years earlier. During Ch'en Tu-hsiu's trial, the Communists alone had demanded the death penalty, for the former secretary-general had committed the unforgivable sin of allying himself with the Left Opposition, whom the Stalinists hated more bitterly than the most brutal of their Rightist opponents.

* * *

As Ch'ü moved closer to Moscow in the years from 1927 to 1932, Ch'en was drifting ever further from orthodoxy. In July of 1928, he refused an invitation to Moscow for retraining. In November of the same year he was formally expelled from the Communist Party of China. By the end of 1928, Ch'en had been converted to the Trotskyite heresy by a group of Chinese students just returned from Moscow, where they had, uncharacteristically, come under Trotsky's influence. With these apostate students, Ch'en Tu-hsiu organized the Proletarian Club, which was to grow through a series of metamorphoses, into the Left Opposition Party, affiliated with the Trotskyite Fourth International.

On December 15, 1929, Ch'en made public a letter addressed to "The Revolutionary Comrades," signed by himself and eighty other prominent non-Stalinist leftists. Violently anti-Moscow in tone, the letter analysed the mistakes of the Chinese Communist movement, affirming the gospel according to Trotsky. Ch'en wrote of his own activities:

"I, who was not clear in perception or decisive in upholding my opinions, sincerely carried out the opportunistic policy of the Comintern, and became an instrument of the narrow Stalinist faction. I could not save the Communist Party of China nor the Revolution by these tactics. For this, I and the other comrades are responsible. But we should objectively and definitely recognise that all opportunistic policies, at present and in the past, come from the Comintern, which must bear the real responsibility."

The immediate task, Ch'en declared, was the reorganization of the Communist Party and the Comintern to restore them to their proper role as agents of liberation rather than enslavement. The Left Opposition put forward a four-point program for the accomplishment of this aim: (1) Trotsky must be restored to his former rank, and a healthy opposition must be created within the Comintern; (2) the writings of the Trotskyites must be circulated as an antidote to the counter-revolutionary tendencies of the present leadership; (3) practical policies must be examined and redefined; and (4) those members of the Party who have been expelled must be restored to membership, and *free discussion* of policy must be permitted within the Party.

The Comintern showed no particular concern with Ch'en's program, nor did it display any haste to reform. But Moscow was dissatisfied with the Chinese Party, which was about to be split by a repetition of the old controversy, with Mao Tse-tung championing rural Soviets and Li Li-san for seizing the cities. In February, 1930, the Comintern once more invited Ch'en to Moscow for an investigation of his expulsion, to be conducted by the Political Secretariat. Ch'en Tu-hsiu declined the opportunity to purchase restoration to leadership at the risk of his principles and his neck.

Ch'en felt that he was needed at home because imperialism, having put off the frock coat for the kimono, had once more set out to dismember China. He denounced both the Kuomintang and the Communists for appeasing Japanese imperialism. After Trotsky's letter affirming Ch'en as his chief Chinese deputy, Ch'en Tu-hsiu was named secretary-general and chairman of the Political Committee of the Left Opposition Party. From that position, he mounted his attack on his most persistent enemy, imperialism, while continuing to exhort his former followers of the Chinese Communist Party to mend their ways. In September, 1931, the Japanese annexation of Manchuria added urgency to his warnings, but the Kuomintang continued to play at diplomacy. However, the Communists, isolated in the south where they would be under no necessity to implement the policy actively, began to advocate more strenuous opposition to the Japanese. They did not yet desire cooperation with the Nationalists to that end, for the Comintern had not yet proclaimed the Popular Front.

The second entente between the Kuomintang and the Communists, when it did come in 1937, came too late to allow of more than a suspicion-haunted rapprochement between Ch'en Tu-hsiu and the Party he had founded. When he was tried by the Kuomintang in 1933, the Communists demanded his head, for he had completely alienated the orthodox left as well as the right. After the organization of the Left Opposition Party, Ch'en had proposed to raise the city workers in a non-Stalinist Communist revolution. He anticipated Mao's method of 1945-1950 in urging that the strength of the peasant Soviets be used to seize power in the cities. Weakening in his antipathy to Moscow, he called for an alliance of all Communists to protect China and the Soviet Union from imperialism. But the Chinese Communists were not interested in such an alliance, for they had received no appropriate directive from the Comintern.

* * *

On October 15, 1932, Ch'en Tu-hsiu was arrested at his residence, 11 Yung-hsing Lane, Yo-chow Road, by police of the Shanghai International Settlement. He had just been discharged from the Hospital of the Shanghai Municipal Council.

Ch'en was indicted by the Shanghai Higher Court for endangering the Republic through his political activities. After being taken to Nanking for trial, he was finally remanded to the Kiangsu Province Superior Court. Chiang Kai-shek had suggested that it would be more "efficient" to try Ch'en before a military tribunal, but pressure of public opinion forced him to submit the case to the cumbersome machinery of the civil law.

While Ch'en Tu-hsiu waited trial, former colleagues like T'ai Chi-t'ao and Ch'en Li-fu came to his cell to urge him to rejoin the Kuomintang, whereupon all his sins would be forgiven. But Ch'en was weary of changing his political affiliation. He refused all offers, and stood before the Superior Court on February 20, 1933, to plead his innocence.

Sinister-looking with his long, drooping mustache, Ch'en stood before the bar to deliver a virtual *apologia pro vita sua*. Reading from a lengthy document, he reviewed his career in the light of the charge that his activities had constituted a threat to the Chinese Republic. Soon he moved to the offensive against his opponents of both the left and the right.

The Chinese government, he thundered, must be based upon a thoroughly representative democratic National Assembly, which neither the Kuomintang nor the Chinese Communist Party desired. The doctrine of "enlightened paternalism" was treason to the Chinese people.

"How can we call ourselves a modern nation?" he declaimed. "How can we call ourselves a modern nation, when the people are deprived of freedom of speech, assembly, and publication, and a National Assembly is not elected by universal suffrage to put an end to the traitorous oppression of militarists and officials? How can we call ourselves a modern nation, when there is no National Assembly to return all power to the people so that they may themselves solve the urgent problems which confront them?"

In England, France, and the United States, he continued, the existence of the Communist Party is taken as a matter of course, because those nations recognize the necessity for an opposition party.

The only threat to the Republic, Ch'en declared, lay in the lack of success which had attended his activities on behalf of democratic Communism. China still needed democratic Communism, and not the brand put forward by the Kremlin.

62

Despite the intervention of Hu Shih, Ts'ai Yüan-p'ei and Madame Sun Yat-sen, Ch'en Tu-hsiu was found guilty. He had made that verdict inevitable by the manner in which he had conducted his defence. The sentence was fifteen years— surprisingly light in view of the gravity of the charge. The Kuomintang could not afford to be too vindictive toward the old revolutionist, whose claws were already clipped.

Ch'en Tu-hsiu died ten years later in Chiang-ching near Chungking. He had been released from prison in 1937 by a general amnesty granted political prisoners at the beginning of the Japanese war. He spent his later days completing a philological treatise based on research begun in prison. During his four years in prison he had studied the characters engraved on bones used in divination by the ancient Chinese, and his last work was entitled *On the Meaning and Classification of Characters.*

*　　*　　*

In prison at Ch'ang-ting, waiting for the decision of the miltary authorities, Ch'ü Ch'iu-pai also reverted to a traditional occupation of Chinese scholars. A reporter named Li was permitted to interview him on June 4, 1935.

Correspondent Li entered the cell to find a man of medium height, clad in a pair of blue shorts, bent over a table engraving stone seals. When he turned to greet the reporter, Ch'ü presented a smooth face topped by hair worn *en brosse* over a broad, low forehead. He looked fat, but correspondent Li saw that his face was swollen and his eye-balls dark-yellow through their black-rimmed glasses. Ch'ü had the aspect of "a man who rests after carrying a hundredweight burden over a long trail."

"Sir, can you engrave seals?" Li asked.

"I've had nothing else to do here, so I've taken it up again. When I was in middle school, I had a teacher of Chinese culture who tutored me in the art, but this is the first time in years I've had a chance to practice."

"How have you been feeling since your imprisonment?"

"Chiefly, I've been glad to rest from political activity. When I was captured, I was exhausted in both body and mind. For years I've been subject to attacks during which I vomited blood, and there were times when I went blind for nearly a week. . . . But recently I've been feeling better."

"Sir, many reports have been circulated about your personal history. I wonder if it would be possible to check them against your own account?"

"I call Wu-chin [an alternate name for Ch'ang-chou] in Kiangsu Province my home. By ordinary reckoning I'm thirty-eight years old, but by Western reckoning only thirty-six. My family were scholars for generations. They served as officials in the 300-year period from the fall of the Ming dynasty to the fall of the Ch'ing dynasty. One was promoted to the post of provincial treasurer and served for a time as a provincial governor in the Kuang Hsü period [1875-1908]. My uncles were well thought of in Hsiao-shan and Ch'ang-shan Counties in Kiangsu Province, but my father, in the aristocratic manner, became an opium smoker and did not work. After the Revolution of 1911, my grandfather and uncles died one by one and our family finances were completely disrupted. My father found that he could barely provide for himself alone, and left the family to fend for itself. My mother was left with the responsibility of caring for me and my four younger brothers and sisters. At the time I was studying at Ch'ang-chou Middle School, while my mother was being borne down by poverty and my brothers and sisters were being strangled by misery. . . ."

The questioning took Ch'ü Ch'iu-pai through the course of his life up to the day of his arrest, pausing for a moment at the case of Ch'en Tu-hsiu.

The question: "What relation, if any, did the arrest of Ch'en Tu-hsiu have with the Communist Party?"

The answer: "Ch'en Tu-hsiu had been cut off from any relation with the Party for some time before his arrest. After

64

General and Madame Chu Teh. They were married in 1929 when she was seventeen and he forty-three.

General Lin Piao who holds almost all power in the Central China Administrative Area. His Fourth Field Army attacked in Korea.

Vice-commander of the "People's Liberation Army" P'eng Te-huai. P'eng also serves as chairman of the Northwest Administrative and Military Areas.

TRIANGLE

General Ho Lung, who "emerged from banditry" to command the Red Army's Second Area Army. The illiterate general is now in semi-retirement as chief of staff of the Southwest Military Area under Liu Po-ch'eng.

TRIANGLE

his name was stricken from the Party roster, he engaged in independent activities. His arrest was therefore not reported as a matter of intra-Party significance."

On June 17, thirteen days after this interview, a telegram from Nanking ordered Ch'ü's execution.

He made a good death.

At eight on the morning of the eighteenth of June, Captain Liao of the Special Service Detachment went to Ch'ü Ch'iu-pai's cell to lead him to the execution ground in Sun Yat-sen Park. There he was photographed, murmuring, if newspaper accounts are to be believed, "Death is the greatest rest given to man!"

Ch'ü Ch'iu-pai's last request was granted by Captain Liao. He wished to return to his cell to finish a poem he had conceived during the night. That poem, preserved for us, is quite conventional. Written in classical style, it bespeaks barren tranquility unmixed with revolutionary ardor.

After finishing his poem, Ch'ü was taken to Sun Yat-sen Park, and given a cup of wine in a pavilion. He sang "The Internationale" in Russian and "The Red Army Song," while being conducted to a round, grassy plot nearby. He sat there with an easy manner until just before the order to fire. Then —crying "Sacrifice in the cause of the Chinese Revolution is the greatest honor given to a man!"—he died.

Ch'ü thus composed his own epitaph, but Ch'en Tu-hsiu, eight years later, uttered no apt last words. It might not be improper to select a passage from his writings to serve at his epitaph here.

In 1937 he wrote: "Man has historically been a rational being who could find the path to his own salvation. The present darkness is but a short phase in the progress of mankind. As long as there are men who can see beyond the present chaos, there is hope."

3. TECHNICIANS, GENERALS, AND BANDITS

On March 19, 1947, Yenan, the cave city which had been the capital of Red China for ten years, fell to the Nationalist troops of General Hu Tsung-nan. Mao Tse-tung and his fellow Communist leaders went to earth in the yellow Shensi mountains. In Nanking, Kuomintang leaders congratulated each other; in their book of strategy the capture of the Red capital marked the beginning of the final stage of their twenty-year war of annihilation against the Communists. Superstitious apprehensions which had nagged at the Nationalist leaders were set at rest. Shensi Province, lying in the four-hundred-mile bend of the Yellow River, was the traditional jumping-off spot for China's conquerors. With Mao and his henchmen wandering in the hills, the Red threat seemed to have been laid at last. The Chinese Communist revolution had been deprived of its strategic base, and only Manchuria remained unpacified.

The fugitive Mao disagreed. The fall of Yenan was an incident in his eyes. Since the city had served its purpose, it might be abandoned for the moment. While the Kuomintang armies exhausted themselves striving to consolidate their gains in the Northwest, an order went out from the secret headquarters of the "People's Liberation Army." Mao swung the mace of Communist military power against the Nationalist armies.

The spikes on the mace's head were the Manchurian Army

of General Lin Piao, the Shantung Army of General Liu Po-ch'eng, and the Central Army under Nieh Jung-chen. The head itself was the headquarters of Commander-in-Chief Chu Teh and Deputy Commander P'eng Te-huai, strengthened by the tactical cunning of Chief of Staff Yeh Chien-ying, and shielded by the garrison troops of aging General Ho Lung. In May, 1947, the first spike bit home as the forces of Liu Po-ch'eng crossed the Yellow River in Shantung Province. Soon afterwards the other prongs began to tear at Chiang's armies. A year later, Central Government troops were pulling back in a general retreat, and two years after the crossing of the Yellow River, Nanking was taken by the People's Liberation Army.

Mao's mace had been a long time at the forge. From the time it became clear that power could not be gained by political weapons alone, the chief concern of the Chinese Communist Party had been the creation of a powerful armed force. The costly Long March was forced by the necessity of preserving the core of the Red Army and finding an adequate territorial base for its expansion. After the arrival in Shensi Province in October, 1935, the best shoes, horses, and food went to the Red Army, and its leaders sat high in Party councils. The war with Japan tempered the weapon, and the civil war from 1947 to 1950 proved its fitness for its task—the conquest of China for Communism. Today the prestige of Commander-in-Chief Chu Teh is second only to Mao Tse-tung's, and Chu is held in greater affection by the rank and file, for the grandfatherly general is a more appealing figure than the Olympian political chief.

The "Chinese People's Liberation Army" is the youngest major military force in the world. Chu hammered the weapon while Mao worked the bellows. The forging began in the summer of 1927 when the Communist cause was at its lowest ebb. Before that time, the Communist line, laid down by the Comintern from Moscow, had been cooperation with the national bourgeois revolution of the Kuomintang, until the proper time came "to toss them aside like a squeezed lemon."

The Nationalists squeezed first. Chiang Kai-shek struck in Canton and Shanghai to destroy Communist strong points, and later moved to establish a rightist government in Nanking and split the Communists from their liberal allies in Hankow. By the end of July, 1927, the Communists found themselves adrift on a sinking raft. Acting on the orders of the Comintern, they had been gulled, out-maneuvered, and finally set adrift. ›

Hysterical in failure, the Chinese Communist Party set a course which should, in logic, have brought them to destruction, but instead proved their salvation. Instead of drawing off to tend their wounds and recruit fresh forces, they cried defiance to the military might of Chiang Kai-shek. If it had not been for the ultimate success of Communist arms in China, this foolhardy gesture would have served Communist schools in Moscow as a horrible example for aspiring Asian leaders. But today the anniversary of the Nanchang Rising is a sacred day, for it marks the birth of the Chinese Red Army.

*　　*　　*

Nanchang lies in northern Kiangsi Province about 400 miles southwest of Shanghai. In July, 1927, the city was in the jurisdiction of Chang Fa-k'uei, the liberal Kuomintang general who commanded the "Ironsides" Fourth Army. General Chang and the main body of the Fourth Army were ordered to attack Nanking in mid-July, leaving some fifteen thousand troops to occupy the Nanchang area. Most of them were under the orders of garrison commander Yeh T'ing, a Communist who was commanding general of the 24th Division. The 24th was peculiarly Yeh's own division—and the Party's. Its core was the former Independent Brigade of the Fourth Army, which had been organized in 1925 under Communist supervision. All officers of the rank of captain and above were Party members, who had conducted a program of intensive indoctrination among the soldiers they commanded.

The Independent 2nd Division of the Szechwan National Reconstruction Army, commanded by General Ho Lung, was also at Yeh T'ing's disposal. Military units within the city were under the orders of Chu Teh, a Party member, who had been made commandant of the Nanchang Branch of the Whampoa Military Academy and chief of the city's Bureau of Public Safety in January, 1927.

During the night of July 31, Yeh T'ing raised the red flag over Nanchang. On August 1, a rump of the Communist Party, just expelled from the Hankow Government, proclaimed an independent regime, appointing Yeh T'ing commander-in-chief of the Ninth Revolutionary Army, with Chu Teh and Ho Lung as his deputies. All three generals were close to the age of forty, but their maturity was leavened by the ardor of Chief of Staff Liu Po-ch'eng, who was, quite literally, a battle-scarred veteran at the age of twenty-one. In the lower ranks, Lin Piao, a member of the Communist Youth League, retained command of the battalion which had deserted Chiang's army under his leadership.

The first Chinese Communist regime was short-lived. The Reds just had time to confiscate bank deposits and levy a "loan" on the propertied classes before they withdrew from the city. On the fifth, troops of the Hankow Government approached in force, and on August 6, 1927 the Ninth Army marched out of Nanchang, headed south, where they hoped to establish a Red stronghold.

Yeh T'ing, marching toward Canton City through a web of opposing armies which grew thicker every day, had no time to woo popular support. He and Chu Teh, who directed the right wing, were well-trained soldiers, but unskilled amateurs in political organization. Ho Lung, in command of the left wing, had risen to military rank from the chieftainship of a bandit array in western Hunan. The peasants along the line of march were sympathetic to the professed aims of the Ninth Army, but there could be no popular rising in the absence of concrete measures on behalf of the people. Later Communist commentators have castigated the Ninth Army for its political errors. The first major mistake was the failure to effect land reform, the second was the assumption that the army's "proletarian" character gave it license for indiscriminate plunder. In some areas the brutality of the soldiers repelled the very peasants whose support they sought.

Under constant attack by the Fourth Army of Chang Fa-k'uei and other Kuomintang forces, the Communist army dwindled. In the middle of September, the left wing under General Ho Lung occupied the port of Swatow, about 350 miles southeast of Nanchang. A Revolutionary Committee attempted to channel the revolutionary discontent displayed by the peasants of Canton Province. The new regime formally declared war on the anti-Communist regimes at Nanking and Hankow, and enacted measures providing for the redistribution of the land. Although Ho Lung was driven from Swatow in October by the combined threat of foreign war vessels from the east and Kuomintang armies from the west, he left his mark on the area. In November, a peasant revolt established the first Chinese Soviet Area in the belt of land below Swatow, lying between the cities of Hai-feng (the Riches of the Sea) and Lu-feng (the Riches of the Earth). This First Soviet Area held out until March, 1928, but Ho Lung's army was destroyed by the attacks of the Kuomintang in November, and he fled to Hong Kong.

To the south, Yeh T'ing seemed to be having better luck. On the tenth of December revolt broke out in the metropolis of Canton under the leadership of Chang T'ai-lei. General Yeh, arriving with the remnants of his troops, was appointed commander-in-chief of the revolutionary armies. Once more, however, the people failed to back the Party. Out of the 150,000 workers who had been organized under the Party in 1925, only 10,000 rose to the tocsin. Within three days, the Canton Commune was driven from the city by Chang Fa-k'uei. Yeh T'ing, his army annihilated by four months of continuous fighting, fled the country. He was to return ten years later to command the Communist New Fourth Army in the war against Japan, be imprisoned in 1941 by the Kuomintang, and die in an airplane crash in 1945, just after his release.

Of the fifteen thousand who had set out from Nanchang, there remained only a battered troop of a thousand soldiers under Chu Teh. When they joined Mao Tse-tung's peasant battalion in the sharp mountain range called Chingkangshan, the thousand became the cadre of the Workers' and Peasants' Red Army. P'eng Te-huai, Lin Piao, and Liu Po-ch'eng became Chu Teh's lieutenants. Today these men are the chief generals of the six-million-man Liberation Army, and Chu Teh is commander-in-chief.

*   *   *

Chu Teh was a career officer in the war-lord service until he turned off the highroad of advancement to follow the shrub-tangled path of idealism—and found himself general of a guerrilla band. Professional diligence led him to Berlin to study military science and he joined the Communist Party there. Chu has remained the professional soldier, content to execute the orders of Mao Tse-tung and those Party organs which take the political decisions.

The commander-in-chief was born in 1886 in Yi-lung, the seat of an isolated county in the highlands of northern Szechwan. Yi-lung would lie just thirty-eight miles west of a line drawn on the map from Chungking to Yenan to show the political axis of China during the War. Yenan is over 530 miles north of Chungking; Chu Teh's birthplace is 135 miles north of the wartime Nationalist capital and 410 miles south of the Red stronghold.

When Chu Teh was born, emperors ruled in both China and Russia. The ideological clash of the time was quite simple; passive Orientalism quivered under the thrusts of active Westernism. But the sleepy dragon was beginning to sharpen his claws as China's leaders studied military strength. After China's defeat by the Japanese in 1895, the provincial gentry, too, became aware of the necessity for armed defense of Chinese civilization.

Young Chu Teh was just beginning to acquire the rudiments of that culture. Though his well-to-do home was broken up by his father's death when the boy was ten, he was taken in by his father's younger brother. Chu Teh went to live with his uncle and study the classics under his direction. There must have been some idea of an official career for the boy; he would not have been the first of his family to wear the mandarin's hat.

Official rank was to be reached by climbing a series of sharply hewn steps. First came the acquisition of a thorough knowledge of the Four Books and the Five Classics, the foundation stones of the Confucian ideology. Young Chu Teh memorized and recited them under his uncle's tutelage, and later studied the commentaries, which had been reared on the classics in the two thousand years following their composition. The pace was leisurely, and the young scholar helped work the family farm when not at his books. As he grew older, he went at one time to a school run by a retired official in the city of Yi-lung, to sit and chant the classics in unison with the other students, rocking back and forth as he read. He would soon be prepared to take the first civil service examination. Success would be followed by appointment to a minor administrative post—and another secure career in the bureaucracy would have been begun.

But away from the rural calm of Szechwan Province, where affairs were ordered much as they had been under the Ming dynasty three hundred years earlier, the world was moving in on China. She needed technical skills in order to resist the incursions of the West, but the civil service examinations drained her intellectual vigor into the study of the classics. In January, 1906, the Court determined to end this waste by abolishing the examination system. Chu Teh had spent the first twenty years of his life acquiring a stock of knowledge abruptly rendered useless by the decree. It was obvious that scholarship was no longer the talisman that would win him advancement and there seemed to be no other way. Bewildered, Chu Teh retired to the family farm to brood for a time on his frustrated ambition.

But learning might still serve as an Open Sesame—if not classical studies, then *modern* education, which meant Western-style education. Shun-ching County had established an upper-primary school—roughly equivalent to an American junior high school—in the county seat thirty-eight miles southwest of Chu's home. Early in 1907, the young scholar entered that school to begin his own Westernization. His vigorous, empirical mind had been sharpened by the discipline of classical studies, but had not been rendered brittle by excessive immersion in Confucian texts. He found little difficulty in mastering all the "Western Learning" the local school could offer.

But in middle school Chu Teh discovered that he was not meant to be an intellectual. He enjoyed acquiring solid knowledge well enough, but found no pleasure in juggling abstractions. And his thickset, hardy body required employment; he could not sit for hours with his heavy hands wrapped around a book. Chu left middle school to go to Chengtu, a medieval walled town which was the intellectual center of southwestern China. It was not the ancient university which drew him, but the Chengtu Institute of Physical Training where he might acquire a skill suited to his tastes. After graduation from a short course, he returned to Yi-lung to become director of physical training in the county primary school.

The rural dignity of that occupation soon palled. It was not his intention to grow old teaching little boys to flex their muscles. New opportunities were not lacking, for even remote Szechwan was beginning to quiver as the Manchu dynasty cracked. When dynasties fell, the soldier came into his glory, for at such times a career in arms might lead to the steps of the Throne. Early in 1909, Chu Teh left home for Yünnanfu (the present city of Kunming) to enter the newly established Yünnan Military Institute. His admission was facilitated by the exercise of the small influence his family could bring to bear.

Chu's previous encounter with Western-style learning had been short, and even his instructors were only half-aware of the meaning of the new subjects they taught so inadequately. At Yünnan Military Institute the instructors were deadly serious and fully cognizant of the immediate utility of military training. Chu Teh, somewhat older than his classmates, made an excellent record, for he had finally found the career opened by his talents. Upon graduation in the spring of 1911, he was given command of a company in the modern army of Ts'ai Ao, the chief military figure of Yünnan Province.

The revolutionary spirit was fashionable. Both Chu and his general joined Sun Yat-sen's T'ung-meng Hui. When the revolution reached Yünnan in the fall of 1911, Ts'ai Ao's Western-style army engaged the forces of Chao Erh-feng, a loyalist general, and defeated them with little effort. Ts'ai Ao became *Tu-chün,* military governor of the province, while Chu Teh was rewarded by being appointed commander of the corps of cadets at Yünnan Military Institute.

This, Chu felt, was more like it. In three years he had come a long way—from teaching physical training to an independent command at the wellspring of one of China's best armies. But if the revolution was over, might not the path of promotion become choked off?

He need not have worried. Within a year, bandit trouble on the border between Yünnan and French Indo-China brought him a new command. As a battalion commander detailed to garrison and border patrol duty near Tonkin, Chu Teh learned the rudiments of guerrilla warfare in broken country, which he was to apply so successfully later on. His integrity and professional devotion—both rare in those days of grab-and-run soldiering—were beginning to win him reputation outside Yünnan Province. By the end of 1915, Chu was

74

in command of a regiment, and fresh disorder promised further advancement shortly.

In the first months of the year 1916, Yüan Shih-k'ai's dynastic intrigues came to crisis. Yünnan was the first province to raise the banner of resistance to his usurpation. Colonel Chu Teh fought with the armies of the resistance under Ts'ai Ao against the forces of the Dictator. This time the battle was harder, for Yüan's armies were as "modern" as Ts'ai's. They put up a stronger fight than the *opéra bouffe* Imperial forces had offered, but the decision was clear by the beginning of June. Yüan Shih-k'ai died of uremic poisoning at the historically appropriate moment on June 6, 1916, after his power had been broken.

Disorder again brought rewards to Chu Teh. A brigadier at thirty-three, he was given the 13th Mixed Brigade of the Szechwan 7th Division in 1919. His new command meant greater power for Chu Teh than is suggested by the name, for the 13th was an independent brigade of nearly ten thousand men, organized like a combat team of World War II. He commanded one of the most powerful striking forces in western China, because his brigade was in fact a small army with its own artillery and cavalry.

After the death of Yüan Shih-k'ai, no Chinese leader was strong enough to make a sustained bid for power over the entire nation. Yüan's former lieutenants still commanded his unbroken armies in the North, but their hold was disputed by the forces of "Christian General" Feng Yü-hsiang in the Northwest, and the Manchurian war-lord Chang Tso-lin in the Northeast. In the South, rival war-lords ruled, each impelled by the desire to enlarge his own glory and accumulate wealth. Alliances were made and broken as expediency suggested.

Chu Teh, still a young man, swam agilely through the seas of greed and brutality. He was a minor power in the land, distinguished from his fellow officers only by a keen interest in the theoretical aspects of warfare and a streak of integrity which held him back from wanton brutality and excessive exploitation. But his scruples were not so strong as to interfere with his advancement. Chu Teh grew in power and wealth, always ready to change sides when it was advantageous. He is reported to have maintained a splendid establishment, complete with retainers, concubines, motorcars, and the other appurtenances of position so gratifying to the barbaric pretensions of his fellow war-lords. Some writers have reported that Chu had a strong taste for opium about this time, and, indeed, there is no reason to believe that he violated war-lord social standards by total abstention from the drug. But it is unlikely that he was an addict, for the fire of ambition burned too hot to permit him to relax into opium-induced euphoria.

In 1920, Chu Teh made a good stroke. He returned to Yünnan to ally himself with Ku Pin-chen, the enemy of the military governor T'ang Chi-yao. The alliance prospered, for T'ang was driven out and Ku set in his place. In 1921, Chu Teh was rewarded with the profitable post of commissioner of police for Yünnan Province. With his fortunes made, Chu Teh moved his retainers, his concubines, and his automobiles to a mansion overlooking the city of Kunming, and settled down to enjoy affluent respectability. He had become a pillar of the community.

But his fortunes were broken as they had been made. T'ang Chi-yao, after rallying his forces outside the province, struck to eject his enemies as they had ejected him. Complacent Chu Teh was caught flat-footed. He fled from Kunming at the head of a bare company of his garrison troops, marching through the mountains of what is now called Hsikang Province. The name, which means Western Prosperity, may some day be justified by development of mineral resources, which are, as yet, untapped. But in 1922 the province was rich only in unpathed mountains and racing rivers.

The 600-mile journey was a one-act rehearsal for the Long March when Chu Teh would again pass through the same territory on foot. But this first time his course led north and east to Chungking, where he had friends. The little band of displaced militarists arrived in the Szechwan metropolis to claim refuge of Military Governor Liu Hsiang and General Yang Shen, who ruled the city. They were glad to have Chu Teh, for he had proved that he could be useful. Yang offered him a division, but the terms were not right, and Chu soon left Chungking to follow the Yangtze River downstream toward Shanghai.

He had been badly shaken by his expulsion from Yünnan; he who had defeated so many, was for the first time defeated. Because the road of ambition had led so surely to rewards before 1922, the first detour was especially painful to his self-esteem. Chu was read a lesson in the evanescence of personal power, and he quickly grasped the moral: no matter how high he rose, he might be destroyed in an instant. During the period of leisurely eminence at Kunming, Chu Teh had not thought deeply, for he was living the good life. But when he was stripped by T'ang Chi-yao's stroke, he considered his past course critically. Pursuit of his own star had led to a height from which he was hurled in an instant. He knew that he could follow the road of ambition again, to arrive, perhaps, at the edge of the precipice once more. And there might come a time when he could not clamber out. Pure self-advantage was a false lodestar.

In 1923, Chu Teh joined Chu P'ei-te, a Yünnan general who was in the service of the Canton government of Dr. Sun Yat-sen. For the first time in his life, idealism played a greater part than personal advantage in a major decision. His past membership in the T'ung-meng Hui had been dictated at least as much by expediency as by conviction, for the Man-chu dynasty was obviously toppling when he enrolled, and the republicans were the coming men. But in 1923, when Chu Teh affirmed his adherence to the Kuomintang, Sun's prospects were not bright. The Kuomintang was becoming a more efficient instrument for the conquest of power as a result of its reorganization on the Russian Communist model, but Sun's territorial holdings were small and his military establishment, though growing, feeble compared to the armies that opposed him. The feature which recommended the Kuomintang to Chu Teh was the one which made for its later victory. Unlike most factions in the Chinese power complex, Dr. Sun's group advocated a specific program for the betterment of the Chinese people. Other groups sought only their own advantage.

Chu's flight from Yünnan had brought him, for the first time, out of the provincial smugness of China's western marches into the complex life of her coastal cities. In Canton and Shanghai he mingled with gifted young men who were working to gain for the Chinese people some of the fruits of their own labor by deposing the war-lords. Chief among them were Wang Ching-wei and Chiang Kai-shek, who were later to betray Dr. Sun's Three Principles—Wang the Principle of Nationalism by collaborating with the Japanese, and Chiang the Principles of Democracy and the People's Livelihood by establishing a rapacious dictatorship. On the fringes of the Kuomintang, the Communists, obedient to the fiat of the Comintern, were cooperating with Sun's bourgeois revolution.

Many saw potentialities in Chu Teh, the reformed militarist, but all were skeptical as to the sincerity of his convictions and his professional competence. After an extended visit to Peking—his first—Chu Teh returned to Shanghai determined to improve his professional standing and acquire political sophistication through a period of study abroad. He was quite free to do as he pleased, for his concubines had been abandoned in Kunming, and money was no problem after ten years of successful war-lordism.

At the beginning of the year 1924, Chu took ship in Shanghai for Germany, which was still pre-eminent in military science. He settled in Berlin, the heart-city of Prussian militarism, to study the German language before beginning his technical studies. Chu, an older man, and already a figure of the second rank in Chinese military and political life, attracted a circle of young compatriots. He had been away from his books for some time, and was a slow learner and a bad linguist. He welcomed the companionship and assistance of the Chinese students in Berlin, finding support for his sprouting political convictions in their ardor.

The Berlin branch of the Kuomintang grew up around him in that manner, and his young friends, in turn, drew him into the activities of the Berlin cell of the French branch of the Chinese Communist Party.

In Communism, Chu Teh, weary of striving solely for personal advantage, found a cause only a little more dogmatic than Sun Yat-sen's Three Principles. It was the moderate period of Chinese Communism, when the aims of the bourgeois revolution of the Kuomintang and those of the Communists were officially declared to be capable of integration. The program of the Communists appeared to be an extension in more concrete form of the platform of the Nationalists. Chu Teh joined the Party in 1925, for there was then no contradiction in belonging to both the Kuomintang and the Communist Party.

Encouraged by his new comrades, Chu broadened his interests. He studied sociology at the University of Göttingen, hallowed by the memory of another revolutionist, the poet Heine. Heine had left Göttingen in bitterness after getting off a jibe which has forever smirched the fame of the women of that quiet community. The poet wrote that he had been forced to give up the project of composing an illustrated treatise on feet, because he was unable to find a sheet large enough to take the impression of the right foot of any of the Göttingen ladies, although he had managed to secure paper large enough for an elephant's foot.

Chu Teh, ninety years later, was not concerned with the women of Göttingen or their feet. After enjoying the services of skilled concubines, he was not tempted by the staid dames of the German town. His surplus energy went into politics, the real reason for his sojourn in Göttingen. He joined the staff of the *Political Weekly (Cheng-chih Chou-pao)*, published by a group of Chinese students at the university.

But studies and writing did not satisfy his need for action. In June, 1925, Chu Teh used the classic safety-valve of the expatriate revolutionist—the public demonstration. The May Thirtieth Incident, in which British troops fired on a crowd of Chinese demonstrators in Shanghai, had roused high indignation among overseas students. Their patriotic anger was given an ideological fillip by the desire to protest the assassination of a certain radical in Bulgaria a few weeks earlier. In June, a noisy conference of Communists assembled in Berlin to "cry out for aid to the mother country."

Chu Teh, conspicuous among the demonstrators because of his age, was picked up by the German police. Although he was soon released, he was to be arrested at least once and possibly twice again. Annoyed by police interference—in the past he had arrested others—Chu Teh decided that it was time to go home. He left Germany, travelling by the Trans-Siberian Railroad to North China. (One Communist source states that Chu crossed the Atlantic to New York and sailed again from San Francisco to China, for Manchuria and North China were not congenial places for a lone Communist general in late 1925. Nor is it likely that he made a long stop in Moscow to study at the Red Army Academy, as has also been reported.)

At the beginning of 1926, Chu Teh reported to the Communist Party in China to receive orders sending him to Szechwan Province. In Chungking he reminded General Yang Shen of his earlier offer of a division, and found Yang glad to have the services of the refurbished Chu Teh with the gloss of foreign study bright on his reputation. He was given a division in what was to become the Twentieth Army of the Nationalist Revolutionary Army. Although he guarded the secret of his membership in the Communist Party, Chu began the political indoctrination of the men under his command. When the Northern Expedition started, Chu joined forces with Chu P'ei-te, his former chief and classmate at Yünnan Military Institute. In January, 1927, he was appointed director of the Bureau of Public Safety and commandant of the Nanchang Branch of the Whampoa Military Academy. Few knew that the general who was rising rapidly in the Kuomintang military hierarchy was a Communist.

At Nanchang on August 1, Chu Teh revealed himself as a Communist by rejecting Chu P'ei-te's order to suppress the rebellion. But even when he stood forth as an avowed Red, Chu's reputation was solid enough to win him offers from non-Communist generals more interested in building up their forces than in ideological feuds. After the suppression of the Swatow Commune, Chu Teh went to earth in Lo-ch'ang County, 140 miles north of Canton City on the border between the provinces of Canton and Hunan. He joined the army of Fan Shih-sheng with his ragged, under-gunned troop —not quite a thousand in number, even including walking wounded. Posted to garrison duty in the town of Shih-p'ing as a regimental commander, Chu entered upon the period of his life described by Communist writers as "ten years of preparation; ten years of cultivation." With the instinct of a military man, he initiated the policy to which Party thinkers were later to give their blessing. Chu Teh began to build an army.

During the winter of 1927-28, Chu extended the area under his control to include counties in Hunan to the north, and later in Kiangsi to the northeast. He broke away from General Fan Shih-sheng to pursue his own aim—the creation of the first solid Red military base in China. In the mountains of Hunan and Kiangsi, Chu was left to shape the Workers' and Peasants' Red Army undisturbed. His surest protection was not the impenetrability of the highlands, but the complaisance of the inhabitants. Chu was developing the tactics which were to bring victory to Communist arms. Instead of striving to create an armed force independent of the people, he determined to knit the two into one force. As early as 1928, he had mastered the lesson Chiang Kai-shek could never learn. Chu Teh knew that a political army could not be effective without the people's support. In order to consolidate his base he cultivated the goodwill of the peasants.

Chu's later writings on guerrilla strategy are used as handbooks by the commanders of Asian Communist armies, for they are as applicable to Korea—or Indo-China—as to China. Their refrain is the necessity of binding the people to the army with political ties. Their text is the experience of the years from 1928 to 1934, which Chu passed in guerrilla war in the Kiangsi-Hunan mountains.

Although his previous experience and education had been in conventional warfare, Chu Teh had two sources of information to draw on when he took to the hills. Back in 1913, he had been on the other side of the fence in a guerrilla fight, striving to suppress the semi-bandit troops which operated among the peasants of southern Yünnan along the border of Indo-China Although he had first come to prominence because of his success in countering the activities of those guerrilla bands, he had been unable to put them down completely. The rebels, fighting on home ground, knew the terrain as Chu's regulars never could, and customarily evaded pursuit by assuming the garments and occupations of farmers. That campaign was his practical guide, but his first textbook on large-scale partisan warfare was a short work on the tactics employed by General George Washington in the Revolutionary War. Washington's example was particularly apt, because Chu Teh, too, was fighting with inferior forces for the establishment of a new form of government against an unenthusiastic enemy. Since Washington and his Continentals had modeled their tactics on those of the American Indians, presumably of Asian origin, the lesson had come full circle.

In May, 1928, Chu Teh joined his Workers' and Peasants' Army with a guerrilla troop of insurgent farmers under the leadership of Mao Tse-tung. On Chingkangshan, a peak in the range dividing Hunan from Kiangsi, was formed the Chu-Mao combination that was to lead the Communists to final victory. The two men complemented each other so well that for several years Chu-Mao was thought to be one man. Chu was the military expert, Mao the political savant. Each appreciated the crucial nature of the other's work, but each felt complete confidence in the other, even in the days when failure meant death. On October 7, 1931, the First Congress of Soviet Representatives, meeting in the town of Jui-chin, formalized their positions by appointing Chu commander-in-chief of the New Fourth Army and Mao chairman of the Soviet Government.

*   *   *

Even Chu Teh's personal life was "proletarianized," as the Chinese has it. He had first married in 1912, shortly after graduation from Yünnan Military Institute, but the death of his first wife had left him free again. In 1929, he married K'ang K'o-ch'ing, who had joined the army among a band of rebels fleeing from Wan-an County in Kiangsi. She was a proper mate for a revolutionary leader.

Born in Kiangsi in 1912, the daughter of a river fisherman, K'o-ch'ing was brought up in the home of her first husband in accordance with the Chinese practice of adopting a prospective daughter-in-law whose parents were too poor to give her a proper up-bringing. When her father-in-law was elected chairman of the local farmers' cooperative, an organization with political as well as economic functions, K'o-ch'ing entered the women's auxiliary and became a leader of the Young Vanguards. In 1928, at the age of sixteen, she fled from her adopted home to join Chu's army. The tall, vigorous girl drew the eye of the commander-in-chief, perhaps because she was so different from the women he had known. Her feet were not bound and her hands had grown big at work. In 1929, when Chu was forty-three and she was seventeen, they were married.

83

"From that time onward," says the Communist biographer, "they have always been together. In the twenty years that have passed since then, the time they have spent apart would not total a full year." The success of their marriage offers further evidence that the best bond between man and wife is a common interest, for K'o-ch'ing, too, has been active in military affairs. She became principal of a children's school immediately after her marriage, but soon found her real work, assuming direction of the Special Service Unit attached to Red Army Headquarters. Since that time K'o-ch'ing has been part of the army. Her ambition was to organize a women's unit to fight in the frontlines under her command, but Chu Teh never permitted it. Perhaps he valued her presence more than her valor. Though K'ang K'o-ch'ing has been dubbed the "Female Commander," she has never been allowed to prove the title by commanding a regular unit as did Ho Lung's sister Ho Ying. For a very short time in 1930, K'o-ch'ing did lead a regiment of women volunteers, but she was soon recalled to attend a six-months course at the Red Army Academy.

Even as Chu Teh's wife, K'o-ch'ing was denied the accolade of Party membership until she had proved herself. It was not until after completion of the course at the Red Army Academy that she was allowed to enroll as a full Party member in 1931. In 1934 occurred one of the short periods of separation from her husband. K'o-ch'ing was surprised by a Kuomintang attack while propagandizing in her home county, but managed to stand off the Nationalists with only 300 men. For that exploit she was given the nickname "Female Commander." Soon afterwards she made the Long March by Chu's side, and was ordered to attend the Party School and Resistance College in Shensi. From that time to the present she has been attached to Red Army Headquarters. Most recently, she was the only woman member of the delegation sent by the Headquarters of the Liberation Army to the People's Political Conference of September, 1949.

The Red commander-in-chief and his bride were an impressive pair on the dusty streets of Jui-chin, the mountain town that was the capital of the Kiangsi Soviet Area in 1932. Chu Teh seemed stocky, though he was slightly over middle height. His broad face was burnt red-brown by the mountain sun, and his large eyes seemed small straddling his wide, flat nose, which had been badly set after a youthful fracture. Chu moved slowly, as if husbanding his energy for the recurrent emergencies of guerrilla life. When he relaxed, his heavy hands, with their calloused palms and corded tendons, hung limp at the ends of his broad arms.

K'o-ch'ing was dressed like her husband and his soldiers. She wore a tightly buttoned blue-cotton tunic girdled by a heavy leather belt, and trousers of the same fabric. Her hair was tucked into her peaked cap, and she seemed Chu Teh's aide strolling through the streets by his side, for she was almost as tall as he. But there was a delicacy in the moulding of the big-boned figure which would have been out of place in a boy, and the breadth of the hips under the thigh-length jacket helped destroy the illusion. She wore the expression of a sulky youth, appearing again to be a self-confident middle-school student whom Chu had just reprimanded. The heavy mouth, with its long upper-lip, was drawn tight under the small round nose, and the eyes were slitted against the glare. But when she smiled she looked older and softer.

*　　　*　　　*

In 1932, another figure came to stand by Chu Teh's side as his chief of staff. Young Liu Po-ch'eng, his abilities refined by three years at the Red Army Academy in Moscow, was given the same post he had held during the Nanchang Rising. Liu, a fellow Szechwanese, was an old Bolshevik at the age of twenty-six. He could count his battles by his scars, for he had been wounded in almost every engagement he fought. Later he was to lose an eye and gain the nickname Liu

Tu-yen, Dead-eye Liu. But the periodic blood-letting seems to have fed, rather than sapped his vigor. He not only led the vanguard during the Long March, but commanded the first Communist army to counterattack in China proper in 1947.

Liu is also distinguished as the first Chinese Communist general to undergo a thorough course of training in Moscow. It was his first formal military education, though he had been a fighter since leaving the home of his musician father in early youth. After drifting from leader to leader, Liu Po-ch'eng entered the Communist Party in 1926, and was ordered to join the Twentieth National Revolutionary Army of Yang Shen in Szechwan. Chu Teh was a division commander under Yang at the time. Liu was soon transferred by the Kuomintang to western Hupei Province as a party representative, and was subsequently assigned additional duties as a special representative of the Communist Party in the same area. Since the Kuomintang was officially the parent party, Communist assignments had to be fitted to Kuomintang orders. Liu Po-ch'eng broke with the Nationalists to become chief of staff of the Revolutionary Military Committee which directed the Nanchang Rising. After the march to Canton and the sea, he fled to Moscow to enter the Red Army Academy.

Liu lived in Moscow for three years on a stipend from the Comintern, studying guerrilla tactics and Far Eastern politics. In 1929, he saw a chance to prove his classroom training in battle. He requested and received assignment to the Special Far Eastern Army of Russian General Galen, who was skirmishing with the Manchurian Army of Marshal Chang Hsüeh-liang. Liu Po-ch'eng was the first Chinese Communist general to fight on the side of a foreign power against his countrymen.

Russia's attack on Manchuria in the fall of 1929 gave some hint of her intentions in the Far East. Under the Ku-Karakhan Agreement signed in 1924, she had resigned all extraterritorial rights in China and agreed to joint Russo-Chinese administration of the Chinese Eastern Railroad, built by the Czar. In 1929, Chang Hsüeh-liang, with the backing of Nanking, charged that Russia had violated her promise not to engage in Communist propaganda in Manchuria. He arrested most of the Russian staff of the railroad and declared that he would hold them until Russia promised to behave. Russia countered by breaking diplomatic relations with China and seizing Chinese representatives in the Soviet Union.

Finally General Galen was ordered to march. With him went Liu Po-ch'eng, charged with the task of recruiting Chinese volunteers to fight on the Soviet side. However, Stalin later decided that Galen's mission could be accomplished without rousing the Manchurian people, and, afraid of starting something he might be unable to control, he ordered Liu's recall. Shortly thereafter, Galen took Harbin and presided over the signing of an agreement which was to Russia's taste.

About a year after the Chinese Eastern Railroad Incident, Liu Po-ch'eng returned incognito to Shanghai. He drifted about the city's underground until he made contact with Chou En-lai, who remembered his role in the Nanchang Rising. Chou secured his appointment as a staff officer of the Central Revolutionary Military Committee, and Liu showed his gratitude by translating into Chinese a number of Red Army field manuals, military critiques, and field orders. In 1931, he entered the Kiangsi Soviet Area to become an instructor in the P'eng-Yang Military School. After two months in that job he attracted the attention of Chu Teh and Mao Tse-tung, who made him chief of staff.

As chief of staff of the Red Army during the period of Chiang's "extermination campaigns," Liu Po-ch'eng proved himself a bold tactician. But his talents were bolstered by the political acumen of P'eng Te-huai and the theoretical genius of Lin Piao. Together the three made up Chu Teh's first team.

*　　　*　　　*

As vice-commander of the People's Liberation Army, P'eng Te-huai today stands second to Chu Teh in the Red military hierarchy; he and Chu are the only generals on the five-man Secretariat which is the administrative heart of the Party. P'eng thinks like Chu Teh, always returning in discussions of strategy to the strength of the people, which he holds to be "inexhaustible." Ever since the hard days in Kiangsi, P'eng has maintained that two conditions would guarantee victory: the support of the people, and strong "political consciousness" among the soldiers, who would be invincible when they knew *why* they fought.

Politically the most astute of the generals, P'eng Te-huai is now chairman of the Northwest Administrative Area which takes in the vast areas of the provinces of Sinkiang, Kansu, Chinghai, Shensi, and Ninghsia—China's wild west. A seasoned soldier, he is commander of both the Northwest Military Area and the First Field Army, but even he may wish for greater talents and a thirty-two-hour working-day in his new assignment. A catalogue of his problems would run to many pages, but a partial enumeration may suggest their scope.

There is the minority problem: The population of the area is compounded of many racial strains—Kazak, Mongol, Chinese, and Uighur—who periodically fly at each other's throats. A further complicaton is the constant friction between Mohammedan and non-Mohammedan inhabitants. A long record of Chinese maladministration has made them all suspicious of any government that rules from Peking. Many are nomads who will prove exceedingly difficult to pigeonhole.

The international problem: The Northwest Administrative Area is bounded by Tibet, Russian Central Asia, and the two Mongolias, potential points of friction with India or Russia. Czarist Russia began cultivating her sphere of influence in opposition to Britain, then reaching up from India. In 1946, United States' representation in Tihwa, the capital of Sinkiang Province, consisted of a young consul and his wife crowded into a four-room house. The Russians maintained a staff of over 200, housed in a mansion surrounded by a high, brick wall which extended along the main street for a quarter of a mile.

The economic problem: Though the Northwest is potentially the richest area of China in mineral wealth, it is almost entirely undeveloped. P'eng's domain extends over 2,000 miles from east to west, but the great stretch must be crossed by horse, camel, or truck when available. A railroad to run from Sian in Shensi Province to Lanchow and thence to Hami in Sinkiang has been mapped out, but never built. And Tihwa, the Sinkiang capital, lies 300 miles from Hami, which the Chinese formerly considered the last weak outpost of civilization.

P'eng finds one consolation amid his perplexities. Hami is famous for producing the finest melons in China, and he is a melon addict. In 1937, at Eighth Route Army Headquarters near Taiyüan he used to sit in conference chewing melon between sentences, and spitting seeds on the earth floor. But P'eng is no crude peasant, for at headquarters everyone spat melon seeds on the floor. Moreover, he wears the wound-stripe of civilization. He acquired his stomach ulcer while crossing the grasslands of western Szechwan and Kansu during the Long March, when the Red Army fed itself for a week on handfuls of raw grain and fresh-pulled grass. P'eng Te-huai emerged from that dietary adventure with a stomach complaint which keeps him on a strict diet of boiled millet and milk, except when he indulges himself with a bout of melon eating.

P'eng Te-huai has been Chu Teh's man since they met. Both men look like peasants, but Chu seems to have no temperament, while there is an impatient thrust to P'eng's chin. He is a product of the same Changsha hotbed which bred Mao Tse-tung.

Not circumstances, but his own aggressiveness made P'eng a revolutionary. He was born into comfortable surroundings as the son of a prosperous farmer in Hsiang-t'an County of Hunan Province, but the first indication that the world was not a perfect place to live in came early to him. His mother died when Te-huai was six years old, and her successor was not inclined to coddle the boy, who was a stone in her rice, continually reminding her that she was a second wife. Under her contemptuous neglect Te-huai grew rebellious, lashing out at his complaisant father, who was more interested in his living second wife and the new family they were raising than in the malcontent son of a dead marriage. Matters grew worse, with Te-huai venting his resentment even on the sacrosanct matriarch of the family, his grandfather's widow— a tyrant of no small force. Finally, the P'engs, in solemn family conference assembled, resolved that the boy should be sent out to make his own way, since he had demonstrated that he was unworthy of the family's protection. That was two years before the overthrow of the Manchu dynasty. Filial piety was still the cardinal virtue and the chief prop of the State.

The boy was not wholly abandoned, for a prosperous uncle, his own mother's brother, kept tabs on him. But his uncle could do little more than see that the boy did not starve to death, for he was too proud and resentful to accept substantial assistance. Te-huai was in a snare of his own devising. Not only was he a masterless man, but worse in paternalistic China, he was a man without a family to stand up for him.

For the next five years he worked at a series of jobs diverse enough to qualify him as a practical labor expert. He was assistant to cowherd for a time and then a bunker-boy in a coal mine, but he found the work back-breaking and the reward infinitesimal. After trying a number of other menial occupations, he tossed in the sponge and asked his rich uncle for a home. Te-huai's uncle was pleased, since he had a daughter who would soon be of marriageable age, and the boy's spirit promised much after subjection to discipline. For two happy years, P'eng Te-huai lived in his uncle's home, absorbing the first systematic education to which he had been exposed and eying his pretty cousin. But the interlude ended in new disaster. He was forced to flee from his uncle's home after becoming involved in the looting of a usurer's stores by hungry peasants.

When P'eng left home for the second time he was old enough at sixteen to pursue the one career which required neither capital nor family backing, but only strong legs and a quick hand. He joined one of the roving bands of soldiers which might be engaged in banditry or bandit suppression, depending upon the political situation and their current commitments. His superiors discovered that, in addition to his other assets, he was possessed of the combative instinct and a clear mind, the two keys to advancement in his new profession. At the age of eighteen, he was placed in command of a platoon in the army of one of the Hunan war-lords.

The next ten years were spent in a series of plots, counterplots, failures, and small successes, punctuated by short periods of attendance upon classes at military schools in Hunan and Kiangsi. P'eng was moving up the ladder in the Kuomintang armies. He served for a time under Ch'eng Ch'ien, a Hunan general who finally threw in with the Communists in 1949 and served as a delegate to the People's Political Consultative Conference in September of that year.

The dapper young officer was something of a lady killer. Ting Ling,* the lady novelist, later said, "There is something about P'eng Te-huai which is quite disturbing to females."

P'eng's uniforms were well-tailored and his heavy walk expressed a profound self-confidence. His swarthy features, though stolid in repose, were illuminated with enthusiasm when he talked, gesturing with his large, well-shaped hands. In 1926, he married a young middle-school graduate; his cousin, to whom he had been informally betrothed, had died some years earlier.

---

* See Chapter 6.

Life was pleasant for the young officer in an army which was beginning to win more battles than it lost. Unfortunately for his composure, P'eng Te-huai, like Chu Teh, began to wonder what purpose, outside that of his own advantage, was served by the life he led. He remembered too well for complacency the desperation of his younger years as a drifting laborer. P'eng saw that the Kuomintang army, which had been conceived by Dr. Sun as a "people's force," was beginning to take over the role of the old-time militarists as it forced them from the scene. It seemed to Te-huai that he was watching the revolutions of a garishly lighted carousel. Each time the music stopped, a new set of riders would scramble for the vacated seats, and the carousel would begin to go around again in the same place. Earlier he had read Liang Ch'i-ch'ao and Sun Yat-sen, and had found in their writings some of the answers he sought. But he was forced to the conclusion that the men who proclaimed themselves the heirs of Sun Yat-sen differed from their opponents in their words, but not in their deeds.

P'eng had glimpsed an entirely new system of thought when he read the widely circulated translations of Kropotkin's works. Looking for a concrete projection of political theory into reality, he read Bukharin's *ABC of Communism*. The rigidity of the system was itself a recommendation to a pragmatic mind which desired absolute solutions. During the years from 1924 to 1927, the Communist Party, legitimized by its connection with the Kuomintang, was free to circulate its views. Even non-Communist radical thinkers were turning from the West and looking to the Russian experiment for inspiration. Littérateurs like Lu Hsün, Mao Tün and Kuo Mojo* were engaged in the translation of Russian novels and Marxist political tracts. In almost all the magazines he read, P'eng found the influence of Russian Marxist thought dominant. A translation of Kautsky's *The Class Struggle* came

---

* See Chapter 8.

into his hands, and finally the parent work, *The Communist Manifesto*. P'eng read the *Manifesto* with the same soaring sense of enlightenment it had brought to some Europeans in 1848, for China was no more advanced industrially than Europe had been seventy-five years earlier. In the twentieth century he was inflamed with the same enthusiasm which many Europeans had felt in the nineteenth. Here were the answers.

P'eng Te-huai was guided in his reading by his close friend and political adviser, Huang Kung-lüeh, a Communist. Huang was later to become political commissar of the Fifth Army under P'eng's command and die in battle at Tung-ku in Kiangsi Province. In March 1928, Huang Kung-lüeh stood sponsor to P'eng Te-huai's application for membership in the Communist Party. P'eng soon backed his pledge of allegiance with action.

"In July 1928 [he later told Robert Payne] I had organized an uprising in Pingchiang in northeastern Hunan. I heard about the defence of Chingkangshan [by Mao and Chu], and after the uprising failed, I led about a thousand men to join the mountain soldiers. By this time our forces had grown. I had a thousand men, and the peasants were flocking to the mountain, so that we had between 4,000 and 5,000 men altogether, with a considerable number of rifles and bayonets. But we were still weak compared to the enemy. They said publicly that they had 60,000 well-trained and well-equipped troops. They may have had 45,000. . . . The enemy had good leaders. Their officers were all regular Kuomintang officers. They had three armies with Chu Pei-teh in command of the Third Army. But we defeated them, first in hundreds of skirmishes and later in battle. It was the first time the Kuomintang used radios; we did not even have telephones. Nevertheless we drove them away. Actually we never had radios at all until after the siege of Changsha in 1930. Even if we had had radios we would not have known how to use them.

"We occupied Changsha for ten days in 1930. It started with the anniversary meeting at Pinchiang. . . . Ho Chien's troops arrived, but we routed them about six *li* away, and then decided to follow them. We had nothing to lose, and they were very frightened. Changsha was defended by five regiments—a total strength of about 30,000. To attack Changsha with our 10,000 was technically impossible—the city was difficult to attack and favors the defender—but our morale was high, and we were bitterly determined to show the war-lords that peasants can muster enough force to get through. We got through. We fought a nasty engagement on the Nanling River fifteen *li* from Changsha, and attacked with bayonet charges, since our main weapons were bayonets. It was costly. We had between 2,000 and 3,000 casualties. There was fighting along the approaches to Changsha the whole day and part of the night, and even when we entered the city, there was still fighting going on outside. It was a hard war, and in ten days Ho Chien was bringing so large a force against us that we evacuated."*

In that conversation P'eng Te-huai revealed the true basis of Communist military power. Their friends have boasted, and their enemies have not denied, that the Chinese Communists were carried to victory by spirit. Communist troops dedicated themselves to the conquest of power, putting aside all other aims. Their exuberant morale brought them triumphant through hardship and peril such as few other armies have overcome. But throughout the struggle enemy slackness has been nearly as decisive as Red determination. Most of the troops who were sent against the Communists by the Nanking Government from 1927 to 1949 had no particular desire to fight anyone, and a positive disinclination to challenge the fire-eating Red Army. That attitude manifested itself in desertions among the troops and lack of decision on the part of

---

* Payne, Robert: *Journey to Red China,* William Heinemann Ltd., 1947, pp. 37-38

their commanders. Had the large, well-armed Kuomintang armies had half their spirit, the Communists would have been wiped out. During the Long March, when the Red Army was completely exposed, it escaped annihilation a half-dozen times because the enemy broke, or because the local commander feared that determined opposition to the Reds' passage would force them to settle down where they were. That was a danger to be avoided by passing them through after a token resistance.

4. TECHNICIANS, GENERALS, AND BANDITS (continued)

Weight of Nationalist numbers forced the Communists to abandon their Kiangsi stronghold in October, 1934, and embark upon the Long March, which would take them 7,000 miles to Shensi in the sparsely populated Northwest. They were jarred loose by the Kuomintang's "Fifth Bandit Extermination Campaign" under the personal command of Generalissimo Chiang Kai-shek, who mobilized several hundred thousand troops and planned his attack with a staff of German advisers headed by General von Seeckt. Thus began an epic which may rank with the anabasis.

Though the Communists might well have been broken if Chiang's subordinate commanders had pressed the attack, their own conduct was dauntless. Their course led them through the wildest regions of China, over rivers, between gorges, across prairies, and through mountains. They were harried not only by Nationalist troops, but by aborigines whose lands they invaded. Their numbers were reduced by battle, disease, and accident, but the core of leaders and cadremen arrived safely in the Northwest, even acquiring new adherents on the later stages of the march.

For the Communist generals the Long March was a laboratory in which they matched against reality the theories evolved in six years of close fighting in the Southeast. Liu Po-ch'eng led the vanguard, while Chu Teh and P'eng Te-huai commanded separate units of the main body, but it was the brilliant planning of the young military scholar, General Lin Piao, and the equally brilliant performance of his First Army Group which got the Red Army over rough spots.

Lin Piao in his rumpled cotton uniform looked like a bright young clerk out for a weekend in the country. One wonders why he became a Communist, for he was at the beginning of a promising career in the Kuomintang armies when he led his battalion to join the hopeless rising at Nanchang. It was hardly foreign influence, since he had never been out of China, nor was it the disgust of the disillusioned veteran seeking new illusions. In Lin's case the most obvious answer seems the correct one; idealism, inflamed by the natural extremism of youth, led him into the Party. He is one of the youngest Red leaders, and was not yet twenty when he chose to defy the newly established government of the Kuomintang to join the Communist rebels.

In the Red camp Lin Piao rose to prominence rapidly. During the bleak days following the failure of the Nanchang, Swatow, and Canton Revolutionary Committees, the borning Communist armies were as desperately short of trained officers as they were of arms. Lin Piao was one of the few Whampoa graduates in their ranks—and Whampoa men were the elite of young Chinese officers. His diploma from the Whampoa Military Academy meant that Lin had passed through an intensive course in modern warfare under the most brilliant faculty in China. By the middle of 1936, Lin Piao had won recognition as a teacher and theoretician on warfare and was acknowledged to be one of the foremost strategists in the country; his critique on the battle of P'ing-hsing Pass was used as a text in the war against Japan. In 1945, he was entrusted with the crucial mission of organizing and commanding the armies assigned to consolidate Manchuria as a base for the conquest of China proper. And early in 1950 he was given the job of taking Hainan Island in preparation for the assault on Formosa. At the end of 1950 his Fourth Field Army war in action against the United Nations Forces in Korea.

There is something comfortingly traditional about Chu Teh, P'eng Te-huai, and Liu Po-ch'eng. Chu, the old general, like one of Napoleon's marshals, is a revolutionary militarist. P'eng is a peasant in revolt straight from the pages of an old Chinese novel. Liu is a professional knight errant out of the same novel. But Lin Piao is wholly a modern man. He is an engineer in arms, personally unassuming to the point of diffidence, but professionally a paragon who appears to be without doubt or hesitation.

Like many technicians he is a son of the lower middle class. When Lin Piao was born in 1908, the Lin family had for a number of generations operated a small textile mill in Huang-an, a county seat of about 50,000 in Hupei Province near Hankow. But the process of replacing the Manchu *imperium* with the aborted Republic, created economic dislocation as a by-product. Hankow, the fuse of the revolution, suffered the most severe effects. The competition of foreign machine-made textiles also played a part in making it impossible for the Lin family to market the product of their handlooms. Although the First World War temporarily stimulated Chinese industry, their primitive enterprise was not benefited. As the family concern moved closer to bankruptcy, Lin Piao's father, a man of some education, was fortunate enough to find employment as purser on a vessel which sailed the Yangtze River.

Mrs. Lin was left with the task of directing their young son. It was not an easy task. The boy was bright, but too forthright in protesting against those features of daily life which seemed to him to conflict with logic. His precocity was troublesome, for he began to adopt "revolutionary ideas" at the age of eleven.

The Wu-Han cities, a center of industry, were a favorite field for radical agitators, who found there an abundance of their favorite new raw material— the industrial proletariat. Their exhortations were transmitted to the surrounding countryside, finding an interested audience among discontented youth. Some, still children by conventional standards, were stimulated to forced maturity by the intensity of the political climate.

A current story—highly apocryphal—tells how Mao Tsetung late in 1919 came to the village of Hui-lung Shan where the Lins were living. He set up a school in an abandoned temple to give the children some elementary education and fan the revolutionary spirit. Lin Piao, according to the tale, was one of Mao's students until the local authorities, jealous of the children's loyalty, ordered the school closed. On the door of the padlocked schoolhouse they tacked a sign declaring: "When the students act rebelliously, the country cannot know peace!"

But the damage had been done as far as Lin Piao was concerned. After singing the songs of revolution as Mao called the tune, Lin Piao knew that he must have more education. He studied by himself until he felt that he was ready for middle school. The Lin family could do without the earnings of the fourteen-year-old boy, though they could offer him no financial assistance. With his parents' blessing, Lin Piao set out for the industrial city of Wuchang to take entrance examinations for middle school. He won admission without difficulty, but was forced to work part-time in a cotton mill to pay his way. However, he found time to become an active member of the "Social Welfare Club," a student organization immersed in the cultural waves from the West.

But in reality Lin Piao felt little affinity for cultural studies. He was inclined toward practical politics in their most concrete aspect—the military one. After graduation from middle school in 1925, he gained admission to the Whampoa Military Academy as a cadet of the fourth class, which began its training in 1925 and was graduated a year later. By this time he was already a member of the Communist Youth League. He had come under direct Communist influence as a delegate to a student conference held in Shanghai early in 1925, and shortly thereafter had entered the Youth League. He was not

99

to be admitted to formal Party membership until late 1927.

Lin Piao's class was the first to receive extensive training. The first three classes had been graduated after three or four months, but the fourth remained for a year. They studied military tactics under Japanese-trained Chiang Kai-shek and Russian General Galen, and political tactics under Communists Chou En-lai and Lin Tsu-han. The experience of the Russian Red Army was drawn on for both organizational and tactical lessons, and popular mobilization through political technics was given equal stress with purely military concerns. Tai Li, later to be chief of the Nationalist secret police, displayed so little affinity for these studies that he was expelled, but Lin Piao was an honor student. At the Whampoa Academy, Lin learned that generals, despite their power, were ultimately dependent upon civilian politicians. There could not be a non-political Chinese general.

After graduation in 1926, he was commissioned in the Kuo-min Ko-ming Chün—the Citizens' Revolutionary Army —and rose to command a battalion in the Ironsides Army of Chang Fa-k'uei at the age of nineteen, despite the obstacles of extreme youth and a frail appearance. Service in the Kuomintang armies truly offered "a career open to talent," because the supply of trained officers was lagging behind the rapid rate of expansion. But Lin Piao abandoned his career in August, 1927, when he led his troops to join the Red insurgents at Nanchang.

He marched with Chu Teh from Nanchang to the sea, and went to earth with him in northern Canton Province during the winter of 1927-28, joining Mao at Chingkangshan in May, 1928. Thereafter his rise was even more rapid than it might have been in the Kuomintang armies. He commanded a battalion in Chu Teh's 28th Regiment, half the Workers' and Peasants' Red Army in the early days of its formation, and in 1929 was moved up to command the Red Fourth Army for a short time.

The Communists had learned the uses of psychological

warfare. They employed no standard nomenclature which would reveal the size of their units, but preferred to exaggerate their strength by variations in terminology. That policy has made almost as much trouble for historians as it did for the Kuomintang. It is next to impossible to fix the size of early Red units. It is unlikely that Lin's Fourth Army exceeded a strength of 8,000 or that there were as many as 15,000 men under his command in the column called the First Army Group on the Long March.

*   *   *

Reading the tales told by the Long Marchers, one is struck once more by the disparate character of war. Each soldier knew only what his own unit was about, and even high officers seem to have been in the dark much of the time. It is impossible to arrive at an integrated view of the course of the campaign, though the lines of march are clearly marked on the great wall-map of China. The commander of each column was briefed on the overall plan and his own responsibilities and then turned loose to make his own way to the rendezvous in the Northwest by a route corresponding to a hike from Tennessee to Nebraska by way of Colorado.

Scarred, one-eyed Liu Po-ch'eng, who commanded the vanguard, was fortunate in having an able chronicler named Hsiao Hua among his subordinates. Most of the recorded tales of the Long March tell of the exploits of General Liu and his dare-devil crew. In *Red Star Over China* Edgar Snow has described the desperate valor of the vanguard in the face of natural obstacles defended by superior arms. The most dramatic attack was the hand-over-hand crossing of the Tatu River on the chains of a half-wrecked bridge in the face of machine-gun fire. But Liu Po-ch'eng's best stroke was diplomatic rather than military.

In March, 1935, the Red armies began to enter the mountainous regions of southwestern Szechwan, the home of the Lolos, an aboriginal people who had never submitted to Chinese sovereignty. As far as the Lolos knew, all Chinese, Red or White, were alike enemies. When the Red Army came to the border of the highlands, the Lolo clans began to assemble, armed with broad swords and long iron spears. The Red advance guard had penetrated about ten miles into the mountains when they were blocked by a Lolo force drawn up across a deep ravine. An unarmed work company, which marched behind the Red vanguard, was deprived of its tools and construction material, and stripped of its clothing. It seemed that the Red Army would be forced to fight its way through the mountains, losing much time and suffering heavy casualties on the unfamiliar terrain.

Liu's lieutenant Hsiao Hua and an interpreter advanced to parley with the shouting Lolos. They explained that they, too, were enemies of the Szechwan generals, who had been encroaching on Lololand, and that they sought only permission to pass through the mountains.

"No! No! Don't let them through," shouted the Lolos. "Let them pay a toll for safe passage!"

Hsiao Hua, who had been prepared for this demand, handed over a bag of five-hundred silver dollars. After the money had been counted and passed from hand to hand for inspection, the Lolos showed no disposition to clear the road. They shook their spears and shouted their war-cries. Hsiao Hua shrugged his shoulders and turned away, while the Red soldiers snapped their bolts.

From the far mouth of the ravine rolled a puff of dust, which swelled larger as it approached until the soldiers could make out the figure of a tall man on horseback, followed by a short one on a black-spotted mule. The Lolo warriors became quiet as the mounted figures drew near. The tall man, the interpreter told Hsiao Hua, was the older brother of Shaoyerban, the chieftain of the White Lolos.

Hsiao Hua repeated his story, telling the Lolo leader that the Red Army was the enemy of his enemies, seeking safe passage through his territories. When the Reds had gained their ends, he declared, they would remember the assistance of the Lolos, and in the meantime would be glad to help them against the provincial troops and their hereditary enemies, the Black Lolos. To seal the promise of friendship, Hsiao Hua offered his pistol to the Lolo chief and was presented in return with the piebald riding-mule of the chief's attendant.

Upon hearing Hsiao Hua's report that negotiations were going well, Liu Po-ch'eng mounted and rode out to meet the Lolo captain, who had been joined by his younger brother, the clan chieftain. The two brothers dismounted and knelt before the Communist general with barbaric courtesy. Liu slid off his horse and dropped to one knee to raise the Lolos to their feet. The aboriginal chiefs accepted Liu's presents and agreed to participate in a ceremony binding themselves to him as blood-brothers.

"Then [the Communist scribe writes] by the side of a small lake near the ravine the Red Army representative and the Lolo leaders tied the bonds of brotherhood. They burnt no incense, nor did they light tapers, but between the azure sky and the crystal water, beneath the precipitous mountains with their dense groves, General Liu Po-ch'eng and the brothers Shaoyerban walked to the edge of the lake. They carried three large bowls before them, while youthful comrade Hsiao Hua served as witness.

"When the bowls had been filled with clear water, Hsiao Hua held a cock aloft. After cutting the head off, he allowed the fresh blood to spurt into the three bowls, completing the preparations for the ceremony.

"Liu Po-ch'eng raised the bowl over his head, solemnly reciting the oath: *'Shang yu T'ien, Hsia yu Ti . . . Liu Po-ch'eng yü Shaoyerban chieh wei hsiung-ti!'* [By the sky that has sheltered us, and the ground on which we've stood . . . Liu Po-ch'eng and Shaoyerban pledge brotherhood!]

"And when he had said the last word, he drank the bowl of cock's blood at a single draught. Upon the Shaoyerbans doing the same, the ceremony was concluded."

After these rites, the Red troops withdrew for the night to a village on the edge of Lololand, taking with them the two brothers and six Lolo retainers. They searched the small Chinese village for wine to entertain the Lolos who were "adept at drinking wine," according to chronicler. On the following day the Lolo chieftain and his attendants withdrew, leaving the older brother to guide the Red Army through the mountain passes. When the Red troops emerged into Chinese territory, the local garrison welcomed them as reinforcements, convinced that the Reds were hundreds of miles away. The provincial troops were quickly disarmed.

*　　*　　*

Before the entry into Lololand, the Red Army had won a decisive battle near the city of Tsün-yi, the metropolis of northern Kueichow Province. The First Army Group under Lin Piao and the Third Army Group under P'eng Te-huai performed a classic maneuver to catch the enemy in a pincer.

In January, 1935, the Red Army occupied Tsün-yi, driving out local magnate Wang Chia-lieh, who hurried south to the town of Lan-pan-teng, where he met two divisions under General Wu Chi-wei marching north along the railroad from Kueiyang, the capital city. When Wu was told of the fall of Tsün-yi, he quickened his pace, intending to attack before the Reds could consolidate their position. At a point ten miles south of Tsün-yi he was checked by P'eng's defending Third Army Group. While Wu's Nationalist troops were engaged by P'eng's forces, Lin Piao's First Army Group swung wide to the east to catch them in the rear. Wu Chi-wei found himself encircled.

General Wu, with two regiments, broke through the Communist line on the south and fled by the route he had come in the direction of the Crow River, sixteen miles south. Communist troops in pursuit arrived at the bridge over the Crow to find that Wu and his staff had already crossed, leaving

104

most of his forces on the north bank. General Wu, afraid that the Communists would push their advantage and march on the provincial capital, dynamited the southern end of the bridge.

Eighteen-hundred men were captured on the north bank to be marched to the city of Tsün-yi with the remainder of Wu Chi-wei's two divisions. In the city the captured soldiers were paid three *yüan* each for their rifles, in accordance with Communist practice, and were given the choice of joining the Red Army or being released. Communist propagandists were assigned to persuade the enlisted men, while Chu Teh himself addressed the officers. In the end, a non-Communist observer reports, eighty per cent elected to join the Red Army, while the remainder were given fare and safe-conduct passes to their homes.

*　　*　　*

After the defeat at Tsün-yi, consternation ran through the headquarters of the Central Government Army and the headquarters of the Hunan, Yünnan, Kueichow, and Szechwan provincial armies engaged in the task of "Red bandit extermination." Several divisions were withdrawn from positions in northwest Hunan, where they had been blockading the Communist Second Area Army ensconced in the Hunan-Hupei Soviet Area under the command of General Ho Lung, the Felicitudinous Dragon. Ho seized the opportunity to break through the weakened siege lines and begin his own little Long March toward Shensi.

When Ho Lung joined Chu Teh on the Tibetan border in the late spring of 1935, two of the three chiefs of the Nanchang Rising were once more united.* There had been a strong similarity between the careers of Chu Teh and Ho Lung, the two elder generals of the Red armies. They were

---

* General Yeh T'ing, the commander-in-chief, was in exile outside China.

almost of an age, for Ho was born in 1887, Chu in 1886, and both had been general officers in the Kuomintang armies when the Nanchang Rising directed their lives into new channels. But their early lives had been strikingly different. Chu Teh, the son of prosperous landowners with official connections, had himself been trained for the bureaucracy, while Ho Lung inherited a hatred of officials from his peasant father, a leader of an extra-legal secret society. If P'eng Te-huai came to Communism in revolt against the shape of things as they were and Lin Piao through a deliberate act of choice, Ho Lung was born to the revolution.

That was in Sang-chih County in the northwest corner of Hunan Province, 630 miles from Canton City. The Manchu *imperium* still had twenty-four years to run, but the attacks upon the Empire, which had begun with the Taiping Rebellion, had not ceased with its suppression. Ho Lung's father was chief of the western Hunan branch of the Ko-lao Hui— the Society of Elder Brothers—the dominant secret society of West China.

For at least two millennia, secret societies have been a major factor in the complex social structure which has enabled the Chinese to live in large numbers upon small and ungenerous areas of land. Despite changes in specific functions, they have always been secret governments pledged to guarantee the security of their members. Naturally, there is little definite information available about the character of the secret societies, but it is clear that members are bound together by a system of para-religious rituals and that disloyalty carries extreme punishments.

Secret societies have often exerted great influence on conventional politics. The Ko-lao Hui and the San-ho Hui (the Triad Association) were founded at the start of Manchu rule, dedicated to the overthrow of the alien dynasty. Sun Yat-sen took advantage of this fact to enroll them among his forces. Because the secret society is a sub-government, bound to protect its members against the depredations of both of-

106

ficials and outlaws, it assumes a vigilante character in times of disorder. This is particularly true of the Ko-lao Hui, whose membership is chiefly lower class.

"*Ho Lung,*" the Chinese say, "*shih t'u-fei ch'u-shen ti.*" ("Ho Lung emerged from banditry.") In the decades immediately preceding the collapse of the Manchus and just following the creation of the Republic, central government's feebleness stimulated the growth of marauding bands under the Ko-lao Hui's sponsorship. Introduced by his father, who had been elevated to a semi-official military post, Ho Lung became a leader of bandit troops. He was later to inherit his father's position. Members of the Ko-lao Hui were immune to his attacks, and the poor were spared because the pickings were not worth the effort. But rich merchants and officials—on the highroad or at home in isolated towns—were Ho Lung's game. As the spoils piled up, the band increased. An occasional gift, or chastisement of an oppressive official, cemented the loyalty of the people of the countryside, making the bandits a match for any but a major military force.

Ho Lung organized his own band about 1911, and he participated, under orders from the Ko-lao Hui's high command, in actions against the Manchu troops during the Revolution of 1911. Eight years later, he led his 10,000 men into the service of the Szechwan war-lord, Shih Ching-yang. Remaining in Szechwan for the next five years, Ho became commander of the 2nd Division of the Szechwan National Reconstruction Army in 1925, and in 1927 was commanding general of the 2nd Independent Szechwan Division. His power in the Hunan branch carried over to neighboring Szechwan, the stronghold of the Ko-lao Hui.

After serving under General Chang Fa-k'uei for a time, Ho found his division stationed at Nanchang in July, 1927. When the expulsion of Communists from the Hankow Government, to which he owed allegiance, and the decision to raise the red flag over Nanchang forced a choice upon him, Ho Lung left the Kuomintang to throw in with the Communists, the party of revolt. His choice was influenced by his close friend, Chou Yi-chün, a Party member, but the decisive factor was his self-identification with peasants in revolt, whom the Communists declared they alone represented. After the collapse of the Swatow Commune, set up under his aegis, Ho Lung fled to Hong Kong. There he met Chou En-lai, also a refugee, and was trained in Marxist doctrine until he was judged fit to become a Party member.

In the spring of 1928, Ho was ordered to Shanghai for further indoctrination. In late spring, he was ordered to establish a Soviet Regime in western Hunan, where the power of his name could raise a regiment in a week. The first recruits of the Second Area Army of the Red Army were impelled not by political convictions, but by devotion to the stout, swashbuckling general. He had already demonstrated that he took care of his men, the first requisite of a guerrilla leader, and his position in the Ko-lao Hui was a strong draw. But his personal appeal was more important in attracting recruits. His jaunty walk and the rakish angle at which his pipe was stuck into his square face were a constant delight to the dramatic instincts of the farmers. The little man took on the charm of one of the poor-but-virtuous farmer-soldiers before whom corrupt dynasties trembled in the Chinese drama. And he was a local boy making good, who understood the brusque local dialect. These characteristics and a penchant for practical joking endeared Ho Lung to the Hunan peasants, just as they were later to make him the most popular Communist leader among the farmers of the Northwest. He has never been strong on policy, but his following has always been considerable.

With Ho Lung to Hunan travelled political commissar Hsia Hsi to keep him in line. But the Hunan-Hupei Soviet Area was never as successful as the Red government established in Kiangsi by Mao and Chu. The Nationalist armies maintained a constant pressure which prevented the creation of a strong Red government. Ho Lung was kept moving; he operated in

Hupei, Honan, and Szechwan Provinces, as well as in his native Hunan, in the years between 1930 and 1935, when he finally joined the main body of the Red Army. However, his primary responsibility was efficiently discharged; Ho had no more than 10,000 men in 1930, but he led an army of between 40,000 and 50,000 to join Chu Teh on the Tibetan border in the spring of 1935.

From the Tibetan border the Red Army's hegira continued across the Great Snow Mountains and over the prairies called the Great Grass Plain to Shensi, a ghost province old in history. Songs blaring from the Propaganda Unit's phonograph startled the mountain birds, whose remote ancestors had watched Buddhist pilgrims making their way to India. Shensi and neighboring Kansu were the earliest sites of Chinese civilization. Shensi was the home of the feudal Prince of Ch'in who unified China 220 years before the birth of Christ. Later, the founder of the most magnificent dynasty, the T'ang, egged his father into undertaking the conquest of China from the stronghold the older man ruled as governor of Shensi. But the glory was long departed when the Red forces began to straggle into the territory during the dusty summer of 1935. Shensi was just another sparsely populated farming province, and a particularly poor one, but it had been the site of a very minor Soviet Area since the Yenan garrison revolted in 1930.

On the east lay Marshal Yen Hsi-shan's "Model Province" of Shansi. Yen's disposition promised peace, for he had displayed little desire to extend his power beyond the boundaries of his own province. Shensi's distance from the seat of Nationalist power at Nanking had given rise to the hope that they would be able to develop the Red Army unmolested by the Central Government. A third attraction was the proximity to the Central Asian territories of the Soviet Union.

After the arrival in Shensi, the Red Army began to shift the emphasis of its propaganda. The chief enemy was no longer the reactionary Kuomintang, but imperialist Japan. All Chinese (Party and Army organs declared) must unite

109

against Japanese aggression. Japan had been the Reds' public enemy number two since the Manchurian grab of 1931, but she pushed into first place by her rapacity in North China. But not until after the Comintern announced the strategy of the Popular Front against Fascism at its Seventh Congress in 1935, did the Communist Party of China come out flatly for cooperation with the Kuomintang against Japan.

After the clash at Marco Polo Bridge in July, 1937, the Red Army allowed its name to be changed to the "Eighth Route Army of the National Revolutionary Armies." It was formally reorganized into four divisions. Chu Teh and P'eng Te-huai, as commander and deputy commander, established their headquarters near the city of Taiyüan in Shansi, and retained direct control of one division. Liu Po-ch'eng was given the 129th Division and Ho Lung the 120th. Lin Piao, who also held the directorship of the Red Army Academy, was given command of the 115th Division. He and Ho Lung soon added luster to their reputations, each in his own manner.

Ho Lung led his troops into the area surrounding the T'ung-p'u Railroad in Shansi Province. He avoided positional warfare to send out mobile columns against Japanese lines of communication. The Japanese Army, depending upon heavy equipment to smash the Chinese in conventional warfare, had no tactics to counter Ho's hit-and-run attacks. Ho Lung himself led an attack on the airbase at Yang-ming-pao, where the Chinese went in with bayonets, broadswords, and homemade hand-grenades to destroy thirty Japanese planes.

At the time of that raid Ho had already begun to suffer from advanced tuberculosis, but he did not withdraw from active service for several years. He has seen little field service recently, remaining in the rear to command garrison forces. He also serves as a member of the Party's Revolutionary Military Affairs Committee, where his intimate acquaintance with the peasant on the land outweighs his lack of formal education. He still retains his jaunty air and the bushy mustache, which, with his ever-present pipe, make him a cartoonist's delight. In the year just past, however, age has further reduced his activity. Ho Lung still holds an important post as chief of staff of the Southwest Military Area, but serves under youthful Liu Po-ch'eng.

Technician Lin Piao filled a different role. He drew up the order of battle and composed critiques from battlefield reports. From Lin Piao's scholarship came the standard tactics of the Eighth Route Army.

In October, 1937, Lin Piao's troops trapped a Japanese brigade in narrow P'ing-hsing Pass in northeastern Shansi to win the first major victory against Japan. The Japanese were contemptuous of Chinese forces. *Lin observed that the enemy's greatest weakness was the arrogance which led him to underestimate the quality of Chinese resistance.* A Japanese brigade pursued Nationalist troops into P'ing-hsing Pass, where they were ambushed by Red troops from positions in the heights overlooking the defile. *Lin noted that the Japanese were encumbered by their heavy equipment and leather boots in mountain operations.* The brigade was annihilated and the conquest of Shansi Province delayed for several months.

Lin Piao wrote a critique on the battle of P'ing-hsing Pass which spared the faults of neither the Japanese, the Communists, nor the Nationalists. Its brusque style self-consciously avoids the elegant touches customary in Chinese prose and only rarely slips into Marxist rhetoric. It reads like the product of a tough-minded, apolitical military man.

"A good method [Lin writes] is to harass the enemy's flanks while he is attacking the camps of allied [i.e., Nationalist] troops . . . whose discipline is entirely too lax, so that they [the Nationalists] do not even stick to the plan of battle they themselves insist upon. While you fight, the allied army stands by—and listens. They boast continually that they will win decisive battles, but in practice they make decisions and do not execute them in battle. Or if they do fight, they fight without resolution.

"The enemy fears night attacks because his own tactics are

111

useless after dark. In order to sustain a protracted war we must study and practice the technic of the night attack.

"We, ourselves, must put more effort into the development of our army's technical skill, paying especial attention to the military education of common soldiers, squad, platoon, and company commanders. Although our troops have progressed greatly in the past half-year, their technical training has not been made uniform. In the future we must stress this kind of education."

*   *   *

While Lin Piao directed the education of the troops, other generals took up the supply problem. To avoid ruining the peasants, the army had to become a partially self-supporting unit integrated with the civilian economy. P'eng Te-huai played a leading role in developing the "work and fight" plan, reminiscent of the "work and study" plan for overseas students which had been encouraged by Mao Tse-tung fifteen years earlier. The soldiers became productive members of the economic community by setting up handicraft and agricultural cooperatives. These co-ops bolstered the guerrilla economy, which operated under Yenan's supervision, with a large measure of local option made necessary by constant Japanese raids slicing across lines of communication. Soldier production kept to a minimum the financial drain of maintaining a standing army.

This hybrid economic system—neither Communist, Socialist, nor Capitalist—proved efficient enough to sustain the Red armies after they were cut off from all outside assistance in 1941 by the Kuomintang blockade. P'eng Te-huai, acting on Chu Teh's precept that the army must be as one with its economic base, tied the cord which made the relationship between the military and civilian economies symbiotic rather than parasitic.

Just before the "China Incident" began, P'eng had declared: "War with Japan may break out at any moment, but we are prepared. The fact that our soldiers know exactly why they are fighting will counteract our lack of material resources. Moreover, behind us are reserves of manpower and resources sufficient to sustain a protracted resistance."

P'eng was optimistic, but not excessively so. It took time to harden the peasants' will to resist, but the effort was successful. Dr. George E. Taylor, assessing the Communists' achievements in 1941, wrote: "In some countries every village would have been a fort; here the village was a collection of impoverished and leaderless farmers, at least at the beginning of the war. That the peasantry of North China did not prove such an easy problem in government, and later emerged as the chief obstacle to the extension of Japanese-sponsored administration, was due to the development of a peasant nationalism on a scale broad enough to constitute a political revolution. The main contribution of the Japanese to this development of peasant nationalism lay in their conduct of the war, but the chief responsibility rests with the Chinese leadership which emerged in the hinterland. Most of the energy and finances of the Provisional [Puppet] Government were directed to the struggle with a rival Chinese [Communist] government and its guerrilla warfare."*

The military aspect of the Reds' fight against Japan defies description by the usual pin-pointing method. The course of the war cannot be suggested by describing decisive battles, for the Reds fought few battles, but thousands of engagements. Chu Teh himself admitted that the Communist armies could not defeat the Japanese, but must wait for an outside force to render the *coup de grâce* to an enemy weakened by their harassment. Chiang Kai-shek also counted on the intervention of a third power to bail China out. After 1941 the Chinese contribution to the war against Japan—made at an

---

* Taylor, G. E.: *The Struggle for North China*, Institute of Pacific Relations, Inquiry Series, p. 41

appalling cost—was the immobilization of several Japanese armies, needed to sit down on conquered Chinese territory.

In December, 1940, the New Fourth Army Incident produced a new split with the Nationalists and further isolation of the Red Border Areas. The New Fourth Army had been reconstituted as a unit of the National Revolutionary Armies of the Central Government from guerrilla units left in the Southeast under General Ch'en Yi, when the main body departed on the Long March. General Yeh T'ing, chief of the Nanchang Rising, had returned from exile in 1938 to command the New Fourth, named to honor General Chang Fa-k'uei's original "Ironsides" Fourth Army.

As Nationalist-Communist relations deteriorated in 1938, armed clashes became bloodier. The Communists had set the Kuomintang on guard by expanding partisan activities through north and east China. In 1938, the Kuomintang slaughtered a Communist liaison mission in Hunan at P'ingchiang, where P'eng Te-huai had begun his Communist career. From that time small engagements increased in frequency, until the Kuomintang attack on the New Fourth Army along the Yangtze brought an end to effective cooperation.

Commander-in-Chief Yeh T'ing was captured and confined in Chungking, while General Ch'en Yi took command of the New Fourth. The Kuomintang claimed that the Communist army had refused to obey orders; the Communists counter-charged that the orders were intended to push them to destruction.

*　　　　*　　　　*

With the end of the second entente, the Red armies had once more to rely wholly upon their own resources. During the period from 1941 to 1945, they consolidated their power in large areas nominally under Japanese control, spreading out from their northwestern base.

The end of the war in the Pacific found the Communists in control of most of the North China countryside and the Japanese entrenched in the cities. Sudden victory caught the Kuomintang off base. They had planned a major offensive to be launched simultaneously with the American invasion of Japan in October, 1945. The conclusion of that campaign was to have placed the Nationalists in command of the vital coastal areas. To compensate for the impossibility of executing that plan, Chiang Kai-shek ordered Japanese garrisons to surrender only to Nationalist troops and accepted the allegiance of puppet officers who could deliver strong points into his hands. The American Air Force and Navy moved Chiang's best troops into the major cities of China, from Canton and Shanghai in the south to Tientsin and Peiping in the north, and Changchun and Mukden in Manchuria.

The Communists protested against Chiang's desire to monopolize surrenders. General Order Number One of the Communist Eighteenth Group Army declared over Chu Teh's signature: "It is the right of our army to destroy enemy and puppet troops with armed force." On September 13, 1945, Chu and P'eng Te-huai rejected Chiang's order of the eleventh, which enjoined the Eighteenth Group Army not to expand the territories under Red control.

Communist strategy aimed at the acquisition of Manchuria as a base for the conquest of China. Manchuria was considered so important that the Reds were willing to weaken their position in China proper in order to provide reinforcements for the Manchurian armies. While Mao Tse-tung, Chou En-lai, and others talked peace with Chiang Kai-shek in Chungking, Lin Piao was ordered to Manchuria to unify pro-Communist forces there. The Reds trusted Chiang no more than he did them.

When peace negotiations broke down, Lin had formed the "Manchurian Democratic Allied Army" from guerrilla forces which had operated in that area during the war, reinforced with levies drawn from the Shensi army of General Ho Lung and the New Fourth Army. After "pacifying" Manchuria, Lin's army, renamed the "Manchurian People's Liberation Army," was to take Tsinan, the Shantung Province metropolis, early in 1948 to begin the final rout of the Nationalist armies.

Lin's shoulders were surprisingly frail for their burden. A non-Communist Chinese, who came in contact with Lin Piao during the American effort to mediate in Manchuria in 1947, was shocked to find that the General moved and talked "as if he might fall apart at any moment." Lin Piao is a slight, stooped little man, whom Nationalist representative Tu Yi-ming called "Little brother." General Tu is an earlier graduate of the Whampoa Academy. But Lin Piao did not allow his disgust at this condescension to betray him into abandoning his superior bargaining position. Taunted with the numerical inferiority of his troops, Lin replied with the countryman's proverb, "One spark can consume a hundred-mile prairie."

Despite his bourgeois origin, Lin frequently expresses his concern for the peasants. His use of homely farmers' maxims seemed to one Chinese to indicate a lack of real culture. He felt that Lin's few classical allusions were obviously drawn from a meager stock, while General Yeh Chien-ying,* at

---

* Yeh Chien-ying, whom I have not treated for lack of space, is a man to watch. Suavely handsome, he is the chosen spokesman of the People's Liberation Army. It was Yeh who went to Sian with Chou En-lai in 1936, was later posted at Chungking as the Army's representative, and still later served in Nanking as chief of the Communist Conciliation Mission. The son of a rich Cantonese merchant and a graduate of Chu Teh's alma mater, Yünnan Military Institute, Yeh was longtime chief of staff of the Communist armies. He was made mayor of Peiping after that city's surrender and is now mayor of Canton City, Communist China's chief outlet to the Western world. The organization of the Sixth Field Army under his command began in December, 1950.

another meeting, conveyed an impression of learning, though he said little.

Lin Piao puts one in mind of the student who studies the assigned lesson and then lays his book down. He knows Marxist and military literature, but has evidently no inclination toward general reading. This despite the fact that his pungent, detailed military critiques have been used as textbooks and that he has been justly described as "a scholar in warfare." The Chinese, with his bone-bred respect for erudition and a good presence, is disappointed to find that Lin Piao resembles the village carpenter.

But Lin is not a simple man; his unschooled demeanor is hardly the reflection of a frank, direct personality. His evasive answers, sometimes flatly misleading, were the despair of American representatives trying to bring him and Tu Yi-ming to agreement. Lin would appoint a day for conference and discover, fifteen minutes before the appointed time, that he was too ill to attend. Or he would appear, only to advance the same proposals which had been rejected on the preceding day. He spoke temperately, as if he truly sought conciliation, but at the end of the conference matters would not have moved an inch.

Despite his conciliatory demeanor, Lin was jealous of his prerogatives. He grew sullen when he felt that he had been slighted. Bushy eyebrows, knotted over his beaky nose, and a heavy beard, black under his white skin, made his anger dramatic.

His temper was, however, at his own service, for he could forget his dignity when it was to his advantage. Lin, a nonsmoker, received with thanks a carton of Old Golds and a tin of chocolates from an American colonel, though he might properly have been offended by such a niggardly present. Chinese etiquette demands that gifts tendered a general be of fitting lavishness. Moreover, his displays of temperament may well have been painful to himself as well as to others, for

Lin Piao has not been a well man since he was wounded at the battle of P'ing-hsing Pass and forced to undergo medical treatment in the Soviet Union.

*　　*　　*

Though the manner in which the Communist armies swept over China from 1946 to 1950 has been quite fully treated in the recent press, there have been few reports on the positions the Red generals, all soldiers from youth, hold today.

All China is divided into six parts, but not equally. Economic and geographic boundaries have determined the lines along which the nation has been split into semi-autonomous Administrative Areas. The first, Manchuria, is under the chairmanship of Kao Kang, a civilian, but the remaining five are all administered by soldiers. Number-two area is P'eng Te-huai's Northwest Administrative Area, the base of the First Field Army, and number-three, North China, is ruled directly by the Central Government. But General Nieh Jung-chen, originally installed as Communist military governor of North China, retains much power as "Commander of the North China Military Area" and chief of the Fifth Field Army.

East China is ruled by General Jao Shu-shih as political chairman, and General Ch'en Yi as commander-in-chief of the Third Field Army; Ch'en is also mayor of Shanghai. General Lin Piao, concurrently commander-in-chief of the Fourth Field Army, is chairman of the Central China Administrative Area. The scope of General Lin's authority is shown by his other titles. He is also commander of the Central China Military Area, secretary of the regional Communist Party Bureau, and chairman of the Financial and Economic Committee for the same area.

Finally, Liu Po-ch'eng, commanding the Second Field Army, the "liberators" of Tibet, and Ho Lung divide the authority of the Southwest Administrative Area as political

118

chairman and chief of staff respectively. Chu Teh, who seems to have been pigeonholed for the moment, still retains his prestige as first vice-president of the Central Government Committee.

The men who carry on the detailed work of day-to-day rule in China and also command her armed forces, are supported by a corps of second-rank officials, also brought up, for the most part, in the military life. On paper, they are subject to a high degree of control by the Central Government, which checks on appointments and initiates major policy. But they are all men accustomed to exercising great power on their own responsibility; for Communist military procedure of necessity gave much leeway to the initiative of the individual commander.

Rule by generals is an "emergency" measure. The statutes which set up the system of Administrative Areas ruled by Political and Military Committees, provide that "when military action is completed, land reform enforced, and the peoples of various classes thoroughly organized, People's Government Councils shall be chosen by popular election to succeed the present governing bodies." But today only Manchuria is ruled by an organ called the "Manchurian People's Government Council"—itself appointive. The growth in power of the military, assisted by Red China's involvement in Korea, Tibet, and Indo-China, will long defer the election of Government Councils for the other areas.

The Central *People's* Government sits in Peking, while *soldiers'* sub-governments administer China.

5· THREE OLD MEN, THREE REVOLUTIONS: HSÜ T'E-LI, LIN TSU-HAN, TUNG PI-WU

Mao Tse-tung, an indifferent student at Changsha Normal School, once remarked, "I had many teachers, but of them all I remember only two with real admiration. One was Professor Yang, the other Professor Hsü."

Professor Yang was Yang Huai-chung, who saved Mao from expulsion and later became his father-in-law. Professor Hsü was Hsü T'e-li, who is now an elder statesman of the Chinese Communist Party. Yang Huai-chung is remembered for his mordant scholarship and, assuredly, for his daughter as well. Hsü T'e-li is not distinguished for scholarly attainment, nor did he render Mao any special service. The Communist chief remembers him because Hsü T'e-li's relations with his students were characterized by profound sympathy—the Chinese word literally means "fellow feeling." Hsü was not a scholar but a teacher, more concerned with the student than the book.

Today, Hsü T'e-li, at the age of seventy-four, is a member of the Central Committee of the Chinese Communist Party, though he is too old and too unworldly to be entrusted with major political responsibility. But in Peking, the capital of Chinese Communism, he is surrounded by former students who are engaged in remaking China in the image of their own desires. Mao himself and Liu Shao-ch'i went to school under Hsü T'e-li at Changsha First Normal School, while Ts'ai Ch'ang, sister of one of the early Red leaders, and Ting

Ling, the lady novelist, were his students at Chou-nan Girls' School. Many lesser men and women, distinguished for political or cultural achievements, also studied under Hsü T'e-li, as did an entire generation of younger Communists educated in Party schools while he was commissioner of education of first the Kiangsi and later the Northwest Soviet Area.

A native of the city of Changsha, Hsü T'e-li taught for many years in that metropolis of the northeast Hunan plain, which produced nearly half the chief figures of Chinese Communism. He became a specialist in teacher-training, so that not only his students, but the students of his students, who were legion, have felt the influence of the old humanitarian who has taken part in three bloody revolutions. Hsü has turned his own world topsy-turvy. In antiquity-struck China he would ordinarily expect to be revered for his years, but instead Old Hsü delights in the nickname bestowed by the irreverent peasant youths of the Northwest as a tribute to his vigor. They called him "The Old Geezer of Eighteen!"

Hsü first made his political mark in his own blood. While the Manchu dynasty still endured, Chinese loyal to the Empire demanded that its institutions be modernized. The citizens of Changsha were sending two representatives to Peking with their petition requesting the establishment of a National Assembly. On the eve of departure, a mass meeting gathered to cheer the emissaries on their way. Old Hsü, then young Hsü, stepped out of the crowd to stand before the table bearing the petitions. He cut the tip off his little finger, and, taking a fresh sheet of paper, wrote in eight large red characters: "We beg that a National Assembly be called!"

The Manchus were insensible to the pleas of their loyal subjects, and allowed their power to decay unchecked. And loyal reformers became revolutionaries bent on the destruction of the Imperial system. Sent to Japan on an inspection mission by the Kiangsu Provincial Educational Association in the late 1900's, Hsü T'e-li met Sun Yat-sen and joined his radical T'ung-meng Hui.

121

But Old Hsü was never a *homo politicus,* despite his numerous political affiliations. His concern with the individual entrusted to his care kept him close to his lectern and out of the political mainstream. He was a reluctant rebel from the start.

His parents, who were not wealthy, managed to give T'e-li six years of classical education in anticipation of an official career, but he was forced to forgo that plan at the age of seventeen because the money ran out before he was ready to take the civil service examination. Despairing of completing his orthodox Confucian education, Hsü T'e-li turned to the study of geography and mathematics, two subjects which played little part in the prescribed curriculum. When he was eighteen, young Hsü opened a small private school for the sons of well-to-do farmers, who were aware that learning bred wealth, but were not so ambitious as to aspire to official careers. For himself he received 3,000 *wen* a year, just enough to live on with the *wen* roughly one cent.

Old Hsü was later to be grateful, not for his poverty, but for the effects of it. He had been prevented from completing a classical education, already rendered obsolescent by external developments, and had been forced to acquire the beginnings of a Western education. After the Russo-Japanese War, China was shocked out of her resignation by the Japanese demonstration that Orientals could manipulate Western engines of war. Shaking off the pathological conviction that they could not possibly master Western technics, many Chinese began to seek Western-style educations.

Russia's defeat by Japan in 1904 did more to impel Chinese authorities to action than China's own defeat in 1894. The tide of reformist enthusiasm, which rose in old China after the signing of the Treaty of Shimonoseki in 1895, had been checked by the Empress Dowager. That enthusiasm, officially diked, turned into the channel of revolution. But the *déclassé* revolutionists plotted in foreign countries, and Chinese officials went back to their pallets and their opium pipes. After the Treaty of Portsmouth in 1905, even the slothful Court turned

122

to reform. One of their first measures was the abolition of the civil service examination system, and with it the impetus to Confucian education.

Although he was already teaching when he was confronted with this comprehensive change in the Chinese educational system, Hsü T'e-li felt that his own training was inadequate. A crop of Western-style schools was springing up with the left-handed encouragement of the Imperial authorities, and two Hunan teachers returned from Japan to establish the Short-Course Teacher-Training School at Ning-hsiang near Changsha. Hsü enrolled in the six-month course with his friends Chiang Chi-huan, who was to head the Civil Government Section in Kiangsi Province during the late 1920's, and Ho Ching, a gifted orator. In addition to pedagogical technics, Principal Chu Chien-fan had carried a cargo of radical political convictions home from Japan, for he was a member of the T'ung-meng Hui.

T'e-li, who had never been out of Hunan Province, was exposed to ardent special pleading for the doctrines of the most radical of Chinese leaders, Sun Yat-sen. But he did not burst into flames of revolutionary ardor. Indeed, his mild reaction was quite disappointing to his teachers, for they esteemed him highly. Hsü would not be pushed into political activity; he was too eager to get back to his teaching. Unmarried as far as the record shows, Hsü gave his students the love which might otherwise have been given to his own children. He was later to found a boarding school for orphans, and become known throughout the city of Changsha as "Grandmother." Still later, old friends, remembering that nickname, were to call him the "Old Grandmother of the Eighth Route Army."

His first political indocrination was not wholly ineffective. Returning to Changsha after completing the teacher-training course, Hsü started a school for young men, teaching according to the methods he had learned from Chu Chien-fan. The first class was treated to a course of revolutionary lectures, in addition to the conventional training in ideographs and composition and the unconventional mathematics. At least two of the students were deeply impressed. One was to be editor of the *Hsin Hua Jih-pao,* the Communist journal in Chungking during the war years, and another to become a well-known writer in the vernacular.

Shortly after the establishment of this small school, Chu Chien-fan called Hsü T'e-li to Changsha to be instructor of mathematics in a girls' school he had just established. It was later to become Chou-nan Girls' School and graduate a score of prominent "new women." But Hsü did not teach there long. Chu Chien-fan's recommendation won him an appointment from the Shanghai branch of the Kiangsu Provincial Educational Association. Sent to Japan to study primary education, Hsü met Sun Yat-sen and joined the T'ung-meng Hui.

He returned to Hunan with a new enthusiasm—pedagogical, not political. A shortage of teachers made it impossible to teach all the children of rural families who could be spared from the fields. Hsü discovered the solution to that problem in a Japanese practice which had been imported from the West. He wished to bring the little red schoolhouse to China, setting one teacher to manage several grades in one classroom. (The same method which was on the point of being abandoned in the West was suggested as a significant advance in educational practice for China.) To indoctrinate instructors in this method, Hsü set up the Short-Course Teacher-Training School at Changsha, and prepared a series of elementary texts for single-classroom schools. Missionary-like, he toured neighboring counties to lecture on his method, and became nearly as well known for his pedagogical contributions as for his symbolic blood-letting in the cause of parliamentarianism.

Old Hsü, in his enthusiasm for single-classroom teaching, had discounted a problem which was to prove most annoying. With the acute shortage of Western-style teachers, young men entering the profession preferred to teach in middle school, where social prestige provided some compensation for

124

meager wages. They sneered at Hsü's proposal for training "two-grains-of-rice scholars"—an epithet provoked by the miserable salaries paid primary-school teachers. But there were enough poor young men, anxious for any kind of training, to make the project a partial success.

At the same time, Hsü T'e-li, his pedagogue's appetite unsated, began to offer night courses for laborers. His old schoolmate, Chiang Chi-huan, assisted him in the project, and there is a picture of the two young men lecturing to their middle-aged pupils in a Changsha shop they had borrowed for the occasion. Bricklayers, carpenters, and rickshaw-pullers sat in rows, their big bodies twisted on wooden benches. One barefoot coolie had his long bamboo-pipe propped against the leg of the bench as he bent over his primer.

The characters were hard to make out, because the deep-yellow light of the swinging bean-oil lamps was dim on the gray paper. *And sometimes the lessons seemed silly,* the coolie thought, sliding his hand under his battered felt hat to scratch his head. *But tonight's lesson looked useful if it would save the public scribe's fee when a letter had to be sent.*

The young teacher was talking in the earnest way he had: "Now this is the form you'd use for a letter to your father. It starts 'Honorable Father'—that's the common form. But when we write 'Honorable' it isn't the kind of stupid flattery that many men use toward magistrates and prefects, who often don't deserve the title. It's just natural respect for the older generation."

Sometimes these young men didn't make much sense. All this talk about officials, what did that have to do with writing a letter to your father? And what did he mean by running down officials? True they were often robbers or thieves, but they were still appointed by the Emperor.

*   *   *

The concentration of propaganda in the reading and writing lessons was low, for Hsü was more concerned with teach-

ing than with agitation. Agitation was important in its place, but that was other men's work.

After the Revolution of 1911, Hsü T'e-li was rewarded for his services to the victorious T'ung-meng Hui by being appointed director of the Changsha First Normal School. His eight years as director there and adviser to other normal schools in the city were the highwater mark of his pre-Communist teaching career. The fiery Hunanese had backed the revolution all the way, and the teacher who had broken so many lances against the champions of tradition enjoyed a vogue. His students, at the same instant released from service to an oppressive monarchy and an outmoded cultural tradition, gave their new allegiance to the glorious ideals of the West, whence Sun Yat-sen had come to liberate them. In classrooms and public meetings they shouted the magic slogan, "Freedom, equality, and civilization!" Through the open windows the streets echoed their hopes, as the fruit peddler on his rounds cried his wares: "Freedom plums, buy my freedom plums! Fine, fresh civilization peaches! Equality melons are the best melons!"

Although Yüan Shih-k'ai's counter-revolution of 1913 sent revolutionaries fleeing to Japan, Old Hsü was able to continue his work in Changsha. One of his first pupils was T'ien Han, who was later to become famous as a poet, playwright, and associate of Kuo Mo-jo* in the Revolutionary Literature Movement. T'ien Han was a poor boy, and to Hsü's way of thinking a gifted student, though he was lackadaisical in his studies. Detesting mathematics, he filled his notebook with landscapes enlivened by grotesque human figures, freak flowers, and monstrous insects. Despite his literary predilections, T'ien Han rarely turned in his weekly composition, and at the end of the term his average was far below passing. But Hsü refused to expel him, presenting to the faculty the same argument which was later to save Mao Tse-tung's scholastic career.

---

* See Chapter 8.

Rules, Hsü declared, were made for the guidance of the school authorities in dealing with ordinary students. But the faculty could not, he argued, allow those rules to supersede good judgment, or permit them to circumscribe the free development of the extraordinary student. T'ien Han was not expelled.

Old Hsü's disregard of rules was to get him into difficulties with the civil authorities, who footed part of the bill for the school's maintenance. His carelessness in financial matters horrified the proper officials of Changsha's Education Commission, particularly because it was their job to keep the books in order. It was Hsü's habit to throw his own cash and the school's funds into one pot to be drawn on at need. One of the most pleasant anecdotes told about any of the Red leaders hinges upon this characteristic of his.

A student approached Hsü asking for money to buy books and ink.

"How much do you need?" Hsü asked, reaching into the cash-box.

A few days later an agitated inspector of the Education Commission walked into Hsü's office.

"Did you," he asked, "give book money to Li Chi-wen?"

"Yes, I did. What's he been up to?"

"Eating and drinking at the best restaurant in town. I thought it was funny seeing him there when he usually hasn't enough for a bowl of noodles—and no way of getting any money. . . . Look here, you'll have to stop handing money out to the students. We can't afford it, and besides, they'll begin to think they can get anything they want just by lying a little."

"No I don't think that will be necessary," Hsü replied. "A good meal won't do Li's studies any harm. And he won't fool me again; next time he asks for money he'll really want it to buy books."

*　　　*　　　*

Old Hsü's former students like to tell a dozen stories illustrating his disregard of "bureaucratic" regulations in favor of the individual. But his semi-official biography does not mention this trait. The Communists laud rebellion against constituted authority in the cause of Communism, but flat disregard of authority in the interest of the individual is not a characteristic which they desire to encourage.

In 1918, Hsü T'e-li clashed with Changsha authority for the last time. The newly installed military governor, Chang Ching-yao, was even more oppressive than the usual run of Hunan war-lords, but he looked with a tolerant eye on "Old Grandmother" Hsü, who was so busy with the affairs of his school and the orphanage he had founded two years earlier, that he seemed politically inconsequential. But even so, Hsü was a strange type, who might be dangerous. He was always so poorly dressed that it was hard to believe he really held offices of some importance. Wearing a robe he had patched himself, he would buy his dinner from a street-vendor and eat with the coolies.

General Chang Ching-yao's secret service soon reported that the feckless school teacher was a leader of the popular movement which sought to depose him. Chang moved his hand and Hsü T'e-li was forced to flee to sanctuary in Shanghai.

Shanghai, the stewpot of revolution, was abubble over the fire of a new enthusiasm. China's chief contribution to the Allied war effort had been labor battalions, employed behind the lines in France. A few students had gone abroad with them in the hope of finding time to study outside working hours. The stories of students returning from France, and particularly a book called *A Work and Study Student in France—His Own Story,* had roused China's middle-school students. Almost all wanted to go to France, to study and pay their own way by working part-time. After the May Fourth Incident, the Work and Study Movement became an organized drive, despite the revulsion against the West implicit in the Peking rioting. Companies of students sold their belongings to buy tickets to Marseilles—and some professional men gave up their careers. It was another Gold Rush, but the rivers at the end of the trail flowed with knowledge and not with gold.

Forty-two-year-old Hsü T'e-li sailed on a Marseilles-bound ship, a bedraggled old rooster among the young cocks just out of middle school. He told himself that he was going to study European educational technics at first hand, but chuckled in a most unscholarly manner. His expulsion at General Chang's hands had been most opportune. He was going stale in Changsha, but might never have left the city if he had not been forced to go.

Like Chu Teh, who was to go to Berlin soon afterwards, Hsü became the center of a coterie of younger Chinese in Paris. But unlike Chu, who was well provided with funds, Old Hsü had to work his way just like the youngsters. The French were glad to avail themselves of the influx of Chinese cheap labor, though they themselves were resentful of the dollar millionaires who strutted through Europe, secure in the purchasing power of American currency. Some of the boys worked as waiters and cooks, but Hsü, with no menial talents at his command, was an unskilled laborer in a Parisian factory between periods of attendance upon classes at the Universities of Paris and Lyon.

Attacking the French language, he found that he was his own worst student. The pure memory work of learning arbitrary meanings for new sound combinations was not easy at forty-three, when he knew no cognate words to help him along. He annoyed his French friends by demanding that they repeat the simplest words again and again, so that he could get the feel of the language, but his efforts were quite unsuccessful. He had never learned to speak Chinese clearly enough so that northerners were not baffled at first by his furry Hunan accent—and French was no easier. Now that he has lost his teeth, the problem has become acute, and some Chinese complain that half the effect of Hsü's oratory is lost in the effort to understand him.

129

Hsü T'e-li probably met Chou En-lai and Li Li-san in France, for they were students in Paris at the same time. There is no direct evidence to that effect, but one writer comments, "in France were laid the intellectual foundations for Hsü's later loyalty to the Communist Party."

Hsü had been pleased to get away from Changsha, but by 1923 he was eager to get back to work. Governor Chang Ching-yao had been removed and it was safe to return. But the three years in France had altered Hsü, and the situation in China had changed so as to make it impossible for him to resume his old way of life. He felt impelled to supplement his teaching with semi-political public lectures. Urged by his old T'ung-meng Hui comrades, Hsü enrolled in the Kuomintang and became co-leader of the Executive Committee of the Changsha branch with his old teacher Chu Chien-fan. The French experience had accelerated his swing to radicalism; he was soon identified with the extreme left wing of the Nationalist Party. When Chiang Kai-shek ordered the execution of labor leader Ch'en Tsan-hsien, both Hsü and Chu signed a telegram protesting the action.

During the spring of 1927, it was obvious that Kuomintang-Communist cooperation could not continue, and even the left wing of the Kuomintang was alarmed by Chiang Kai-shek's thirst for personal power. Old Hsü, counseled by former students who were Communists, made up his mind during that uneasy springtime. When the red flag was raised at Nanchang in August, he joined Ho Lung's army in the march to the sea and fled with General Ho to Hong Kong after the overthrow of the Swatow Commune. He was formally inducted into the Communist Party on the march.

In the spring of 1928, when Ho Lung was ordered to Shanghai for political training, Hsü T'e-li went with him. Afterwards, the two travelled to Hankow to receive 200 rifles from a Red officer in the government service, and then went to western Hunan by river steamer. Shortly afterwards, Hsü was detached from Ho Lung's command and ordered to Moscow.

At the age of fifty-one, Old Hsü went back to school for the second time. He was, however, finished with "cultural" studies. He attended Sun Yat-sen University in Moscow, the training center for revolutionary leaders of the Far East. The Chinese Section was in the process of expansion as the Comintern called her erring children home for instruction. Young Liu Shao-ch'i had reported for indoctrination, but Hsü was more intimate with two men nearer his own age: dapper Tung Pi-wu and hearty Lin Tsu-han.

* * *

The three were to become a Little Triumvirate, administering the domestic affairs of the Soviet Areas while Mao Tse-tung and his generals turned their attention to the struggle with the Kuomintang and the Japanese. Tung Pi-wu, Lin Tsu-han and Hsü T'e-li were the civil affairs specialists of the Red regime as director of legal affairs, commissioner of finance, and commissioner of education respectively. They were responsible for the day-to-day management of the primitive Communism which prevailed in the backward areas under Red rule until the Communists hurled themselves from the fourth century to the twentieth behind their conquering armies.

Tung Pi-wu and Lin Tsu-han were to rise higher in Party circles than the less sophisticated Old Hsü. Today, both are members of the Party's Central Committee, and the Politburo as well. In the Central People's Government, Tung is principal assistant to Premier Chou En-lai, with the title "Vice-Premier for Political and Legal Affairs." Lin holds the pivotal post of secretary to the Central Government Committee, the body which rules China. The two were straw-bosses of the crews which erected the present governmental structure.

Lin Tsu-han and Tung Pi-wu are optimists. Their careers have been characterized by the dominant trait of hopefulness, for they have been confident since 1910 that they could find the proper fulcrum and a lever long enough to move the world. Their fanatical assurance shines through every crack in the new government's structure.

The men who brought Western democracy to birth were pessimists. They knew that a monolithic government was an invitation to corruption—and feared that the invitation would speedily be taken up. In revolt against the tyranny of monarchs, they feared to replace it with the tyranny of an uncrowned king. Code and custom therefore stipulate that rulers hold their authority from the governed, while the mutual jealousy of various factions and the different arms of government ensures against usurpation of power by any one group.

But Lin Tsu-han and Tung Pi-wu are optimists. Because of their faith in Red virtue, they have placed no such restraints upon the present rulers of China. Their design for a governmental system follows the principle of "democratic centralism" enunciated by Liu Shao-ch'i.* The word "democratic" is justified by provision for popular elections, but at this writing no body chosen by popular election rules in China. The principle of "centralism" is more secure, since all power is derived from and funnels back to the sixty-three man Central Government Committee, whose secretary Lin Tsu-han is.

Yet neither man's experience of life has been such as to inspire faith in the integrity of rulers.

Lin Tsu-han—also known as Lin Po-ch'ü—was born in 1882, in the city of Ling-ling, Hunan Province, near the Kwangsi border, 200 miles southwest of Changsha. Although his father was a primary school teacher—one of the company of "two-grains-of-rice scholars"—income from landholdings kept the family comfortably well off, and it was early decided that young Lin should be a teacher too. After graduating from Ch'ang-te Normal School near Changsha, he was shipped off to Tokyo to attend higher normal school on a

---

* See Chapter 7.

government stipend. Later he studied at Japan's *Chuo Daigaku*—Central University.

At home in Ling-ling, the Lin family were shocked by his letters: they had sent the boy abroad to get a respectable education, and he was hobnobbing with radicals. In Japan, Lin Tsu-han met Sun Yat-sen and Huang Hsing, the patriarch of the revolutionary movement. He joined the Hsing-chung Hui (Raise Up China Society), and in 1905, when that group was reorganized as the Ko-ming T'ung-meng Hui (Revolutionary Unity Society), Lin was a charter member. The following year, he was ordered to Manchuria by the T'ung-meng Hui, to teach school at Kirin and win his conspiratorial spurs. The T'ung-meng Hui, which had its financial roots among the overseas Chinese, was just beginning to grow into China proper in preparation for the overthrow of the Manchus.

The work was dangerous, for the headsman's sword had become the basis as well as the symbol of the authority of the jittery Manchus. Never bound by their own elaborate legal codes, they took the Empire's peril as sanction for dispensing with legal process. The finger of suspicion pointed directly to the grave.

Lin proved expert at evading it. After teaching for two years in Manchuria, he was engaged for a third year in what one biographer calls simply "secret work." It was more of the same, probably inside the Great Wall after he had proved himself in Manchuria. In 1909 he was ordered to return to Ling-ling. The T'ung-meng Hui, like the Communist Party afterwards, preferred to use its agents in areas where they were well known. Both groups utilized the social, business, and even bandit connections of their members. When the 1911 Revolution broke out, Lin was one of the leaders of the Hunan branch of the T'ung-meng Hui. As such he became a charter member of the Kuomintang, when that party was created by the union of the T'ung-meng Hui and other groups in 1912.

In 1913, the abortive Second Revolution against Yüan Shih-k'ai forced Lin to flee to Japan. Another refugee was Tung Pi-wu, fleeing his position as salt tax commissioner at the Yangtze River port of Ichang. Tung, who was also the son of a teacher, had not been abroad before 1913. Born in Huang-an, Hupei Province, in 1886, he attended Wuchang Middle School in the industrial heart of China. His father, sprung from the gentry, held with the old ways, urging his son to improve his classical scholarship. But young Tung Pi-wu preferred to become an assistant-instructor in the school from which he had just graduated. While teaching, he formalized his divorce from the orthodox tradition by joining the T'ung-meng Hui. His membership in that organization won him the tax post, from which he was soon expelled because of that same affiliation.

Tung Pi-wu took advantage of his enforced absence from China to complete his education in the law at the Institute of Political Science and Law in Japan. Lin, four years older, received his first practical lessons in the economics of revolution in Japan, while assisting Sun Yat-sen in fund-raising in preparation for a new bid for power. Tung was to remain in Japan until his graduation in 1917, but Lin, already a finished conspirator, was ordered to return to Hunan in 1915 to become secretary to the Kuomintang sympathiser, General Ch'eng Ch'ien. He was to stay with General Ch'eng for several years and become his chief of staff, a promotion dictated more by political than military considerations.

While Lin Tsu-han was becoming a political soldier, Tung Pi-wu was a propagandist in Szechwan Province from 1917 to 1920. In the latter year he returned to the Wu-Han area to open a middle school, which provided an excellent cover for his Kuomintang revolutionary activities. In 1921 it was to become the center-point of Communist agitation in the pivotal province of Hupei, for Tung Pi-wu was a delegate to the meeting in Shanghai's French Concession in July, 1921, where the Communist Party of China had its formal beginning. There he met Mao Tse-tung for the first time.

In 1922 Lin Tsu-han followed Tung Pi-wu's lead, to become a member of the Chinese Communist Party after talking with Secretary-general Ch'en Tu-hsiu. Chosen an alternate member of the Central Executive Committee of the Kuomintang in 1924, Lin was identified with the left wing of the Nationalist Party. He taught at the Whampoa Military Academy in the Political Training Department under Chou En-lai. On the Northern Expedition, Lin Tsu-han served as Kuomintang representative in General Ch'eng Ch'ien's Sixth Army, and was a member of the Revolutionary Military Committee and finance commissioner of the left-wing Hankow Government of Wang Ching-wei, Borodin, and Madame Sun Yat-sen.

Tung Pi-wu was on a parallel track. An obedient Communist, he turned to the proletariat at the Comintern's order, participating in the organizational work for the railroad strikes of 1923. After politico-military assignments in Szechwan and Manchuria, he was elected an alternate member of the Kuomintang's Central Executive Committee in 1926, and served on the Hupei Provincial Committees of both the Kuomintang and the Communist Party.

In the summer of 1927, when the die was cast at Nanchang, both Tung Pi-wu and Lin Tsu-han went left. They quit the Kuomintang and fled to Japan, whence they arrived in Moscow in the spring of 1928 to meet Hsü T'e-li.

*   *   *

There is no precise record of the character of the training given to these three and to Liu Shao-ch'i, Liu Po-ch'eng, and a dozen other Red leaders who were in Moscow at the same time. It was a period of confusion. Theoretical justification and dialectical name-calling could not sweeten the Comintern's defeat in China, nor restore the shattered cornerstone of its Asian policy. Nor could they disguise the fact that the Chinese at Sun Yat-sen University were refugees as well as students. While the Third International was casting about for a new China policy, the Chinese comrades were certainly called upon for suggestions. However the deliberations in Moscow were quite meaningless, for Mao Tse-tung, at home in China, was making his own China policy. Lin Tsu-han, for one, seems to have tired of the futility of these councils, for he soon left Moscow to open a school for Chinese refugees in Khabarovsk, north of Vladivostok.

In 1931 and 1932, the refugees began to drift back to China through the meshes of the Kuomintang blockade. The wheels of the underground railroad, greased with bribes, carried them safely into the Reds' major stronghold in Kiangsi Province. There they took up the tasks which were to occupy them for years to come.

Lin Tsu-han became commissioner of finance. In his rumpled cotton tunic, his spectacles repaired with string, Lin would have shocked even the liberal economists who were beginning to run the show in Washington at the time. They would have been appalled at his problems, for he had few resources with which to carry out two antagonistic tasks. He had first to extract from a poor, predominantly agricultural economy, funds to maintain an army. At the same time, the peasants had to feel that their lot was being improved, in order to insure their loyalty to the Red regime.

In 1934, Lin Tsu-han summarized his own problems: "For the economic reconstruction of the Soviet Areas we must raise agricultural and industrial production. By promoting trade with the outside we must make our Soviet markets prosper. We must develop the cooperative movement, and collect capital to back Soviet currency. An especially grave problem is the accumulation of foodstuffs.

"Moreover, the social consciousness of the inhabitants of the Soviet areas must be heightened; we must increase the guidance by the agencies of economic reconstruction and, above all, we must ferret out all elements who plot to nullify or retard our economic reconstruction through sabotage."

Lin came to a partial solution of his problems by doing

away with corruption, thitherto an inescapable feature of Chinese financial administration, and by utilizing to the utmost the labor power available to him. He may have received some financial assistance from the Comintern and used the funds in his dealings with the White regions, for, by his own testimony, the Chinese Soviet was not entirely cut off from trade with the outside. But the region was too small to be self-sufficient in any real sense. When the blockade was tightened in the Nationalist "Fifth Bandit Extermination Campaign," acute shortages of such staples as salt and cloth forced the Red Army to move its base.

On the Long March much of the Red's small stock of capital goods was lost. Heavy machinery from the arsenal and printing presses were jettisoned in the first stages of the march to the Northwest. Despite these losses, Lin met with greater success in Shensi, because the area was larger, the population smaller, and battle lines more fluid. Soldiers who were not in the lines were employed in production in accordance with the plan worked out by General P'eng Te-huai.

After the Seven-Seven Day (July 7, 1937) when the Japanese provoked the "China Incident," Lin Tsu-han, Tung Pi-wu and Hsü T'e-li were all tapped for missions to the outside, but life in the cave city of Yenan changed little, though the Reds had become allies of the Kuomintang in the war against Japan. Chief Justice Tung Pi-wu, a member of the Central Committee and soon to be elected to the Politburo, committed criminals to a prison carved into the yellow cliffs, and Old Hsü conducted the business of the Education Commission from a cave office.

Official rank had not worked any change in Old Hsü's nonchalant personal habits. Students hurrying to get out of the rain would meet the Commissioner of Education walking barefoot in the mud, his shoes slung around his neck. He told them that wearing shoes in the rain cut their life, and he was determined to make his pair last for at least two years. "My feet," he added, "won't wear out."

137

In 1937 Old Hsü went home again. He was assigned to the Eighth Route Army mission in Changsha, where he was worth a library of propaganda tracts to the Communists. It had been ten years since the old man left town, but he was well remembered. One newspaper reported that "friends, students, and the students of his students flocked to see him." He still loved to talk and was happiest when lecturing a crowd of attentive youngsters.

But he was still a maverick, too independent to be elected to the Politburo. The man who had copied out *Das Kapital* from beginning to end to train his memory—and reinforce his theology—seems never to have arrived at complete orthodoxy. Pro-Communist writers say that Hsü's strong point is harmonizing doctrine and reality in the manner of Mao Tse-tung himself, but the explanation reads like a euphemism for a lack of complete conviction. An incident in Changsha led an ex-student named Shu to wonder whether the Communists might not have doubts as to the old man's fidelity.

Shu entered the Changsha office of the Eighth Route Army to find Old Hsü sitting at a small table, in the path of the sunlight shining through the small window. A pair of reading glasses rested on the flat bridge of his nose. His heavy body was bent over a tattered wadded-jacket, which lay in his lap, as he worked a length of coarse thread through the cloth with a large needle. With his left hand, he brushed his thin, straggling hair away from his small eyes. He looked like an old Mongol horseman repairing his riding gear, for the skin of his face was weathered to a ruddy brown, and the long wrinkles, which creased the skin of his cheeks, extended to his chin to frame his broad mouth.

After they had chatted for a while, Old Hsü accompanied his former student to the door. Stepping outside, he said, "It's not really convenient for you to come here to see me. After this I'll come to your house, and we'll be better able to converse."

Each Saturday for the next three months, Old Hsü came to

138

Shu's home after dinner. The two sometimes talked until one or two in the morning, for the old man dearly loved to lecture, though he was an impatient listener.

Later, Old Hsü went back to the Red areas to assume the presidency of the Academy of Natural Sciences and take up housekeeping in his cave once more. At the present time, he is a member of the Central Government Committee, which holds all authority in Communist China. That body is the creation of Tung Pi-wu and Lin Tsu-han. The two began experimenting with government-making in 1937, when Tung became chairman of the Shensi-Kansu-Ninghsia Border Area, the formal governmental unit of the Red stronghold. Lin followed Tung in that post.

After the second entente was concluded in 1937, Tung and Lin were posted to Sian as Communist representatives to the Nationalist Government. They were to take part, until 1947, in the fruitless negotiations between the two parties to the Chinese civil war, which paused for the first half of the war against Japan and then resumed *pianissimo* in 1941, to swell *forte* in 1945. Lin and Tung also served as members of the Political Consultative Council, which met under Central Government sponsorship to discuss the creation of a government satisfactory to both sides.

In Sian on May 4, 1944, Lin Tsu-han began a series of discussions with Nationalist representatives General Chang Chih-chung, now a member of the Peking government, and Dr. Wang Shih-chieh, who is now in exile on Formosa. Three problems occupied their attention: (1) the disposition of Communist armies with regard to the Nationalist forces; (2) the relationship between Communist-controlled local governments and the Central Government; and (3) the position of the Communist Party with regard to the Central Government, and the linked question of civil rights. Talk continued into September, but there could be no agreement on any one of the three points.

Judgment of intent is hazardous, but, at a venture, it

would appear that both parties sincerely desired to effect a compromise in 1944. However, their basic premises made effective cooperation impossible, as did the accumulated bitterness and distrust of two decades. Each party yearned for peaceful cooperation—on its own terms. Lin Tsu-han played a major role in negotiations from 1937 to 1947, but Chou En-lai was diplomat-in-chief. The problem will therefore be discussed at greater length in the account of his life.*

*   *   *

Tung Pi-wu's signature appears on the Charter of the United Nations Organization, signed at San Francisco in June, 1945. His presence at the San Francisco Conference was a concession granted by the Nationalist Government at the insistence of American Ambassador Patrick J. Hurley. But Tung was at San Francisco as a Communist member of the Chinese Government delegation, not as a representative of the Communist regime.

As a representative of the Communist regime, he took part, in 1946, in negotiations for a coalition government, an aborted project, and was chief delegate in Nanking from the time of Chou En-lai's departure until the Central Government ordered him to leave on February 11, 1947.

With this preparation behind them, Tung Pi-wu and Lin Tsu-han entered the most important period of their service to the Communist Party of China. On May 1, 1948, the Central Committee passed a resolution calling on representatives of "united workers, farmers, soldiers, students, merchants, and all oppressed classes, every people's organization, each democratic party and faction, all minority races, overseas Chinese in all lands, and other patriotic elements" to assemble in the "Liberated Areas."

They were to prepare for a People's Political Consultative

---

* See Chapter 9.

Conference, which would determine the structure of the "coalition government" to be established after the greater part of China was "liberated." In August, 1948, representatives began to arrive. (One was Ssu-t'u Mei-t'ang, eighty-four-year-old delegate of American Chinese.) In Harbin, Manchuria, on November 25, 1948, the delegates met representatives of the Central Committee to discuss the composition of the Preparatory Commission for the People's Political Consultative Conference. Delegates acceptable to the Communists were made members of the Preparatory Commission. Lin Tsu-han, his face smoothly youthful under thick white hair, hurried from committee-room to conference-chamber, keeping the delegates in line. As secretary-general, he was responsible for coordinating their decisions, a function he continued to fill when the Consultative Conference was formally convened in September, 1949.

Since the full session of the People's Political Consultative Conference did little more than hear and approve the recommendations of the Preparatory Commission, the latter body really determined the governmental structure through which China is now ruled. Most decisions had already been taken when the Preparatory Commission was formally created on June 15, 1949, with Mao Tse-tung as chairman and five vice-chairmen: Communist Chou En-lai; Li Chi-shen of the Kuomintang Revolutionary Committee; Ch'en Chün-ju of the Democratic League; Kuo Mo-jo, an independent; and Ch'en Hsü-t'ung of the "commercial and industrial world." Communist Li Wei-han was secretary.

The ratio of three Communists to four non-Communists was roughly the same as that which was to prevail in future bodies. However, any estimate of the extent of Communist control must take into account the fact that Kuo Mo-jo, a non-party Marxist, could be depended on to follow the Party line. Moreover, the Communists were the only party which could present a full program, and the Party's Central Committee had controlled the composition of the Preparatory

Commission, the parent cell from which all other organs of the People's Government were to proliferate. Nevertheless, the Communists stoutly maintain that the People's Political Consultative Conference, acting on the recommendations of the Preparatory Commission, created a "coalition" government.

Slack-mouthed Tung Pi-wu voiced the Communists' views on both coalition government and opposition parties in his address to the plenary session of the Conference on September 22, 1949. As chairman of the Preparatory Commission's sub-committee which drafted the Organic Laws, Tung reported from a silk-draped table supporting six microphones. Behind his bald head hung the seal of the Consultative Conference, flanked by photographic portraits of Mao Tse-tung on the right and Sun Yat-sen on the left. The skin of Tung Pi-wu's jaws hung loose, and his moth-antenna mustache worked up and down as he read from papers clutched in his left hand:

"The principle of *democratic centralism* is in opposition to the three-power principle of old-line democracy. In the legislatures of old-line democracy, a small controlling group drawn from the capitalist class, permits another small group, the so-called opposition, to posture on the platform and bawl out empty words. But the group in control retains a tight grip on the actual administrative power, which it manipulates in its own interest. This is, in truth, play-acting before the people; the exploiting class divides the spoils behind the façade of democracy, erected to deceive the people. The judicial arm is independent in name, but in reality serves the ruling circles in the same manner. We do not desire this set [of pretences]. In our system, legislation and execution are unified; all power is concentrated in the Government of the People's Representative Council.*"

Characteristically, Tung Pi-wu lumped together the concepts of the loyal opposition and the division of powers, to

---

* A body not yet formed.

dismiss them in a single phrase. The new Chinese government does without either check upon its exercise of power. This extreme "centralization" makes it possible for the Communist Party to control the government, as it does the organs of public opinion.

The Central Government is indeed "centralized." The font of authority is the People's Central Government Committee, whose roster was approved by vote of the captive Consultative Conference. Lin Tsu-han is secretary-general of the Government Committee, which rules through four subordinate agencies.

The first is the State Administrative Council (Cabinet), the highest executive organ, with Premier Chou En-lai at its head. Vice-premiers head the three sub-committees of the Administrative Council: Tung Pi-wu for Political and Legal Affairs; Ch'en Yün for Financial and Economic Affairs; and Kuo Mo-jo for Culture and Education. Li Wei-han is secretary to the Administrative Council. Of the six top administrative officials, only Kuo Mo-jo and Vice-Premier (without portfolio) Huang Yen-p'ei are not Communist Party members.

The People's Revolutionary Military Committee, chaired by Mao Tse-tung, but with a membership drawn chiefly from among professional soldiers, is a separate agency. Two other sub-bodies are the Supreme Court and the Censorate. The Court is the "highest legal authority," while the People's Censorate is charged with the task of seeing that "officials and private citizens discharge their proper responsibilities."

The Chinese Communists have erected an edifice which resembles the English more than the American model. However, it lacks the twin safeguards of custom and party responsibility, and the only sovereign is the state. (Mao is not president of China, but of the People's Central Government Committee.) Nor was the Central People's Government chosen by popular election. The people made the revolution, pricked on by the Party, but they have not made the government.

143

The Organic Laws provide that the Central Government Committee shall "prepare for and convene a conference of representatives of the entire nation," the representatives presumably to be chosen by popular vote. Though no date is prescribed, the implication is that elections will be held when the present emergency ends and the period of transition passes. Optimists Lin Tsu-han and Tung Pi-wu are obviously confident that the people will eventually rule, while old Hsü T'e-li has made no public declarations. But non-Communist Chinese, remembering that the "transitional period" of Chiang Kai-shek's rule lasted from 1927 until a constitutional convention finally met in 1946, wonder: "How long is a transition?"

6. LOVE, DEATH, AND RADICALISM:
TING LING

Changsha, the capital of Hunan Province, lies in a valley shaped like a shallow basin. Natives of the Changsha plain are known throughout China for their addiction to hot peppers and their fiery dispositions. In addition to the small red peppers clustered in every free space, the valley produces two other crops in abundance: rice and revolutionaries. Mao Tse-tung was born in Shao-shan Village about ten miles south of Changsha; the grand old man of the Party, Hsü T'e-li, is a native of the Changsha area; and General P'eng Te-huai was raised in Hsiang-hsi, not far from the city.

In 1905, another revolutionist was born in the town of An-fu, just south of Changsha. Her father was a member of the Chiang family, and she was given the personal name Ping-chih, but it is not as Chiang Ping-chih that she is known to-day. Though Chiang Ping-chih is familiar to few, the name "Ting Ling" will draw a nod of recognition from even the illiterate peasants of northwest China, for she has written simple propaganda plays for their consumption, as well as more conventional novels and short stories.

Ting Ling made her reputation as the chronicler of the "new woman," shaped by the revolution in Chinese society. Her writing, though matter of fact in style, is dramatic because of the sexual and political tensions which work upon her characters. She has evidently given valid expression to the experience and desires of Chinese women, for within three years after she began to publish in 1928, she had gained wide popularity. Her life has been as dramatic as those of her characters, but her artistic career has been comparatively smooth. ' Ting Ling's position as China's foremost woman writer has been beyond challenge since 1931.'

Ting Ling was secretary of the League of Left Wing Writers, formed in Shanghai in March, 1930, by Kuo Mo-jo, Lu Hsün and Mao Tün, to unite socially conscious writers against the government—and the publishers. The *Dipper*, a monthly under her editorship, was a major organ of the League until its suppression, just before her arrest in 1933. Upon her escape from prison in 1936, Ting Ling entered the Northwest Soviet Area, where she was received as a long-lost comrade, for she had joined the Communist Party in 1931.

Immediately after her arrival in Paoan, the capital of the Soviet Area, she was named vice-chairman of the Red Army Guard Unit. At that time Mao Tse-tung, whose second wife had been a schoolmate of Ting Ling, wrote a poem to welcome her:

> An hour past a personage to Paoan came.
> In our caves we feted her,
> To hail her escape from jail;
> In the past a literary miss,
> She is now a general of armies.

* * *

Ting Ling was blessed—or cursed—with remarkable parents, who put upon her the burden of living up to them. Her mother, one of the earliest students at Changsha First Women's Normal School, became a primary-school principal in 1916. Her father, who studied in Japan before becoming an official in the Imperial civil service, was a young man of excessively generous temperament. He had a passion for horses, which Ting Ling has inherited without inheriting his skill in managing them. It was his custom to tuck a long whip under his arm and ride out on the highway to exhibit his mount. He sometimes returned on foot, cheerfully flicking his boots with his riding-whip.

Ting Ling's mother would ask: "What about your horse?"

"Oh," her father would reply, "he's a fine horse."

"And where has he flown away?"

No answer.

She would answer for him: "You sold him, didn't you— or gave him away? You met a fine upstanding fellow who admired the horse, and you felt that such a splendid horse should be mounted by a remarkable man. Then you practically forced the horse on him. Didn't you?"

"Not at all. He wasn't a remarkable man, just a fellow who understood horses. I don't see what you're angry about. Here I come home feeling fine after a generous deed—and you get angry."

"I? Angry? It's not I who should be angry, but you. You're a grown man and yet you act like an infant. Just because you have a few extra acres and a good wife, there's no reason for carrying on so. If you feel generous, you might sell a few acres and do something useful with it, like founding a school."

Ting Ling's father died at the age of thirty-one, leaving his widow to care for the ten-year-old daughter and a younger son. The three moved to Ch'ang-te, twenty miles north of An-fu on the Changsha plain, where the mother devoted herself wholly to the children's education, keeping aloof from the neighbors. After a year, tired of inactivity and eying her dwindling capital, she decided to make work for herself. Assembling a number of graduates of Changsha Women's Normal School to serve as a faculty, she set up a girls' primary school.

Ting Ling received her early education under her mother's supervision in an atmosphere quite advanced for the day. Most striking was the militant feminism the widow displayed in running a school with an all-female faculty—and without male sponsorship. Twenty years earlier it had been unseemly for a Chinese woman to display interest in scholarship—or even write a good hand.

The males of the Chiang family were a sickly lot; before long the little brother died of a fever, while Ting Ling came through a bout with the same illness rosier and fatter. Mother and daughter were left to mourn their dead together, but Ting Ling's own departure from home was not long delayed by her brother's death. The break seemed minor at first. She entered the Second Girls' Normal School of T'ao-yüan County at Hsiang-hsi, thirty miles from home. Her record at school was, her Chinese biographer delicately puts it, "not of a character to evoke surprise." She got by, complaining of the inadequacy of the faculty and the library, both of which were, in truth, somewhat outdated.

Despite the opposition of the conservative school authorities, the students were given a full dose of radicalism, for Hsiang-hsi was well within the range of the libertarian hotbed at Changsha. The brave slogans of the May Fourth Movement inflamed the little girls' imaginations as they squirmed under the discipline of their old-fashioned teachers. Catchwords like "Self-awareness and Self-determination!" and "Freedom and Equality!" echoed in the dormitory. They made a lovely sound in Ting Ling's ears as she discoursed, her ribbon-tied pigtails bobbing around her plump face. The sounding phrases set her blood pounding, and the rapt attention of her schoolmates made her feel profound indeed. The torrent of words swept over sorrow for her brother and father, and the cravings of adolescence were fed by promise of magnificent fulfillment. Political intoxication palliated personal frustration and pain.

Inflammatory talk led to ostentatious action. Put on their mettle by the news that a boys' middle school in Changsha had agreed to admit female students, Ting Ling and three schoolmates defied parental and pedagogical disapproval to

148

steal away from the school they had so often denounced. She was a fourteen-year-old sophomore at the time.

With Ting Ling travelled a girl named Wang, whose home was in eastern Szechwan, and two youngsters from Hupei Province. The four were welcomed by the faculty of the Changsha middle school, who were a little discomfited to find that their grandiloquent gesture had conjured up four eager young ladies out of the interior.

But the inoculation of enthusiasm had taken too well. Changsha was just a waystation for the four. They soon decided that their new freedom was still too constraining—and were off again. This time the destination was Shanghai, the wellspring of advanced ideas for all of southern China. The girls hoped to enter Shanghai University.

By this time, almost two years after the incident of May 4, 1919, Shanghai had become the radicals' haven. The foreign concessions, where the Chinese law did not obtain, offered sanctuary from the repressive measures of an alarmed government, and the city was the *entrepôt* for literature and visitors from the West. The roster of professors at Shanghai University for the years 1920 to 1924 is studded with the names of Red leaders. Ch'en Tu-hsiu was Dean of Letters and Ch'ü Ch'iu-pai was chairman of the Sociology Department. Shao Li-tze, Li Ta, and Mao Tün, delegates to the People's Political Consultative Conference of September, 1949, were all members of the faculty. Later Communist writers have called Shanghai University "a training school for Party cadres."

Shanghai was not only a political nursery, but also a literary seedbed. Ch'en Tu-hsiu was already famous for his advocacy of the New Literature Movement in the *New Youth* magazine, and Ch'ü Ch'iu-pai was to become a leading Marxist theorist on the function of art in revolution. Mao Tün had already had some success in imaginative writing, and was later to become one of the five chief figures of modern Chinese literature. Today Ting Ling also stands within that charmed circle.

149

When she came downriver from Changsha with her entourage, little Ting Ling would have been loath to predict such future eminence. Not because she had any doubts about her abilities or opportunities, with the wide world before her, but because she had not yet selected the field in which she would excel. All enthusiasm, she descended upon Shanghai, to be checked before she had started. The girls, too young to enter college, were forced to attend the People's Women's School, a "proletarian" preparatory school, before they were permitted to register for classes at Shanghai University. In the interim, one died, and another, frightened of the Bohemian life, went back to Hunan, leaving only Ting Ling and Miss Wang from Szechwan to sit at the feet of Ch'en Tu-hsiu and Ch'ü Ch'iu-pai in the Literature Department of Shanghai University.

After class, the girls, enchanted by the leftist doctrines, sought the company of their instructors. They lived for a time in the same boarding house as Ch'ü Ch'iu-pai and Shih Ts'ün-t'ung, another charter member of the Chinese Communist Party. The Party had already been formed. Those men were its leaders, and Shanghai was its headquarters. There was much furtive coming and going of Party functionaries in the drab boarding house, while after dark, policy debates stretched into the morning hours. The plump little girl from Hunan was sometimes allowed to listen to the arguments, occasionally throwing out a timid opinion, which was received with either exaggerated deference or quick laughter. She was hardly permitted to sit in on discussions of major policy, but the atmosphere in the boarding house was charged with Communist ardor. Her instructors lived only for the revolution and propagandized as they breathed—spontaneously and continuously. During the years at Shanghai University, Ting Ling's general reformist enthusiasm was turned into the specific Communist channel.

But she did not enter the Party at that time, either because she did not yet know her own mind, or because she was too young to be asked. Ting Ling was just nineteen in 1924 when she left Shanghai for Peking, the traditional hub of Chinese culture. She enrolled in the Chinese Literature Department of Peking University, the intellectual storm-center of transition China. Her objectives were not clearly defined. She only knew that one ought to study to perfect one's self for service to the people, and the study of literature appealed to her. Peking University, shaped her life as it did Mao Tse-tung's. But in her case the influence was oblique.

A fellow student at Pei-ta was the hotheaded young editor of the *Mass Literature* magazine, Hu Ye-p'ing. He had resigned as a cadet at the Naval Academy to devote himself to the cause of left-wing literature. The Communist leaders, thinking well of him, recommended Hu to Ting Ling. He in turn was smitten with the tiny girl from Hunan, whose wide eyes looked out of a classic "moon face," beloved of Chinese poets. The lady Yang Kuei-fei, the most famous beauty of Chinese history, had such a face above a plump body like Ting Ling's. Despite these advantages, Ting Ling was rather pretty than beautiful, but her vivacity overweighed a lack of physical perfection.

Emotionally, she had not come far from the bright-eyed little girl who had set out from Changsha four years earlier. Given to moments of exultation and despair, she needed someone to share her enthusiasms and cushion the fall into depression. Despite her aggressive feminism, she showed the traditional dependence of the well-bred Chinese lady; her will required external stiffening. Ting Ling had drifted away from her travelling companion, Miss Wang, and felt alone in the city. She was just beginning to manifest those intellectual traits which would later make her famous, but, for the most part, she must have seemed invitingly plastic. To Hu Ye-p'ing it seemed that she was a worthy comrade to be won for the cause, and a congenial woman to be won for himself.

Although she needed a comrade, Hu's ardor at first repelled her. She was cool to him amid her tears. She wailed that she would not be alone in the world if only her little brother had lived. Hu Ye-p'ing saw the opening, and presented himself to fill the place of her dead brother. Whatever the reason, they soon became lovers. She was lonely; he was attractive and importunate. Therefore the classic formula must serve: they met, they loved, and—after a time—they married.

Like so many of her contemporaries, Ting Ling's emotional and political lives were entwined root and branch. She married Hu to serve her emotional needs, but their political affinity was decisive in her choice. Even before they began to live together, they had agreed that two persons working together could exert a greater social effect than they could as individuals. Her Chinese biographer remarks that "the two had already felt a desire to perform some function in society. They didn't really care about the nature of the task, as long as it was something they could do well. The two ached to *assume a social role.*"

This gravely responsible attitude toward social duties is a primary characteristic of the modern Chinese intellectual, one which the present Communist government is attempting to broaden and exploit. But Ting Ling's dedication to social service did not purify her of personal desire. Like the rest of humanity, and more particularly G. B. Shaw's Englishman, who " . . . supports his king on loyal principles, and cuts off his king's head on republican principles, his watchword . . . always duty," the Chinese is adept at finding a public reason for the satisfaction of a private want. She married Hu Ye-p'ing the better to serve China—she said.

Life with Hu was pleasant, but not easy for Ting Ling. Aside from the occasional sale of a manuscript and frequent remittances from her mother, they lived by borrowing from friends and pawning their belongings. Always pinched for money and searching for an outlet for his stories, Hu had a pet project guaranteed to solve all their problems. He wanted a magazine to take the place of *Mass Literature,* a financial mortality. Ting Ling sometimes tired of his obsession, though she had promised to do the clerical work once the magazine was underway. When Hu and his friend Shen Ts'ung-wen urged her to try her hand on a piece for the magazine, she invariably declined.

"One writer in the family is enough," she would say. "I'm no writer and never will be. You two take care of the artistic side and I'll manage the business end."

In spite of her lack of enthusiasm, she was to be impelled to enter upon the practice of literature. Ye-p'ing's impetuous spirit often carried him to the edge of disaster, and it fell to Ting Ling to abate the effects of his recklessness. That responsibility, and the fight to keep rice money in the family cashbox, left her little time to think of writing. She complained loudly, but was happy, for Hu's staunch optimism provided the support her unstable spirits needed. But the task of maintaining the family budget was beginning to overwhelm her. Finally she decided to take a fling at the writing business, encouraged by her literary friends, who felt that a woman writer treating women's lives might attain some financial success.

The editor of the *Short Story Monthly* had pressed her to do some stories for him. One day in 1928, impelled more by hope of cash returns than by artistic necessity, she sat herself down to compose a short story. "Yellow Jade" took its material from her efforts to break into motion pictures in 1922. She described the tumultuous world which engulfed the young girl come to Shanghai from the provinces to make her fortune. The *Short Story Monthly* published "Yellow Jade" and asked for more stories. Ting Ling obliged with "Sophie's Diary," which she is reported to have written in one week's time. She was paid 140 *yüan,* a respectable price for two stories. More important, they were well received and all literary Peking wondered who "Ting Ling" could be.

Her success bolstered the family finances, and not long thereafter she and Hu Ye-p'ing were formally married. Ting Ling continued to write for the *Short Story Monthly,* while

Hu began to earn some money from his contributions to the literary supplement of the *Peking Morning Post*. In their sudden prosperity, Hu saw a chance to put through his favorite project. Ting Ling, Hu Ye-p'ing and Shen Ts'ung-wen banded together to publish the *Red and Black*, a magazine which was an artistic success—and a financial failure.

In 1928, the Northern Expedition seemed to have succeeded in uniting the nation under the rule of Chiang Kai-shek. The repressive policy which the Kuomintang adopted toward leftists in general and writers in particular, forced radicals to seek refuge in the foreign quarters of Shanghai once again. Ting Ling and Hu Ye-p'ing joined the southward migration early in 1929, taking up residence in the French Concession. In November, 1930, a son was born to them.

They had joined the League of Left Wing Writers in March, 1930, and were quite active in its support. But Hu, tired of restricting himself to words, wanted direct action. The details of his career as an agitator are obscure. He was rumored to have organized the Rickshaw Pullers' Union and to have led its strikes. At any rate, the effects of his underground activities were evidently worthy of the Kuomintang's attention.

*   *   *

On January 17, 1931, Hu Ye-p'ing disappeared. He had visited Shen Ts'ung-wen that morning to ask assistance in preparing a formal funeral scroll for his landlord's nephew, in lieu of rent. At the apartment in the French Concession that evening, Shen found that Hu had not returned. Ting Ling and he waited through the night for Ye-p'ing's homecoming. The next day they began to make enquiries of their friends. They could learn little besides the fact that thirty-four men and women had been arrested in a raid on the Far Eastern Hotel in the French Concession. Among the thirty-four, it was rumored, were seven writers.

On the evening of the second day, Shen Ts'ung-wen returned to his lodgings to find a note. He read:

TS'UNG-WEN:

I've run into some trouble. Yesterday, after our chat, I left your rooms and went to the Hsien-shih Company, where I met a girl I know. She insisted on dragging me off to the Far Eastern Hotel to see another friend. How was I to know that I'd be arrested by mistake as soon as I got there?

Will you beg Messrs. Hu [Hu Shih] and Ts'ai [Ts'ai Yüan-p'ei, former president of Peking University, in 1931 director of the Academia Sinica] to help get me out of here. Also hire Wu Ching-hsiung as my lawyer, and have him start an action before they take me off to Lung Hua [Prison].

You know my position—things must be done quickly. If you let things slide, anything can happen. And please see Ting Ling and the kid. Tell her not to worry.

The thing can't be put off. If it is, matters may become serious. I'm really jumpy.

YE-P'ING

But there was no news from official sources. Ting Ling and Shen Ts'ung-wen went to Nanking in search of information. But in Nanking, as in Shanghai, they were met with protestations of ignorance.

"Oh, is he in jail? I hadn't heard," was the typical response, even in the Ministry of Justice.

"But you must know of his case. He was arrested on the seventeenth at the Far Eastern Hotel with thirty-three others," Shen would reply. "Hu Ye-p'ing is too well known to just disappear. The government would be doing itself an injury if it did away with him in secret. Won't you look again?"

After a half-hour: "Sorry, I just can't find any record of the arrest of Hu Ye-p'ing. Maybe he just took off for a while. I certainly hope you find him; it would be a shame to lose such a fine writer. . . . Well . . . good luck!"

Another note, more desperate, was smuggled out of Hu's cell, but responsible officials still denied knowledge of his arrest. Hu Shih and Ts'ai Yüan-p'ei did what they could, with little effect. Finally the curtain parted a trifle. The father of Ting Ling's old schoolmate, Miss Wang, who was a representative in the National Assembly, turned up with a story.

155

He said that Hu was in Lung Hua Prison with the others arrested at the Far Eastern Hotel. He could arrange for Ting Ling to see Ye-p'ing—with bribes. They scraped up several hundred *yüan* for old Wang.

On the appointed day, Ting Ling and Shen Ts'ung-wen were at Lung Hua at seven in the morning. They waited in the cold rain until noon for an entry permit. By four in the afternoon they had progressed to an inner court, where they were told that their entry permit bore the notation: "Not to be permitted to see the prisoner."

Enraged, they protested, shouting at the stolid guard. He shrugged his shoulders and turned away, but the governor of the prison strolled by to see what the commotion was about. When he heard Ting Ling's name and learned whom she had come to visit, he declared that something might be done, and then vanished through a small door. At five o'clock, Ting Ling and Shen Ts'ung-wen, peering through a heavy grating, saw a dim figure enter the adjoining courtyard. Though he was manacled and in leg-irons, the jaunty walk was Hu Ye-p'ing's.

"Why, he looks quite well," Ting Ling gasped.

After ten minutes, Hu was led away through an iron door, which slammed behind him. Ting Ling left the packages she had brought for him, and went home.

Armed with the knowledge that Ye-p'ing was still alive, Ting Ling once more attacked the wall of official denial. On February 8, she and Ts'ung-wen again went to Nanking. A high Nationalist official had expressed his willingness to discuss Hu's case with them.

Shen went to see the official alone, because Ting Ling was afraid that she, too, would be arrested if she were seen in Nanking. On February 9, Ts'ung-wen and the Nationalist official had a long talk. They discussed the latest novels and the new forms in Chinese poetry, and exchanged gossip of the literary world. As Ts'ung-wen was leaving, the official expressed a desire to see him again, hinting that they might get to Hu Ye-p'ing next time.

Returning to his hotel that evening, Ts'ung-wen received a letter which sent them scurrying back to Shanghai. Twenty-three men had been shot in Lung Hua Prison on the evening of February 8. Rumor held that Hu Ye-p'ing had been among them.

For three days they heard nothing more. Then there was a leak—unofficial again. Ts'ung-wen carried the story to Ting Ling, whom he found feeding the baby.

Hu had been among those executed. He and twenty-two others had been marched into a courtyard and told to prepare for a trip. Sure that he was going to Nanking for trial, Ye-p'ing had scribbled a note to Ting Ling, urging her to follow him to engage lawyers. That note he had slipped to a friendly guard before the prisoners were taken into an adjoining courtyard. Rifle-fire kept the prison awake for a half-hour.

Ting Ling smiled thinly, looking at the baby. "I should have known that it was all over!" she said.

"What shall we do about—him?"

"Do? We'll do nothing. He's dead—and the dead rot in their graves. Why should we worry about a corpse? Let's think about the living. Those who are still alive must exterminate the knaves and fools. Our real problem is how we shall live on—and how we shall continue to die!"

Shen interposed: "He may still be alive. Remember I talked to that Nanking official on the ninth. If Ye-p'ing's case had been closed on the eighth, he would have known."

Ting Ling did not reply. Bending over the baby's cradle, she whispered: "Little monkey, your father's life is over, but his work is not yet done. Sleep well and eat well so that you may grow strong and put your hands to the task your father left undone."

*   *   *

A decent respect for dramatic convention would require that Ting Ling's Communism be traced to the events of January and February, 1931. Unfortunately, the evidence bespeaks no sudden conversion. Her revolutionary ardor was fanned by Hu's execution, but it was hardly ignited in an instant. She joined the Communist Party in September, 1931, after his death, but she had been an active member of the League of Left Wing Writers while Hu Ye-p'ing was still alive. Chairman Lu Hsün was her mentor.

Lu Hsün occupied a unique position in modern Chinese letters, before his death in 1936. He was both Maecenas and Horace, encouraging young writers with patronage as well as by superlative example. His genius expressed itself like Voltaire's, for his satirical essays had the greatest social effect. Lu Hsün's fictional masterpiece *The Story of Ah Q,* like *Candide,* stirred the age by the biting accuracy of its observations.

There is irony in the Reds' adulation of Lu Hsün as their artistic prophet, for he was a great individualist. Yet the Communists named the literary academy at Yenan the Lu Hsün Institute, and Mao Tse-tung invariably presents Lu Hsün as the perfect model in directives to artists. But the real Lu Hsün spared no political faction in his bitter protests against social inequity. Worse yet, from the Red viewpoint, he delivered a scathing comment on the craze for "proletarian literature as a tool of revolution" when he remarked: "Even though literature may be propaganda, all propaganda is not necessarily literature."

The Communists seized upon Lu Hsün's sponsorship of the League of Left Wing Writers as reason enough for enshrining him as their god of letters. Tired of struggling alone, he had come to that alliance late in life because he felt that, as a social critic and satirist, he must join ranks with the left to be socially effective.

With Lu Hsün's guidance, Ting Ling came to full growth as a realistic writer. She had no rival as the painter of the "new woman." In an access of feminism, she organized women factory workers and hoped to make her magazine, the *Dipper,* a platform for China's young women writers. Despite this public busyness, her own life was sad and confused after Ye-p'ing's death; Shen Ts'ung-wen wrote that she had never passed a thoroughly happy day after the arrest. Ye-p'ing's sturdy optimism had sustained her flexible spirits. When he was gone, her self-confidence wilted, and only her political convictions remained rigid. "My experience of life is too meager," she wrote, "and my scholarship too shallow to make for any real literary accomplishment."

A year after Ye-p'ing's death, Ting Ling took a new lover, identified only as "that fellow Feng, a young upper-clerk." Shen Ts'ung-wen is authority for that fact, which is strenuously denied by Communist sources. But if Ting Ling did indeed live with "that fellow Feng," he was not of great importance to her. Shen reports her saying of Feng, "We're very polite to each other, just like casual friends."

Seeking compensation for the aridity of her emotional life, Ting Ling became a political activist. The *Dipper*, started just after Hu's execution in the summer of 1931, became a chief organ of the League of Left Wing Writers, and continued publication for two years despite occasional interference by the police. Details of her conspiratorial life are lacking, but it is likely that she worked underground organizing working women. The mills and factories of Shanghai employed a large proportion of female workers because they were more docile than their brothers. Ting Ling, who had worked as a factory hand, was valuable to the Party because she knew her way among them. But her writing was still her first duty.

Early in 1933, the *Dipper* was suppressed by government order and on May 14, 1933, Ting Ling, working late alone, was bundled into a police car, betrayed by "that fellow Feng." She was driven to a Nanking hotel, for the secret police hoped that she would reveal details of Communist plans. Although she was not subjected to physical torture, Ting Ling, abandoned to despair, begged her captors to kill her. But she withheld the information they sought, and after a few weeks she was taken to an empty house on the outskirts of Nanking.

159

As the automobile passed through the deserted streets, she heard one of her guards say, "Well, I guess we'll finish this business right now."

The business was not finished, because the Kuomintang still hoped to gain her cooperation, even if they could not force her to betray the Reds' secrets. She was held in the suburban home until the middle of 1936, under surveillance which gradually slackened. Toward the end of her confinement, she was permitted to have her mother and son live with her, and to take them about in Nanking. On September 16, 1936, Ting Ling eluded her guards and escaped to Shanghai. The underground smuggled her to Sian, dressed in the gray uniform of a private in Chang Hsüeh-liang's Manchurian Army. From Sian she entered the adjoining Soviet Area, arriving in Paoan, the Red capital, in the middle of November, 1936.

The street crowds in the little town of Paoan were eager to see her, their curiosity stimulated by the reports of her progress which had been circulating through the Soviet Area for months. Mao Tse-tung himself turned out to welcome her, for, aside from critic Ch'eng Fang-wu, she was the only major writer in the Red areas. He also had a personal reason for the warmth of his welcome; Ting Ling had been a schoolmate of his dead wife. He wrote a poem to welcome her, as did Ch'eng Fang-wu, who hailed her as "China's greatest woman writer."

After the dry years, Ting Ling was once more bathed in hearty approval. The Communist leaders urged her to write, but she demurred, saying that she could not report on the Soviet Area before she had seen it. During the first two months, she travelled through Red China, mounted on a scrawny horse and accompanied by one of the ubiquitous Little Red Devils, a war-orphan attached to the Red Army. She complained, with her habitual half-smile, that she really needed the small pistol she carried, since she was responsible for the horse, the Little Devil, and herself. Later she retraced a portion of her journey as escort to Agnes Smedley, whom she had known in Shanghai.

June, 1945: Tung Pi-wu signs the United Nations Charter at San Francisco. Then a Communist member of the Central Government's delegation, he is now a vice-premier of the People's Republic.

Left, Hsü T'e-li — the teacher of Mao Tse-tung and Liu Shao-ch'i — is a member of the Party's Central Committee and the Republic's Central Government Committee; *right,* Lin Tsu-han, the third "old man," is secretary-general of the Central Government Committee, and a member of the Party's Political Bureau.

Ting Ling, the lady novelist, escaped from prison in Nanking to join the Reds in 1936. She joined the Party in 1931, after her husband's execution by the Nationalists.

TRIANGLE

Mesdames P'eng Te-huai, Chou En-lai and Chu Teh, (*left to right*). Mme. Chou — Teng Ying-ch'ao — is an alternate member of the Central Committee; Mme. Chu — K'ang K'o-ch'ing — a member of the headquarters staff of the Army.

TRIANGLE

When she returned from her travels, Ting Ling was fitted into the Red cultural and propaganda machine. She took part, with Teng Ying-ch'ao, Chou En-lai's wife, in the Women's League, and lectured on literature at Resistance College, the university at Yenan. As vice-chairman of the Red Army Guard Unit, and later as chief of the Service Unit, she was responsible for information and education work among the troops and the civilian population. Despite her duties, which included production of plays for the edification of the populace, Ting Ling found time for a flirtation with P'eng Te-huai, deputy-commander of the Red armies. But their affair was smothered by the zeal of their match-making friends. Ting Ling finally told them that she admired P'eng Te-huai tremendously, and Mao Tse-tung even more, but had no intention of marrying either man.

After her entry into the Soviet Area, Ting Ling's creative work fell off. She produced chiefly "reportage," which made good propaganda. Although the Red leaders urged her to take time off for literature, she preferred "practical" activities, and allowed herself to write only in the evening, when her energy was lowest. Perhaps her contentment was too perfect. She once wrote: "I began to write because I was lonely and dissatisfied with society, and could find no outlet for my energy." Working for a cause she wholly believed in, she felt no need to exercise her imagination.

Ting Ling was even busier during the later years of the Japanese War and during the civil war. She became feature editor of the *Liberation Daily* in 1941, and visited the Soviet Union three times in the 1940's, flinging herself into the work of international women's organizations and Communist literary associations.

As Ting Ling stood among the delegation sent by the All-China Conference of Writers and Artists to the People's Political Consultative Conference on September 21, 1949, she must have thought back to Hu Ye-p'ing's death. It had been eighteen years between his execution and the realization of his dreams.

161

7. A SNAPSHOT—UNDEREXPOSED: LIU SHAO-CH'I

LIU SHAO-CH'I: A Hunanese, born 1905. After graduation from a Hunan middle school, studied in Moscow. In 1933 assumed chairmanship of the All-China Labor Federation; then secretary of the [Communist Party] Bureau for the Labor Movement. A member of the Political Bureau of the Central Committee, he is also a theoretician.
—*Important Figures in the Chinese Communist Party*

A pamphlet devoted to biographical sketches of Chinese Communist leaders offers only this note on the second most important man in Red China. Although the critic Ch'eng Fang-wu spreads over seventeen lines, the architect of the 1945 revision in the Communist Party's structure is dismissed in one and a half.

As the distance between Moscow and Peking shortens on the political map, pale-faced Liu Shao-ch'i becomes more powerful, for he is the chief conduit between the yellow-tiled roofs of the Imperial City and the tulip-bulb towers of the Kremlin. Yet Peking evidently does not desire that outsiders should look too closely at the man who fills that function. He is better known inside China, but has never been ballyhooed as a popular hero.

In every back-alley in China, Communist bill-posters have slapped up the approved picture of a beaming Mao Tse-tung: Great Buddha in a sun-helmet and felt boots. But only a few

162

underexposed snapshots of Liu Shao-ch'i are available. Usually taken in a bad light, Liu always seems to be hoping that he is outside the camera's range. After twenty years in the half-world of the underground, ducking publicity must be a conditioned reflex. To Mao's Buddha, he plays the role of a minor attendant-deity, busily adjusting the Great God's robe.

⸎ The official portrait of Liu Shao-ch'i, murky as it is, presents a man who comes as close as is humanly possible to the ideal of the Iron Bolshevik—the professional revolutionist who lives only for the Party. He resembles that fictional hero more than any other Chinese Communist does. Liu has written that the Communist Party is the highest expression of human capabilities, and would obviously prefer that a description of his life confine itself to his public career, ignoring the non-essential individual analysis. And unfortunately, that method is almost mandatory in his case, because of the paucity of available personal data. ⸎

Most Chinese Communist chiefs are specialists in one area —the army, culture, or foreign affairs—but Liu Shao-ch'i, like Russian Politburo members, has played every position on the field. He broke in as a labor leader and later switched to Party organization. His was the chief hand in drawing up the Party Constitution, promulgated in June 1945. His lectures, *On the Party,* and *On the Education of a Communist Party Member,* have become the Bible of aspirants and old Bolsheviks alike. He had had little experience in foreign affairs, but when it became necessary in 1948 to express the Chinese Party's loyalty to the Soviet Union, Liu produced *On Internationalism and Nationalism,* an affirmation of Stalinist conformism. As if to demonstrate his versatility, he now takes a hand in military matters through his vice-chairmanship of the Revolutionary Military Affairs Committee, an organ of the Central Government rather than the Party.

The roll of his honors was filled by his appointment as one of the six vice-presidents of the Central Government Committee. To prop the "coalition" façade of the government,

163

only three of the vice-presidents are Communists. Old General Chu Teh was given the title in deference to his prestige as a popular hero second only to Mao Tse-tung, while Kao Kang, the second vice-president, is fully occupied with his duties as chairman of the Manchurian government. Liu Shao-ch'i therefore appears to be the Party's watchdog at that level. Yet in 1945 he was almost completely unknown outside the Red brotherhood, though he had played a major role in the Party's inner circles for some time.

Even today the substantiated facts on his career are few. One Western specialist on China suggested, half seriously, that the Communists were anxious to keep Liu under cover because he was really a Russian or a native of Russian Asia. He was reassured only when a Chinese friend reported that he had met Liu in Shanghai in 1938, and found him to be quite obviously a Chinese, who spoke in the velvet-furry accent of Hunan Province.

There is no doubt that Liu Shao-ch'i was born in Hunan Province, for all that he faces Moscow as consistently as a Moslem turns to Mecca, but it is difficult to determine exactly *when* he was born. Though the pamphlet already quoted places his birth in 1905, other authorities give 1898, and the facts of his career bear out the impression that the earlier date is more correct. Youth is no bar to advancement in the Chinese Communist Party, for much younger men, notably Lin Piao, hold jobs nearly as important as Liu's, but it would have been chronologically unlikely for him to have taken part in the formation of the General Labor Secretariat in 1920 if he had been only fifteen at the time.

To lay the facts on the table: Liu Shao-ch'i was born in Hunan Province, probably at the turn of the century, and probably in the vicinity of Changsha, the revolutionists' incubator. His father was a farmer, but a "rich" or "middle" farmer like Mao Tse-tung's, rather than a peasant. Young Liu Shao-ch'i, after graduating from primary school, entered a middle school somewhere in Hunan. His interests at the

164

time have not been reported, but his studies were probably quite general, in preparation for a teaching career. After graduation from middle school, he entered Changsha First Normal School. Mao Tse-tung was a student there from 1912 to 1918, and the two probably met at that time. But Liu was a very junior under-classman while Mao, older than most of his classmates, was an upper-classman in 1916, at which time Liu might have begun his studies at the age of sixteen. The basis of a later intimacy could hardly have been laid while they were schoolmates in Changsha.

Nevertheless, Liu Shao-ch'i, staying longer in Changsha, must have received his first injection of "revolutionary thought" there. Ting Ling, the lady novelist, has reported the electric effect exerted upon the city's discontented students by the news of the riots of May 4, 1919. After receiving his diploma from Normal School, Liu Shao-ch'i went to Shanghai to seek life and the revolution. He found them in the Socialist Youth Group, which had been founded in the spring of 1920 by Ch'en Tu-hsiu at the behest of Gregory Voitinsky, the Comintern's representative in China. Liu was probably one of the earliest members of the Socialist Youth, for in the winter of 1920-21 he moves up a step to participate in the formation of the National General Labor Secretariat.

Liu did not become a professional revolutionary at the time, perhaps because he still had no specialty of positive value to the cause. Instead, he returned to Hunan to teach in primary school and continue his Party activities on the side. But in his teaching, as in everyday social conversation, he was the Party propagandist first and the human being second. And Party assignments left him little free time.

Mao Tse-tung, on his walking-trips through Hunan Province, had assayed the quality and needs of the peasantry, and was ready to organize them for revolutionary action. Liu may have been involved in this phase of the Communist Party's work, but he was more interested in labor unions as revolutionary cadres. This bias had the blessing of the Party.

165

There was already a strong labor movement among skilled workers in central China, but its leaders were primarily concerned with welfare rather than political action. As craftsmen they felt infinitely above unskilled industrial laborers. It was Liu's task to convince them that their interests were identical with those of the mass of the proletariat, rather than those of the middle class.

In 1922, Liu Shao-ch'i was called to full-time revolutionary work. The First National Labor Congress, convened on May 1, 1922, had voted for a political emphasis. Liu Shao-ch'i's first assignment was to the coal mines at An-yüan in P'ing-hsiang County of Kiangsi Province, just south and east of the Hunan border. The mines were not of major importance quantitatively, for the entire province produced only 0.3 per cent of all China's coal. But they were of great strategic value because of their proximity to the heavy-industrial heart of China in the triangle formed by the cities of Hankow, Hanyang, and Wuchang—the Wu-Han cities. Since the strongest unions, outside those in the transportation field, would be built in the Wu-Han area, it was necessary to organize the proletariat on the periphery for their support. The assignment was perfect for a young man trying his hand while the Party watched. Important enough to engage all his loyalty, the task was not so vital as to make bungling irreparable.

Liu showed a knack for dealing with the miners which won him quick promotion. Working under the brutal conditions characteristic of the mining industry in all but the most technically advanced countries, the miners were politically sensitive beyond the degree Liu might have hoped for in consideration of the education they had not had.

The pale, self-contained young man, who went down into the mines with them, although obviously not a real miner, could still make good sense to them. He started by agitating for improvements in working conditions and went on, after his elevation to the union's presidency, to demonstrate that

166

the miners' misery was enforced by the same social forces which kept the entire laboring and peasant classes in subjection. Party tacticians felt that laborers must realize their community of interest with all the "exploited" classes, before they could be organized for direct political action.

Liu Shao-ch'i lived with the miners until the autumn of 1923. Having proved himself, he was then transferred to the headquarters of the Labor Secretariat, which had been forced to go underground because of the opposition's alarm over its success. During this period Liu was a travelling delegate and professional trouble-shooter among the unions of the great coastal cities like Shanghai and Canton, and in the Wu-Han industrial area. In 1924, the Kuomintang-Communist coalition allowed the labor organizers to walk in the sunlight for a time.

Liu Shao-ch'i later complained that the restrictions imposed upon Red labor agitators by the requirements of Kuomintang membership nullified the advantages derived from the legalization of their activities. As a loyal Moscow-liner, he blamed the Party's lack of success upon the vacillating leadership of Ch'en Tu-hsiu, whom he charged with submission to the Kuomintang's orders in defiance of Comintern directives. But that was Moscow's policy as well as Ch'en's; subordination of the Chinese Communist Party to the Kuomintang was the will of the Communist International. During the acute crisis of early summer, 1927, Borodin, the Comintern's representative in China, rejected Ch'en Tu-hsiu's request for 5,000 rifles from a shipment going to the Kuomintang forces. Borodin held that the Comintern did not desire to see the Chinese Party dissipate its strength in independent action.

Intra-Party dissension notwithstanding, and despite Liu's later complaints, the activities of the Labor Secretariat produced large, militant unions. The May Thirtieth Incident of 1925 was followed by a highly effective boycott and a wave of strikes which seriously embarrassed the British, whose troops

167

had fired on a Chinese mob. The Second National Labor Congress, meeting in Canton City from May 1 to May 7, 1925, voted to organize the All-China Labor Federation. Liu was named vice-president of the Federation, so that times were not so lean for him.

After the entente between the Kuomintang and the Communists was ended by a series of coups and massacres in the spring and summer of 1927, Liu once more burrowed underground. He had been engaged with Ch'en Tu-hsiu and Chou En-lai, in organizing the "street" unions of Shanghai and arming them for military action, when Chiang Kai-shek's troops crushed them in April, 1927. If Liu took part in the Emergency Meeting of August 7, 1927, which purged the Party of "deviationists," his was a minor role, for he had not yet been admitted to the Party's inner circles.

Liu Shao-ch'i's movements from 1927 to 1931 are not recorded, but he probably chose to make a retreat in Moscow. The Comintern, recognizing a major setback in China, was calling in its disciples for retraining. It is, therefore, likely that Liu went to study in the Holy City, for his services as a labor expert could be spared by a Party that was changing its emphasis upon the city proletariat to a dependence upon the peasants.

Liu visited Moscow twice, but the dates of his trips are not available. If history did not have such an annoying way about her, forever ignoring the logical process, it could be stated with certainty that Liu was in Moscow in 1928, 1929, and 1930, studying at Sun Yat-sen University and taking additional courses in the Red Army Academy with Liu Po-ch'eng. The Sixth Congress of the Chinese Communist Party, held in Moscow in 1928, named Liu chief of the Labor Bureau, and it is probable that he was in Moscow to press his campaign in person. He may also have been involved in the Russian expedition against Manchuria in the fall of 1929, for the Party later assumes a connection between Liu and the Manchurian guerrilla forces, requesting him to draft communications to the Manchurians. Regardless of the accuracy of these details, it is clear that Liu's primary loyalty to international Communism was fixed during his training period in Moscow. He would not waver from that stand thereafter.

In 1931 and 1932, Liu's trail once more becomes clear, although he was at great pains to cover it at the time. With Chou En-lai and the orthodox rump of the Party, Liu organized underground unions in Shanghai. In 1932, he was smuggled into the Kiangsi Soviet Area to become commissioner of labor in the provisional government. When the All-China Labor Federation moved its headquarters to Jui-chin, the Kiangsi Red capital, Liu Shao-ch'i assumed the chairmanship of that organization too.

* * *

On January 22, 1934, the Second Congress of Soviet Representatives was convened in Jui-chin. Before the meeting opened, the delegates assembled at the Central Government Parade Grounds to review units of the Red Army. The parade began at five o'clock on the morning of the twenty-second, as troops from the Red Army Academy, the First and Second Infantry Schools, the Red Army Specialists' School, and the Central Guard Unit paraded for three hours. Then the Red Physical Training Association ran off a field meet, which was followed by a parade of the delegates themselves. Afterwards they adjourned to watch a performance by the Workers' and Peasants' Dramatic Club.

At two in the afternoon, amid the echoes of a three-gun salute, the delegates filed into the Great Temple, appointed as the meeting hall. From the walls hung red, yellow, white, and green banners bearing appropriate slogans of felicitation and hope. Their duplicates decorated all the streets of the mountain town, where Young Vanguards had worked all night to place them. Beside the steps leading into the temple were assembled nearly fifteen-hundred spectators.

The first item on the agenda was a report by Chairman

Mao Tse-tung on the progress of the two years which had gone by since the first Soviet Congress. The next item was the selection, from among the 693 representatives, of a seventy-five-man steering committee. This committee, having taken all major decisions, would present resolutions to the full Congress for ratification, in the manner habitual to the Chinese Communists, whose notions of parliamentary procedure vary considerably from the Western standard.* Mao Tse-tung, Ch'ü Ch'iu-pai, Liu Shao-ch'i and others were named to the steering committee from the Kiangsi delegation. Liu's name stood fourth on the list in token of his importance in the Party, but he addressed the Congress in his capacity as chairman of the All-China Labor Federation rather than as a Party representative.

On the afternoon of January 31, 1934, he delivered "A Summary of the Labor Union Movement in the Soviet Areas During the Past Two Years":

"Governmental power in the Soviet Areas [he declared] is wielded by the workers, peasants, and soldiers under the guidance of the proletariat. . . . During the past two years, we have solved many basic problems of a theoretical nature. In addition we have implemented our decision to *reshape the leadership of labor unions* by completely proletarianizing their guiding organs. We are bringing over ninety per cent of the laborers in the Soviet Areas into our unions, which are organized in three categories: (1) peasant unions, (2) unions of sales-clerks and handicraft workers, and (3) unions of coolies and transportation workers. Moreover, we have encouraged the development of the democratic character of these unions, improved the condition of the laborer, and raised his position to the end that he may participate in the Soviets and *assist positively in the creation of the Red Army.*"†

---

* The Kuomintang, it must be said, has always employed similar methods.
† Italics mine.

170

The Communists would make sure of the obedience of the unions by *reshaping the leadership*. Nor did they ever lose sight of their objective amid the mists of social betterment. Their goal remained the complete conquest of power, and every action moved them toward that goal. The improvement of working conditions was not an end in itself, but purely a means of moving the laboring class to *assist positively in the creation of the Red Army*.

Machiavellian or not, the Communist program won the loyalty of workers by giving them better conditions and higher wages. There is no reason to doubt Liu's report of maximum-hour laws and guaranteed holidays and vacations, or to reject his favorable comparison of pre-Communist wage scales with those fixed by Red decree. He concluded by promising "liberation" to those workers who groaned under the brutal repression of the Kuomintang in White areas. The text notes that his speech was followed by "Prolonged applause!"

Despite success in winning the workers and peasants by promising them a fair break, Chiang's military pressure on the circumference forced the Reds to embark on the Long March in the fall of 1934. Liu Shao-ch'i, just beginning to break into the Party's front rank, was too valuable to leave behind with men who had outworn their usefulness like Ch'ü Ch'iu-pai. Available accounts of the Long March do not mention Liu's role, but he probably marched with the political commissars in the Political Unit. After arriving in the Northwest, Liu once more drops from sight. Edgar Snow, who visited the Northwest Soviet Area in 1936, one year after its establishment, makes no mention of Liu Shao-ch'i, nor do the Chinese reporters who toured the Red areas in 1937, after the formation of the Popular Front.

He was probably in Moscow again, for, as has been noted, a reliable source indicates that he visited the Soviet Union twice. Since his tracks do not show up again until 1937 or 1938, it is likely that Liu Shao-ch'i made his second visit to the Soviet Union from the beginning of 1936 until the end

171

of 1937. He could have been spared, for once more his special talents were not of particular value in barren, agricultural Shensi. Moreover, his authority as the font of orthodox doctrine would seem to have been derived from recent close contact with the Holy City. It is therefore likely that Liu spent a year or two in Moscow, working for the Comintern, studying, and perhaps teaching.

Returning to China in haste in the autumn of 1937, he found that the labor field had once more been opened for exploitation by the formation of the Popular Front. With Kuomintang sanction, he undertook the task of rallying the Shanghai workers against the Japanese, but was soon forced underground again. Unperturbed, he continued to run the All-China Labor Federation, working toward two objectives: effective opposition to the Japanese, and preparation for the Communist Party's eventual seizure of power.

After the split between the Reds and the Kuomintang in 1941, Liu returned to the Communist areas. As partisan activity enlarged the Red regions to take in semi-industrial areas nominally under Japanese control, his position became more important.

In 1942, the Communist Party, though still on the defensive, turned its attention to post-war politics. In 1940, Mao's *New Democracy* had given them a blueprint for the conquest and retention of power, but it was necessary to train *kan-pu* (cadres) to follow that plan. The year 1942 was set aside for the *Cheng-feng Yün-tung*—the Movement to Order the Winds. Drawn from a classical text, the name signified that the Reds were remaking their weapons for the conquest of power. The men who would rule China were indoctrinated with the aid of a textbook called *Documents on Ordering the Winds*. The anthology of twenty-two documents presented the proper view on a variety of subjects. It included articles by Mao and Stalin, and also featured Liu Shao-ch'i's "On the Self-cultivation of the Communist Party Member," written as a speech in August, 1937.

172

In 1943, Liu was elevated to the Secretariat of the Central Committee, the tight innermost circle which, according to the Party Constitution, conducts the everyday business of the Party. In 1934, he had been given a seat in the Political Bureau which controls the Party, policy and administration alike. The ten-to-fifteen-man Politburo stands in relation to the five-man Secretariat as did the English Cabinet to the War Cabinet. The two organs are nominally responsible to the Central Committee, which fills the function of the House of Commons, without its power to disavow the Cabinet.

Liu had arrived. He had previously served as secretary of a number of Party Branch Bureaus, but his elevation to the Secretariat was the conclusive accolade. It was also an indication that the Reds were preparing for intensive operations among labor at the end of the war, for Liu was the chief labor expert in the Party's tutelary organs.

In 1945, he was serving as chief of staff of the 5th Division in the New Fourth Army and concurrently as political commissar. With the regrouping of forces at the end of the war, he was reassigned to the labor movement, operating out of Shanghai.

At Yenan in June, 1945, the Seventh Congress of the Communist Party of China was convened; the Sixth Congress had met in 1928. The Party, on the final lap of its drive to power, paused to overhaul the machine. The first order of business was the adoption of a revised Party Constitution. Liu Shao-ch'i, who had been foremost among the designers of the new mechanism, was chosen to exhibit it to the Congress.

The chief structural principle was what Liu called *min-chu ti chi-chung chih-tu*—the system of democratic centralism. In practice the self-contradictary term means that all members of the Party are "unconditionally" bound to execute the orders of the Central Committee. That is "centralism." The word "democracy" is included by virtue of the fact that the Party Constitution provides for the election of the Central

Committee by the Party Congress. It is further justified by the fact that candidates for office are permitted to campaign freely, and open discussion of all issues is allowed until the responsible organ has taken its decision. Thereafter, no dissent is permitted and Party members must endeavor in all ways to implement the decision. That is "centralism on a democratic foundation, and democracy under the guidance of centralism."

In unpleasant fact, the Party Constitution of 1945 provides for a rule of good intentions rather than law. The Party Congress, which chooses the Central Committee, is to be convened once every three years, but the Central Committee may postpone sessions of the Congress as it sees fit. A seventeen-year lapse between the Sixth Congress in 1928 and the Seventh in 1945 did not prevent the Central Committee from recruiting new members or making crucial decisions. The Party leaders are, in effect, given complete discretion to utilize or ignore the Congress. Since the Constitution further provides that the same individual—at present Mao Tse-tung —shall be chairman of the Central Committee, the Politburo, and the Secretariat, the Party's extreme centralization insures that the ruling circles will remain in control as long as they desire to do so. Democracy exists only on the tolerance of "central" authority.

In his commentary on the Constitution, Liu adjures the faithful to guard against "extreme democratization." He quotes Mao Tse-tung on this danger: "When the heterogeneity of the *petit bourgeois* is introduced into the Party, we call it *extremely democratized thought*. Such thought is basically incompatible with the militant responsibilities of the proletariat, for, objectively viewed, it is a species of counter-revolutionary thought. All persons who permit themselves to indulge in that kind of thought tread the road of counter-revolution."

Having chosen his text, Liu expounds: "Anti-democratic, dictatorial tendencies within the Party, and the phenomenon

174

of extreme democratization within the Party, are the two extremist phenomena in the Party's internal life. However, the phenomenon of extreme democratization, when checked and reprimanded, often gives rise to dictatorial tendencies, and on the other hand, when dictatorial tendencies run into difficulties, they often undergo a transformation into the phenomenon of extreme democratization."*

A facile conclusion might be drawn from the foregoing extracts, i.e., the leaders of the Chinese Communists are doctrinaire mediocrities, who exercise dictatorial power in China through a kept Party. That conclusion would be wholly erroneous. It is true that the mechanism of the Party is devoid of those safeguards against usurpation of power which the West understands to be the essence of democracy. Yet Mao Tse-tung and Liu Shao-ch'i have learned better than to attempt the imposition of a wholly arbitrary sway. They hope to prevent decay by providing for a measure of flexibility within the Party, but pride in their own virtue has prevented their erecting adequate barriers to their own will.

Though the Party is hardly democratic by Western standards, it has displayed a remarkable sensitivity to the wishes of the Chinese masses. Mao Tse-tung came to power because he understood the popular will and gave in to it—made use of it, if one prefers. He has won his victories not by imposing his will on the people, but by turning their aspirations into the channels most advantageous to him. He cannot, however, thwart their wishes, and one phase of reform which will not be slowed down is redistribution of the land, as Liu Shao-ch'i testified in a statement issued in June, 1950.

In domestic matters, the leaders of the Chinese Communist Party can make their own way, deferring to Moscow, or

---

* The translation is literal; the exact import may well evade the reader as it has the translator. It does, however, serve to convey an impression of the quality of Liu's style and the manner of his thought.

175

seeming to, when necessary. But they have had no qualifying experience of foreign affairs. Before the establishment of the Central People's Government a year and a half ago, the Chinese Communists had been restricted in their foreign relations to negotiations with the Kuomintang and infrequent intercourse with Moscow, neither of a nature to prepare them to direct the affairs of a potential great power on the world scene. They have displayed much less originality in international affairs than in domestic policy, and have manifested a growing dependence on Moscow.

Since the administration of international relations properly lies within the sphere of Foreign Minister Chou En-lai, it will be discussed in the chapter devoted to him. But Chou En-lai has written little, and the chief theoretical document treating China's world role is from the pen of Liu Shao-ch'i. *On Internationalism and Nationalism* is not a major work in the Lenino-Stalinist library, for it contains little that is original. But it is important for its indications of the attitude the Chinese Red hierarchy holds on world affairs.

Dated November 1, 1948, the document, had it been read by some of our more persistent optimists, might have spared us much enthusiastic speculation on the likelihood of Mao's becoming another Tito. It opens with a round endorsement of the Cominform's resolution condemning Tito's nationalism. Liu Shao-ch'i proposes to tell "Why Tito's anti-Soviet stand is likely to lead to Yugoslavia's becoming the dupe and victim of aggression by American imperialism, and why it will destroy Yugoslavia's independence, to convert her into a colony of imperialism."

The bourgeoisie conceive of nationalism, Liu declares, as an extension of their class interest. Unsated with the fruits of their exploitation of the domestic working class, the bourgeoisie seek to extend their sway to other nations. That is the core of bourgeois nationalism, finding its natural development in imperialistic denial of the valid national aspirations of other countries.

176

Proletarian nationalism is wholly different. It desires, according to Liu Shao-ch'i, only to extend the hand of friendship to the proletariat of other nations. Liu reaffirms the orthodox Marxist conviction that a capitalist nation must become imperialistic, while it is impossible for a Communist nation to indulge in self-aggrandizement at the expense of other nations. Therefore, proletarian internationalism is the logical outgrowth of proletarian nationalism. Communist nations, taking a righteous pride in their national cultures and history, will cooperate for the benefit of the proletariat of all lands. A bourgeois nation, on the other hand, cannot give selfless assistance to other nations, since it is compelled by the nature of its economic system to seek profits through exploitation.

Marshal Tito's fundamental error, in Liu's view, is his belief that the nationalism of the Soviet Union is indistinguishable from the nationalism of the West. The Soviet Union, because it is a Communist nation, cannot seek to use other nations for the benefit of its ruling circles. It should therefore be plain to Tito, as it is plain to Liu, that all Socialist nations must align themselves with the friendly Soviet Union against the hostile West. That is the course China will follow. *Also sprach Liu Shao-ch'i!*

Such a theoretical projection often finds itself at variance with the hard facts of international politics. In their internal administration the Chinese Communists have displayed a remarkable capacity for altering doctrine to conform to expediency's dictates. But in 1948, they saw no reason to change their preconceived notions of international politics. Continued American support of Chiang Kai-shek after State Department observers had reported as early as 1944 that Chiang had lost all popular support, led the Chinese Reds to give complete credence to what Moscow has told them of evil American designs.

The Chinese have, therefore, turned to Russia for material aid and ideological comfort, despite their knowledge that only the United States can provide sufficient material assistance to advance China's industrialization substantially. This swing has been made despite the ingrained distrust of Russia in the Chinese mind, and despite the friendly feeling toward the United States which occupied a strong position in that mind until 1945. (It is, of course, true that those two attitudes were long ago reversed in the minds of the Red leaders.)

If Russia can refrain from attempting to impose her will upon China, as she has attempted to reduce the "People's Democracies" of eastern Europe to slave-nations, China's leaders, secure in their Marxian analysis, will go along with the Soviet Union. There is small prospect of any immediate split between the colossi of the Red world. If the Russians can behave with a trifle more than their usual discretion, there is no discernable reason why the bonds between China and the Soviet Union should not remain firm until China has grown strong enough to frighten Russia in Asia. However, a display of bourgeois imperialist tendencies by the U.S.S.R. could very easily upset the ideological balance of the pragmatic Chinese Communists.

These eventualities are all ungratifyingly remote. As to the immediate future, Liu Shao-ch'i's speech before the People's Political Consultative Conference on September 22, 1949, provides a good draft. (Repetition, so characteristic of Communist rhetoric, has been drastically cut in translation.)

"The Chinese Communist Party will uphold the People's Political Consultative Conference, and fight to put its Common Program into effect. The Communist Party's present policy is aimed at effecting certain minimum measures, all of which are accepted in the People's Political Consultative Conference Program. That is the present situation.

"However, as you all know, the Communist Party of China, apart from its minimum program also has a maximum program, which has not been included in the Common Program of the People's Political Consultative Conference. During the process of consultation, a number of representatives suggested that the Socialist future course of China be delineated in the Common Program, but this was not considered necessary, because pure Socialism is still a matter for the far distant future. There is no doubt that China's future course will be Socialistic and Communistic, because a non-Communist industrialized China must inevitably become an imperialist nation. And that is something which neither the Chinese people nor the people of the world could countenance.

"The People's Political Consultative Conference can discuss those matters in the future. China's progress toward Socialism must be based on the practical requirements of her social and economic development, and the desires of the overwhelming majority of her people. When the time comes, China's Communist Party will consult with the various democratic parties, the various people's organizations, the minority peoples, and other patriotic, democratic elements in order to reach a joint decision. The Communist Party of China will go forward hand in hand with all men who desire to achieve Socialism. We know that the unity of all the people is necessary for the realization of the New Democracy at present, and that such unity is also essential to the creation of Socialism in the future.

"*Long live* the revolutionary unity of the Chinese people!

"*Long live* the Chinese People's Political Consultative Conference!

"*Long live* the Chinese People's Republic!

"*Long live* the Central People's Government!"

8. CONFUCIUS TO SHELLEY TO MARX: KUO MO-JO

Many statesmen have thought themselves poets, but few poets have been statesmen. Since the traits common in literary men are not those which make for administrative efficiency, a poet in office is like a fireplace in a munitions factory—a pretty, but dangerous luxury. The Central Government of the People's Republic of China has hazarded that chance in appointing Kuo Mo-jo, a lyric poet, to one of the three key administrative posts in Peking. As Vice-Premier for Culture and Education, Kuo shepherds Chinese minds along the paths chosen by the Marxist regime. Kuo, who has frequently affirmed his opinion that literature is a tool of class interest, must now see to it that Chinese art serves the interests of the new ruling classes. He is qualified, by his experience as a historian and lecturer, for the task of gearing the educational system to the same interests. Under a Marxist system, which treats all human endeavour as an extension of politics, his chief duty encompasses the other two. Kuo Mo-jo directs both the foreign and domestic propaganda of Red China.

Kuo was not cut to the same pattern as most propagandists. He is not a disappointed journalist, but a respected artist, whom Lao Shaw, the author of *Rickshaw Boy,* called the "second most important figure in modern Chinese literature." Lu Hsün, by acclamation the most important, died in 1936. Kuo's appointment to the post of vice-premier was tantamount to a declaration that the Communists considered the mantle of Lu Hsün to have fallen on his shoulders. But Kuo achieved that eminence by his own efforts. He has published six novels and collections of short stories, three plays, five volumes of poetry and essays, and more than twenty translations of Western classics. For most of his life he took no major role in politics, preferring the study of archaeology to Marxist agitation during his long periods of exile from China.

Kuo's lack of humor is his chief literary fault; no laughter leavens the unremitting intensity of his poems and stories. The Chinese say that his life and works are pervaded by a spirit of "resistance," a word which might well be rendered "resentment." He has resented the predatory West, the tyranny of native "feudal and bourgeois elements," and his own hard life.

But his resentment is now abating, for he has come into his kingdom. Kuo was chairman of the Chinese delegation to the Communist-sponsored Paris Peace Conference in the spring of 1949. On June 15, 1949, he was appointed one of the five vice-chairmen of the Preparatory Commission for the People's Political Consultative Conference. After having been elected a member of the sixty-three-man People's Central Government Committee on September 29, he was given the post of vice-premier on October 20.

* * *

Kuo Mo-jo in the chair of authority is a strange sight, for he has stood opposed to the established order for most of his life. Kuo has presented an example of a phenomenon prevalent in our time: he has been a modern rebel in search of a cause. For half his days, his chief need was a purpose which would give stability and meaning to his life. He could find neither in the chaotic society of contemporary East Asia. It therefore became imperative for him to fabricate an emotional and intellectual purpose as a hub around which the spokes of his eccentric existence might revolve in harmony.

His first solution was artistic egocentricity after the manner of Byron or Nietzsche. But it was difficult for him to find sufficient comfort in literary self-adulation, particularly since he was burdened with a conviction of social responsibility, inherited with the Confucian tradition. He went through a period of sentimental Marxism—the "infantile leftism" of the Communist lexicon—and has finally found a snug niche as an orthodox prophet and literary high priest of Chinese Communism.

Though he became a radical, Kuo Mo-jo started life in an atmosphere of extreme reaction. He was born in 1892 in Chia-ting, a town about 180 miles due west of Chungking in Szechwan Province. For the first twenty years of his life, he lived under the Manchu dynasty in the snug comfort accorded a younger son of the small gentry. He received a thorough classical education and loved "to read the *Odes of Ch'u,* the *Shih-chi, Chuang-tze,* and T'ang poems," works esteemed by the literati who ruled China until the Revolution of 1911. It was not until his middle-school days that Kuo Mo-jo came into contact with the forces which overthrew the Empire and shattered the social and political bases of traditional Chinese culture. Before that time, he had little chance to learn of the new thought imported from the West, for rock-girt Szechwan, regretting the Ming dynasty's collapse, had never given full allegiance to the *arriviste* Manchus, and was almost as conservative as nearby Tibet.

Kuo's father was a landowner who also served as an untrained country doctor. When the provincial government offered six scholarships to Tientsin Medical College, Kuo was moved to compete, as much by his desire to get away from home as by his father's example. He was awarded a scholarship and sent to Tientsin in northern China, but shortly after his arrival in late 1913, the arrangement fell through, and his older brother, an official in Peking, sent him to Japan to acquire modern medical training. On his arrival in Tokyo in January, 1914, Mo-jo was struck by the realization that there were modes of thought and life wholly different from those current in his native province—and perhaps better.

The years between Kuo's twentieth and thirtieth birthdays were spent in China in an atmosphere of chaotic war-lordism and in Japan, where the native or "Asia for the Japanese" brand of imperialism was coming to the forefront. These two environments produced in him that inspired, and almost fanatical, nationalism characteristic of Chinese of his generation. He smarted under the arrogance of the West, and the patronizing contempt which the Japanese affected toward a dissolute China.

In the summer of 1918, Kuo Mo-jo came down to the city of Fukuoka to enter the Medical Department of Kyushu Imperial University. He was twenty-six, and had just been graduated from the Sixth Higher School at Okayama. When he remembered that he was much older than his fellow students, Kuo was oppressed by a sense of urgency. (Ch'eng Fang-wu, three years his junior, had been graduated from Okayama Higher School the previous year.) Nor was it comforting to recall that his government allowance of thirty-two *yüan* a month was insufficient to support his wife and seven-month-old son. For he had acquired a wife in characteristically impetuous fashion.

While visiting a tubercular friend, Kuo met a Japanese nurse called Anna. When the friend died, Kuo convinced himself that Anna had been sent as consolation for his loss. He married her; she left her job, and she too enrolled in the pre-medical course. They then made a shocking discovery: Kuo's allowance, just adequate for the support of one student, would not do for two. After the first child arrived, they were desperately short of funds, and Anna gave up her studies to take care of the boy.

Kuo Mo-jo thereafter entertained a grievance against himself, which he was later to transmute into a grievance against the social order. He wrote in a letter to a friend that he had "destroyed his Anna." For a number of years he continued to torture himself with the belief that he had failed as a husband. Later, Marxism provided absolution, permitting him to transfer the guilt to the system.

While pursuing his pre-medical studies, Kuo made up his mind to ignore literature. He would, he decided, even give up reading for pleasure, so that all his time might be free for scientific studies. That decision, though taken with his accustomed ardor, was not carried through. In place of the classics he had discarded, Kuo began to study the literature of the West. He was much attracted by the romantic writers of the eighteenth and nineteenth centuries. Shelley, Heine, the younger Goethe, and Nietzsche evoked the strongest response, for Kuo felt in their impassioned libertarianism release from his own bondage under the petrified Confucian social ethic.

Their affirmation of the moral necessity for the subordination of society to individual development was a revelation to Kuo Mo-jo. He, who had been seeking in vain for stability in a transition society, was at once presented with a faith, a doctrine, and a mission. The mission was service to the doctrine of individualism through the creation of literature which expressed his own individuality. His vocation, he concluded, was for art rather than science.

Though Kuo Mo-jo, unlike Lu Hsün, did finish medical school, his new orientation was reflected in his changed attitude toward the practice of medicine. A few years after determining that he would devote himself single-mindedly to science, he reflected that being a physician was advantageous only because it relieved him of complete financial dependence on his pen, which might have exerted an unhappy effect on his art.

After graduation from medical school, Kuo was to reject the proffered directorship of the Szechwan Provincial Hospital. He wished to give himself over entirely to the cultivation of his artistic ego. Through *creation*—the sacred word in his creed—he would exalt himself and attain to the full development of his *individuality* and *liberty*. As a lyric poet, he felt he need not worry about society, but must rather devote all his attention to the creation of beauty. The "elevating" effect on the public of the beauty in his verse was a desirable by-product, but hardly his chief concern. The artist need only be true to himself.

* * *

These convictions were several years shaping. Kuo's literary career began with a casual conversation on the shores of Lake Hakozaki in the late summer of 1918, which Kuo recounts in his autobiography. Chang Tze-p'ing, a classmate at Okayama Sixth Higher School, came up from Kumamoto to spend a few days. Chang and Kuo met on the beach of Hakata Bay near Fukuoka, where the Mongol invaders had been repelled in 1281 by the Japanese and the *kamikaze*— the divine wind. After inspecting the shrines commemorating the victory, the two wandered through a pine grove, and finally seated themselves on a large root overlooking Lake Hakozaki.

Chang Tze-p'ing, just returned from home, complained that there was not one magazine worth reading published in all China.

"What about the *New Youth?*" Kuo asked.

"The *New Youth* is all right—as far as it goes. But it publishes simple didactic articles—and not much else. It's the same with other magazines. They're all too highly specialized, or too diversified. The way I look at it, what China needs is a magazine devoted to literature alone. You won't find anything in China like the purely literary magazines here in Japan."

"Do you think there's any demand for such a magazine?" Kuo asked.

"No doubt about it. There certainly is a demand," Chang

replied. "Students at home are as dissatisfied as we are. Look at the *New Youth*. Even a superficial magazine like that got a tremendous reception."

"You know, I've been thinking along the same lines," Kuo said. "A few of us might get together to publish a magazine devoted to pure literature. We could use a simple format, and specialize in *belles lettres*. Not in the classical style, but the vernacular."

"I like your idea, but where would you find the others to go in with you?" Chang asked.

"Well, there's Yü Ta-fu who was in our class at prep school. . . ."

"Fine, fine. Old Yü isn't a bad poet; I've seen some of his verses in the Shanghai papers. And he writes short stories too."

"That's right. I think he'd be interested. And there's also Ch'eng Fang-wu from Okayama. Last year he started at Tokyo Imperial University. He's studying munitions manufacture, but I know he's much more interested in literature— and he writes English well. Can you think of any others?"

"I'll try, but I don't think so."

"Well," said Kuo, "four should be enough. We've got Yü Ta-fu, Ch'eng Fang-wu, Chang Tze-p'ing, and Kuo Mo-jo. If we can scrape up four or five *yen* a month each, we'll have enough for the printer's bill."

When Ch'eng Fang-wu came to Fukuoka, Kuo told him of the plan. Ch'eng was not enthusiastic. He liked the idea, he said, but felt they should go slow.

Ch'eng's attitude prevailed. It was two or three years before anything came of the discussion alongside Lake Hakozaki. The four did organize themselves into a literary society called the Creative Club while they were in Japan, but it was not until Kuo's return to Shanghai in 1922 that they issued the *Creative Quarterly*. Once introduced, the magazine received a strong welcome, although there was no hope of drawing any money from it. The *Creative Quarterly* was fol-

186

lowed by the *Creative Monthly,* and later by the *Flood,* in which Kuo published some of his most significant works. But he did not wait until he had an organ to begin his writing. The necessity for service to the cause of individualism pressed too hard to permit of delay. He published a book of lyrics called *The Goddess,* and a volume of essays under the title *Starry Space.* The two were well received, but his first triumph was *The Falling Leaf,* a novel in a series of letters, which sketched the development of a Japanese girl from adolescence into womanhood.

Canton University, impressed by Kuo's growing reputation, asked him to become dean of the Department of Letters. But Kuo soon left Canton, returning to Shanghai to resume the hand-to-mouth existence of the professional writer. He would not practice medicine because it would leave him no time to write, and there were no further offers of academic positions. When he could no longer support them, he sent Anna and the children back to Japan while he stayed on in Shanghai alone.

* * *

Kuo Mo-jo, like many of his colleagues, was possessed of the self-pitying and lachrymose disposition that Professor Chi-chen Wang of Columbia University regards as the bane of the modern Chinese intellectual. He swore that the world had been unjust, denying him *freedom* to develop his *individuality.* Romantic individualism, it seemed, required a firm financial base. In 1924, Kuo finally found the solution to all problems—social, personal, and aesthetic: Salvation was to come not from the exaltation but the surrender of individual liberty.

The gifted individual, Kuo now believed, must not strive for the development of his potentialities at the expense of the masses. Rather must he submerge his individualism in the struggle to gain for all human beings the right to full development in an atmosphere of freedom.

187

This formula for the abnegation of freedom in the cause of freedom is the rationale which has enabled Kuo Mo-jo to justify the paradoxes of the Party line. He has now arrived at the inevitable end of such thinking. With the victory of the Communist revolution in China, he personifies the classic contradiction of successful revolutions, for he has become the apostle of law and order and the steadfast opponent of rebels and rebellion—political, economic, or literary.

Kuo's resignation of his prized individualism formalized his conversion to Marxism. He had previously been tormented by the desire to find certainty in belonging to a dedicated group. However, the convert had always been required to surrender something dear to him before he was permitted to find peace in faith. Kuo's renunciation of his individualistic desires was such an act of penance, which lightened the feeling of guilt that lay heavy upon him. He had castigated himself for his fancied failure as a husband and father, and had suffered a generalized guilt feeling for the condition of the nation. His early Confucian indoctrination had implanted the conviction that the educated man was responsible for the masses—and he had done nothing to serve them. His later education instilled an impassioned nationalism—and China was still debased. The refuge he found—Communist orthodoxy—accepted his sacrifice and absolved him of guilt by transferring the onus to the institution of private property. Moreover, his compulsion to social service was exploited by Marxism.

Kuo's declaration that he had pledged his pen to the service of Communism came in a letter to Ch'eng Fang-wu dated August 9, 1924. He wrote that he had intended, upon his return to Japan in the autumn of 1923, to immerse himself in biological studies and the completion of a novel to be called *Pure Light*. But he was prevented from following that plan because of material want, and a restlessness of the spirit which overcame him. Material security and freedom from anxiety, Kuo realized, were prerequisite to a life spent in the pursuit of truth—through science or through art. However, he declared, artists and scientists will find such security only when the economic system has been remade. His own *Communist Manifesto* continued:

"Ah, Fang-wu! We were born into a significant era, the era of the great revolution of the human race! The era of the great revolution in literature! I have become a complete believer in Marxism. Marxism is the only road to salvation in the era in which we live.

"Matter is the mother of the spirit. The highest development of material civilization and equal distribution [of wealth] are together the womb of spiritual civilization.

"Now, Fang-wu, I have awakened. I have cast aside the individualism to which I clung so desperately in the past. . . . I have fully awakened. . . . I have found the key to all past contradictions and all previously insoluble problems."

The universal solvent was Marxism. Kuo, the rebel, had at last found his cause, and was determined to follow its dictates in remaking every phase of his own life and the life of society. Since the practice of literature was his chief concern, literature was first to be coordinated with the new system.

"When Socialism has been made a reality [he continued], literary genius will attain to free and perfect development. . . . Literature will then be able to take pure character as its subject, and then will truly great literature appear.

"Talk of pure literature today is merely hallucination arising in the spring dreams of youth, the stuffed bellies of the rich, the euphoria of the morphine-sotted, the stupefaction of the drunken, or the mirages of the famished.

"There can be only one road for the true life, and literature should be a reflection of life. Therefore, it ought to follow only this road, which is the correct one. . . . We are now in the period of propaganda, and literature is a propaganda tool."

After 1924, it was no longer a desire for the "creation of beauty," which inspired Kuo, but a wish to use literature as a "tool of revolution." The organization of the League of Left Wing Writers in 1930 was more satisfying than the publication of a new novel. His standard for literary criticism was simplified. Works which advanced the cause were "good," non-revolutionary writing "meaningless," and counter-revolutionary literature "bad." He became a firebrand of the left, attacking the native "feudal and bourgeois classes," which joined with foreign imperialism to force China into "semi-colonial" status. Among foreign nations, he declared, only the Soviet Union could be considered friendly to the aspirations of the Chinese people.

Chinese Communism has displayed a consistent Russian orientation since its beginning, as well as ideological solidarity with the Comintern. However, there are in practice, certain unique elements in Chinese Communism which may play an important part in shaping its development. One peculiar aspect is the Confucian origin of the impetus to action. Kuo Mo-jo himself has been described as a "mandarin in modern dress." His aspect and manner recall the sage of Chinese tradition, as does his desire to participate in government and battle. The ideal of the philosopher-king—enunciated at about the same time by Plato and Confucius—was for millennia the ideal of Chinese political thinkers. Following that ideal, Kuo the thinker has at times become Kuo the fighter, and now, it appears, Kuo the ruler.

His first active participation in war and politics came in 1926, when he served as chairman of the Propaganda Unit under the Political Bureau attached to the headquarters of the Southern Armies of Chiang Kai-shek on the Northern Expedition. It was during the first honeymoon of the Kuomintang and the Communists. Kuo met Mao Tse-tung at the home of Lin Tsu-han on the evening of June 24, just before leaving Canton City to take up his duties in Chiang's army. He took part in the siege of the triplet industrial cities of central China, Wuchang, Hankow, and Hanyang, serving for a time in the Wuchang government.

190

On the march, the young poet discovered that soldiering was not to his taste. He wrote an ode describing his companions and himself as "heroes on horseback," but was thoroughly uncomfortable in the saddle. In Changsha he was assigned an elderly white horse of uncertain ancestry and disposition. The horse had one unalterable habit. He had taken to his heart Pope's admonition to be neither the first nor a laggard. Early each morning he would take up his position just behind the mount of Teng Yen-ta, chief of the unit, and would maintain that place through the day's journey. Teng and his Russian adviser were old cavalrymen, exuberant at finding themselves once more in the saddle. In high spirits, they would urge their horses into a gallop, and Kuo's old white horse, faithful to his training, would follow. After bouncing across the Hunan countryside for three days, Kuo decided that an altruistic gesture was in order. His mount became the unit's pack animal.

After Wuchang was taken, Kuo was able to give up his travels for a time. While serving in the military government of the city, he became unhappy over the course the revolution was taking. His protests were answered with soothing words, which stressed the "tactical character" of the measures to which he objected and promised correction after victory. But Kuo finally became disgusted with a revolution he characterized as "a sheep's head on a dog's body." In June, 1927, he left Wuchang on a river steamer bound for Shanghai.

His trail is not clear for the rest of 1927. He was definitely in Canton in September, but is also reported participating in Ho Lung's Swatow Commune in October. Japanese intelligence reports also place Kuo in Nanchang during the August First Rising, but it is unlikely that Kuo was with the newly formed Communist armies in 1927, since he does not mention that campaign in his own writings.

By the end of the year 1927, the Nanking government of Chiang Kai-shek had issued an order for his arrest, perhaps for his service under Ho Lung, but chiefly because of his publication of articles attacking the Kuomintang. In December, Kuo fled to Hong Kong to escape arrest, and shortly thereafter returned to Japan and Anna. His excursion into politics had been most unsatisfactory.

Kuo Mo-jo's exile in Japan—interspersed with short trips to Shanghai and Hong Kong—lasted until the summer of 1937, when the Japanese provoked the *Shina Jihen*—the China Incident. His chief occupation was research into the prehistory of China through the study of archaic inscriptions on bronze and tortoise-shell implements dug up in northwest China. *A Study of Ancient Chinese Society,* the treatise which came out of those studies, is an important contribution to knowledge of early Chinese civilization. He followed it with a half-dozen works treating of various aspects of ancient history and philology.

Kuo began his archaeological studies because a friend wanted to prune his library. When Kuo was about to leave Shanghai for Japan, he asked for something to read on the boat and was offered several volumes on archaeology, which his friend said need not be returned. Kuo accepted the gift, read the books en route, and plunged into the study of archaeology upon landing.

Regardless of incident, his devotion to historical research fits the pattern. Like the classical scholar-statesman he withdrew to study history and literature when in disfavor.

At times his political passion seized the reins, and in the course of a month he delivered five speeches and composed a dozen essays on social justice. Only his literary work was neglected, for he produced little imaginative writing, and that inferior to his earlier compositions. He did, however, publish translations of Upton Sinclair's *The Jungle,* Turgenev's *New Age,* and a number of Galsworthy's plays during the 1930's.

The incident at the Marco Polo Bridge on July 7, 1937, led to China's war with Japan and a truce in old political feuds. Kuo returned to China in the late summer of 1937 to assist in the propaganda of the resistance to Japanese aggres-

October 1, 1950: President Mao Tse-tung celebrates the first anniversary of the founding of the Chinese People's Republic in Peking. Beside him Moscow-trained Vice-President Liu Shao-ch'i shares the crowd's acclamation.

EASTFOTO

Vice-Premier for Culture and Education Kuo Mo-jo signs the Stockholm Peace Appeal as Premier-Foreign Minister Chou En-lai looks on.

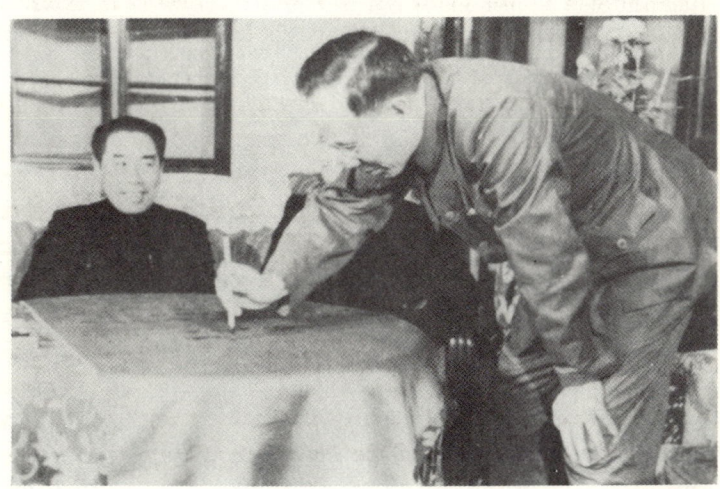

SOVFOTO

Mao Tse-tung visits the Stalin Auto Plant during his visit to the Soviet Union early in 1950.

January, 1950: Chou En-lai acknowledges his welcome at the Yaroslavl Railroad Station upon his arrival in Moscow. On the extreme left is Andrei Vishinsky. Beside him stand Wang Chia-hsiang, ambassador to Moscow, and General Wu Hsiu-ch'üan, who came to Lake Success in November, 1950, as the Chinese Reds' special emissary.

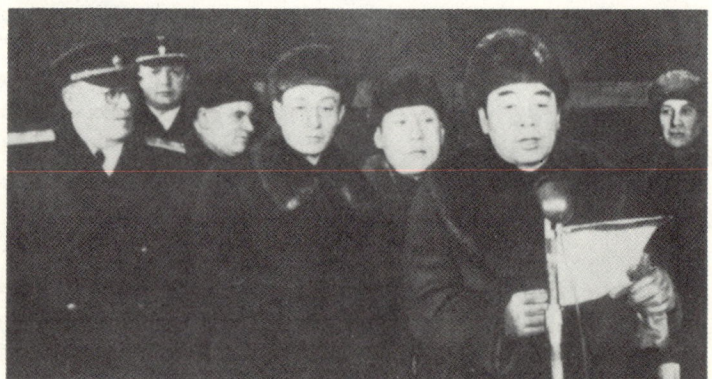

sion. Reaching Nanking about the tenth of September, he indulged in an Oriental version of Christopher Robin's busy day. Within the space of three days, he paid his respects to Ch'en Li-fu and Shao Li-tze, and had long chats with Chiang Kai-shek and Wang Ching-wei. Today no city in this world could hold those five men at the same time.

Wang Ching-wei, the Alcibiades of modern China, infinitely gifted and infinitely corrupt, died in 1944 after turning traitor to become president of the puppet regime set up by the Japanese. Kuo had known him in the days of the Hankow government, when Wang was the leader of the Kuomintang's radicals against the military clique and the rightists under Chiang Kai-shek. Ch'en Li-fu's name is today anathema to Kuo, for with his brother Kuo-fu he is the leader of the neo-Fascist wing of the Kuomintang, the C C Clique. The Communists would like to hang the two Ch'en's, but they have welcomed Shao Li-tze, who had been in and out of the Communist movement since its beginning. Though his last post was minister of political affairs under the National Military Affairs Committee, Shao evidently endeared himself to the Communists during his participation, on the Nationalist side of the table, in Kuomintang-Communist peace negotiations after the war. He is now safe in Peking.

When Kuo Mo-jo called on him, Chiang Kai-shek was quite cordial to the man he had not seen in ten years. He asked about the deafness with which Kuo had been afflicted and questioned him on the progress of his philological studies. They fenced for a time on the reasons for Kuo's long stay in Japan, but arrived at a face-saving truce when Chiang accepted Kuo's allegation of "personal reasons." At the end of the interview, the Generalissimo pressed Kuo to accept an official position in one of the propaganda agencies.

Kuo demurred, saying that his deafness would make it impossible for him to discharge the duties of office. Chiang replied firmly that he wished Kuo to accept appointment. The duties, he continued, would be nominal, for Kuo need only write an occasional article and might spend most of his time at his studies. Embarrassed by Chiang's insistence, Kuo launched a counter-attack. The poet got from the Generalissimo a promise that, when the war was won, he would buy back certain of China's archaeological treasures, which had been carried abroad. That pledge has never been claimed.

Kuo could not reject Chiang's request. In 1938, he became director of the Third Department of the Political Training Board, an agency which operated among the troops under the auspices of the National Military Affairs Committee. In many ways the work was similar to that he had performed during the Northern Expedition. At that time Chinese generals were impressed by the overwhelming victory of Chiang's Southern Armies, distinguished in their eyes from the warlord Northern Armies only by the presence of Political Units in the Russian manner. In this new war, each general felt that a Political Unit in his command would guarantee victory. But fear of insidious Red influence kept the Nationalists from organizing an effective program of political training, and the Political Training Board was gradually deprived of its functions. In time it was allowed to do no more than issue broadsides for distribution to the troops, and despatch a few lecturers to organize meetings.

Kuo Mo-jo stayed with the Political Training Board until the end of the war in 1945, becoming chairman of the Cultural Work Committee in 1940. After 1943, however, the Cultural Work Committee lost most of its remaining functions, and Kuo began to give more of his time to independent political writing. As China and her allies pressed toward final victory over Japan, his views veered sharply from the Kuomintang line. Chungking's only Communist newspaper, the *New China Daily,* printed Kuo's most influential essay in 1944 in a special issue for Double Ten Day—October 10, the beginning of the Revolution of 1911. Its effects were so wide-spread and its thesis so radical that Kuo's new split with Chiang became a chasm.

194

Under the title, "The 300th Anniversary of the Fall of the Ming Dynasty," Kuo extolled the virtues of Li Tze-ch'eng, a popular leader viewed by orthodox historians as a bandit whose marauding weakened the native Ming dynasty, so that it could not resist the invading Manchu armies. Kuo maintained that Li had been neither a brigand nor a traitor, but the patriotic leader of a justified agrarian revolt against a corrupt government. The allusion was necessarily oblique, but the parallel between Li Tze-ch'eng and the Communists was not far to seek.

Because of Kuo's name, and his startling viewpoint, the essay attracted much attention. His argument was highly effective among students and intellectuals, accustomed to viewing contemporary conflicts in the light of historical precedent. Following the first impact, the Communists issued thousands of cheap reprints of the piece. Old prejudices were shaken by Kuo's arguments and set opinions cracked. Intellectuals began to re-examine their attitudes toward modern problems. Kuo's offhand excursion into history was an important factor in the swing of intellectuals toward the Communist camp.

Not long after the publication of his article on Li Tze-ch'eng, Kuo Mo-jo was packed off to Moscow as Chinese delegate to the exercises celebrating the anniversary of the Soviet Academy of Science. But the move came too late to counteract the damage he had done Chiang's regime. Kuo returned from Moscow to find himself *persona non grata,* but stayed on in Chungking until 1946, though he had resigned from his post in 1945. His last political act in conjunction with the Kuomintang was attendance as chairman of the Non-Party Delegation at the Political Consultative Council held by the Kuomintang and the Communist Party at the beginning of 1946. During the session, thugs, allegedly hired by the Nationalists, attacked Kuo Mo-jo in the conference hall, but he was not seriously injured. When the Central Government moved to Nanking in May, 1946, he drifted to Hong Kong, where he wrote and watched developments. Later he journeyed to the Communist-controlled North.

His welcome was all that he could have wished. For the first time Kuo enjoyed not only the acclamation of the impoverished intelligentsia, but also the ungrudging approval of men who actually held power. The sometime iconoclast was still Confucian enough to rejoice at the praise of government officials—and the prospect of holding office himself.

The roll of his subsequent honors has already been called. Kuo Mo-jo's chief assignment during 1950—it will remain his most important task for some time to come—was to convince the Chinese people of the undying friendship of the Soviet Union and the implacable enmity of the United States. The circulation of the Stockholm Peace Appeal in China was his responsibility, and the same assignment took him to the Warsaw Peace Conference in the autumn of 1950 as chairman of the Peking delegation.

In the spring of 1950, an article in one of New York's Nationalist-sponsored Chinese-language newspapers suggested that Kuo was not happy in his official role. It reported a conversation in which Kuo complained that serving on innumerable committees left him no time to write, and that he was surrounded by spies.

That attitude sounds like a recurrence of "individualism," but Kuo continues to discharge his official duties unexceptionably. When the Red United Nations envoy, General Wu Hsiu-ch'üan, landed at the Peking airport on January 5, 1951, Kuo Mo-jo, wearing the regulation floppy cap of the Red Chinese civil official, stepped forward to greet him. Kuo had just been named chairman of the "Committee to Defend World Peace by Opposing American Aggression."

The former Romantic poet had already read into the record of an official proceeding his reaffirmation of orthodoxy and anti-individualism.

On the morning of September 25, 1949, Kuo stood on a platform in Peiping, speaking as chairman of the Non-Party

Delegation to the People's Political Consultative Conference. His manner was calm, almost casual, and he spoke in low tones, occasionally raising his voice slightly for emphasis.

"We are non-party democratic delegates [he declared], and therefore cannot voice the opinions of an organization. It would seem that we are here as individuals. That is true, but there is one statement we most emphatically desire to place before this body: We are very definitely not those men whom American imperialism has been plotting to seduce; we are not *democratic individualists.*"

Kuo straightened his tall, spare body, sweeping his eyes around the hall. His voice was heavy with controlled emotion, and his eyes sparkled behind their black-rimmed glasses. He smiled thinly as he pronounced the phrase from Secretary Acheson's introduction to the White Paper on China.

"*Democratic individualists* were the props of old-line democracy, but today they have become the tools of American imperialism. They have taken selfish profit-seeking as a body, and placed upon it a *democratic* hat. And the more thoroughgoing the individualism is, the more phony the *democratic* hat becomes! American imperialism is the case in point: financial, educational, and cultural control have all been swept into the hands of a small number of individuals, who represent eight great plutocratic concentrations. Because of this, so-called American *democracy* is, in fact, oligarchy.

" . . . as for us, we are disciples of Mao Tse-tung; we are *democratic collectivists.*"

As he neared the end of his speech, Kuo's voice became shrill:

"The heroic age of collectivism has arrived. Our reborn motherland is calling to her heroic sons and daughters, exhorting them to bring to rapid fulfilment the great enterprise of rebuilding the nation.

"*Long live* the Chinese People's Republic!

"*Long live* the people's democratic dictatorship!

"*Long live* the great people's leader Mao Tse-tung!"

197

9. THE ELASTIC BOLSHEVIK: CHOU EN-LAI

Communists worship adamance. Christian doctrine exalts justice tempered with love, but in the Red gospel the paramount virtue is inflexible resolution in attaining the Party's ends. This obsession reveals itself even in the pseudonyms chosen by the Russian leaders: Stalin means "steel" and Molotov "hammer." The persistent theme is metallic vigor.

The ideal Communist is the Iron Bolshevik, his chief quality a massive determination which bears down all obstacles. Quite another kind of Communist is the Premier and Foreign Minister of the People's Republic of China, General Chou En-lai. An Elastic Bolshevik, his outstanding characteristic is the resiliency which has enabled him to retain his seat up front, as the Party Juggernaut whipped around the sharp corners of deviationism, and shattered its timbers against the granite of purges.

Chou En-lai, who has held major posts in both the Communist Party and the government continuously since 1924, is a master of the one accomplishment essential to both successful football players and Red bosses; he has learned how to fall. Relieved of his post as chairman of the Organization Bureau by the purge that wiped the Li Li-san faction from power in 1931, he reappeared as chairman of the Military Affairs Bureau, which was to become the most active Party organ in the years immediately following.

Chou's private life, too, is tied to the Party, for his wife is a leader among women Communists. Nor has he any occupation other than that of professional revolutionist. He must subordinate himself to the Party's rigid discipline, for, like a monk, he has no place to go outside the order. But a monk would probably have a craft—bookbinder, gardener, or vintner—which he could practice in civilian life. Chou En-lai, labeled the Party's "expert on foreign affairs," has none, and until very recently, even his diplomatic experience was limited to negotiations with the Kuomintang and infrequent intercourse with the organs of international Communism.

With no farming experience—his family were officials—Chou has never had the option of returning to the land. Nor is he a professional soldier, though he wears the title "General" by courtesy, through his service on the Communist Board of War. Even journalism, the common refuge of the highly literate professional revolutionist, has been closed to him. Edgar Snow, in *Red Star Over China,* wrote that Chou had displayed "literary genius" as a youngster, but his infrequent writings show none of the sensitive grace which quickens the Marxist rhetoric of Mao Tse-tung. Chou En-lai could only be what he has been, for he is the true son of his dickering mandarin ancestors, and his talents as a negotiator are matched by few Chinese. His medium of self-expression is the conference table; he finds fulfillment in intrigue, and in the complex maneuvering which is the blood of Chinese political life, regardless of party or political creed.

Chou is shrewd, but he lacks the originality and brilliant adaptability shown by Mao Tse-tung. He is a good administrator and a faithful agent, but hardly a maker of major policy. He has avoided identification with any one faction within the Party, and has served whatever group happened to control the organization. Again the parallel with the old-fashioned mandarin: the civil servant who ruled China before the Revolution of 1911 had a simple view of his responsibilities. It was his duty to render faithful service to the Emperor who sat in Peking, be he Chinese or barbarian, but his chief loyalty was given to the state and, presumptively, to the people, rather than to the sovereign. Chou En-lai, having given his allegiance to the Party, showed the same disinclination to question the character of the ruler which had been displayed by his ancestors, who were officials in the orthodox Confucian tradition.

*   *   *

Like Kuo Mo-jo, Chou En-lai came to Marxism by way of Confucianism. When Chou's father began his son's classical education with the *Thousand Character Classic* he was putting the boy's feet on the road to Moscow. From the works of the classical authors Chou En-lai learned not only his ideographs, but the doctrine that the educated man owes service to the masses. As a student at middle school and college during the turbulent second decade of the twentieth century, Chou was forcibly made aware of the flaws in the traditional Chinese political and social structure—flaws which appeared as gaping holes in the light from the West. In obedience to the Confucian ethic, which enjoins responsibility upon the educated, Chou and his contemporaries took as their mission the restoration of China to a place of dignity in the world. The instrument which seemed to them to be best fitted to the execution of that task was Marxism. So, following an injunction of Confucius, they bound themselves to the destruction of Confucian morality.

Chou had spent the early years of his life in Manchuria, away from the center of conflict. The family had moved from the ancestral home at Huai-an in Kiangsu Province near Shanghai when the elder Chou was given an official assignment outside the Great Wall. After the Revolution of 1911, the Chous moved back to China proper, but they did not go home again. Chou En-lai's father chose to manage his business affairs from Tientsin, the mercantile port of the North. In that city, with its large foreign concession, young Chou saw at close hand the forces which had snapped the thread binding him to the career of his ancestors. In 1913, at the age of fifteen, he enrolled in Nankai Middle School, a Western-style institution. His father, having retired from official life with good grace, was determined that the boy should be given the means to make his own way—and be useful to the family—by acquiring the tool of Western Learning.

When Chou En-lai entered this new world, the Confucian tradition was being swept away by torrents from the West, and with it were disappearing the twin pillars of faith which had sustained the official class of non-religious Imperial China.

The first filled the universal human need for sanction for one's own existence from an entity greater than one's self. It was the belief that mankind was, in itself, an eternal unity whose will was apparent in the flow of the generations. This was the faith which expressed itself vulgarly as "ancestor worship," but might more accurately be termed "posterity worship," since the living, themselves a palpable manifestation of the eternal vitality of the dead, looked to the unborn for their own immortality. In short: humanity without end.

A contemporary of Chou En-lai wrote: "The great river, swift-flowing, sweeps down from the horizon's edge. Wave follows upon wave, sails appear and disappear, in an atmosphere of deep solemnity. Here is the true curve of humanity. Mankind exists eternally, through all space and all time. On the hillside lie our ancestors; in their houses close by the Pagoda sleep our parents; and today's current brings down the river those who will be the ancestors of tomorrow. Mankind is one, a unity that is not to be broken by the words ancestor, living person, posterity. Past, present, and future are only modes of endless being, and cannot break the eternal one-ness of Mankind, nor the eternal community of its interests."*

---

* Sheng-Cheng: *A Son of China* (translated from the French by M. McM. Lowes), W. W. Norton and Co., 1930, p. 55.

The second article of faith had been the conviction that China, herself dominant over the known world, would continue to be ruled through the Imperial system, unchanged in substance since 221 B.C. The Empire, motivated by the Confucian state ideology, had enforced a benevolent totalitarianism, coordinating all aspects of human life around a few central precepts. Only the economic phase had been slighted in the ideology, and in practice even economic affairs were governed by custom and the state. To this ideal of China, Imperial and Eternal, the mandarins gave their services. A change of dynasties left that devotion unchanged, for officials merely transferred their loyalty to the inheritor of the Decree of Heaven, and learned to write a new dynastic name on their official papers.

The military, economic, and ideological incursions of the West had demonstrated that China was not supreme in the world, and had forced Chinese revolutionaries to attack the Empire, lest they perish in the attempt to preserve it. Belief in the mystical unity of mankind eternal was shattered by more subtle but no less effective means. The kindly Darwin, who did such violence to Victorian equanimity, could hardly have suspected that his discoveries would wreak spiritual desolation on the other side of the globe. Western science had already begun to eat away the foundations of Confucianism when mordant Darwinism dissolved the mortar. His theory of evolution demonstrated that the human being was merely a highly developed form of animal life, who might be superseded by a higher organism, just as he had won the world from the dinosaurs. Deprived of the illusion which invested the human race with a peculiar divinity, the educated Chinese felt his spiritual life reduced to chaos.

Since he came of an official family, which had lived at the heart of the Confucian-Imperial tradition, these generalizations apply with particular force to young Chou En-lai at the moment of his matriculation at Nankai Middle School. Entering a Western-style school was a step into the camp of the enemy, for the West was a hostile force in the eyes of the young Chinese. If Chou required evidence to bolster that view, he need not have looked beyond neighboring Peking, where Yüan Shih-k'ai was embarked on his career of ambition. Combining in himself the worst of two worlds, the European and the Chinese, Yüan would plunge China into a maelstrom of greed and slaughter. While Chou En-lai was imbibing Western culture, strongly flavored with missionary evangelicism, the machinations of Yüan Shih-k'ai and his Western backers, who wanted a "strong man" to keep China weak, were discrediting the cup-bearers of that culture.

*   *   *

Continuing in the collegiate department at Nankai, Chou was soon arrested for his part in a student demonstration. He had begun his career as an agitator, and was to attain the higher status of organizer when he returned from a year's study in Japan to found the Awaken Club. It was one of the multitude of student clubs founded after the May Fourth Incident with hot purpose and vague designs.

The Awaken Club, like its sister societies to which Mao Tse-tung and Lin Piao belonged, found itself hardly competent to attack any of China's grave political and economic problems, except insofar as it served as a rallying point for future leaders. But it did solve one of Chou En-lai's personal problems—finding a wife. In 1920, Teng Ying-ch'ao, a twenty-year-old girl student from Hopei Province, made application for membership in the Awaken Club. Her political ardor had been stimulated by a course of residence at that agitator's finishing school, the Tientsin municipal jail.

Chinese girl students of the early 1920's were an earnest group, who sometimes seemed even more intense about politics than were their brothers and lovers. The brave new talk of equality and liberty was very personal to them, promising release from the formal subjection under which Chinese women had always lived. Some took it as license for excess, and good burghers drew aside with horror from short-haired girl students, who, it was said, changed their "friends" more frequently than their dresses. Others were less impulsive, but all were determined to "live their own lives." Teng Ying-ch'ao was asserting both her social and political independence when she joined the Awaken Club, for slim, dark Chou En-lai was attractive personally as well as politically. They were to be married five years later in Canton.

If Teng Ying-ch'ao was indeed planning to annex Chou En-lai when she joined the Awaken Club in 1920, her purpose was frustrated. After his graduation from Nankai University that same year, Chou joined one of the troops of "work and study" students who were on their way to France to complete their education in matters Western. Mao Tse-tung, though still small-fry, was interested in the Work and Study Movement, and it is likely that he and Chou met at the time, for Mao was a student in Peking, only a few miles from Tientsin. For the next decade, Chou, who spent four years in Europe, was to be a more powerful figure in the Communist Party than Mao, who remained in China.

Because so many of them later became eminent, the accounts rendered by these "work and study" students, a highly articulate group, are part of Chinese social history. With good reason, the word "work" stood first in their slogan. For most of them, formal study was a diversion to be squeezed in between long periods in the silk mills, automobile factories, or coal mines. Some found employment as waiters, others as pick-and-shovel laborers. Inevitably, they learned as much outside universities and libraries as within them, and inevitably, many grew bitter at the system which worked them so hard for their bread. Young strangers in an alien land, they endured the twin trials of loneliness and young manhood.

The novelist Pa Chin tells of pacing his tiny rooming-house bedroom in a French provincial town on a snowy Sunday afternoon. He cursed the "capitalist" from whom he had been forced to beg work, so that he might "pour flesh and blood into steel to make automobiles in which rich men and women may ride. In resentment, in anguish, and in fear," he bowed his head and nursed his hatred of the capitalist system which imposed such suffering upon him.

Chou En-lai was in slightly better case than most of his fellows, though he did work for a time in the coal mines of the Rhineland. He may have been receiving funds from home or from the Comintern, for he had enough money to study in England and Germany as well as in France. In Berlin, toward the end of the year 1920, he organized a branch of the Socialist Youth Group of China, and in the summer of 1921 participated in the meeting which formally established the Paris Branch of the Chinese Communist Party. Other charter members were Li Li-san, who was later to be boss of the Chinese Party, and Ch'en Yen-nien, the older son of Ch'en Tu-hsiu, the Party's first secretary-general. They were to become the leaders of the "international faction" of the Chinese Communist Party, opposed to both the "Russian faction" under Wang Ming, and the "Chinese faction" of Mao Tse-tung.

Working with the French Communist Party and the International's representatives in Paris, Chou En-lai won recognition in the ranks of international Communism. When he returned to China in 1924, his importance was acknowledged by an appointment as secretary of the Canton Province Branch of the Communist Party. The post was a major one, because the Party was in the process of coming to an agreement with the Kuomintang, and Canton was the base of the Kuomintang's armies. With the aid of Russian advisers and a subsidy from Moscow, the Kuomintang was reorganizing, and building its armed forces along Russian revolutionary lines. This new-model army was to be the instrument with which Chiang Kai-shek would win control of China in 1927 and 1928.

One of the first steps was the creation of an officers' training school, the Whampoa Military Academy, in May, 1924.

Chiang Kai-shek, who had attended a Japanese military academy prior to a short term of service in the Japanese army, was made commandant. His inspection tour of Russia in 1923 was a strong recommendation, for Russian funds were to support the academy. Although he had no particular use for Communists and did not get along with high-strung Chou En-lai, Chiang was forced to accede to the young Communist's appointment as chairman of the Political Training Department of the Whampoa Academy.

In conformity with Russian practice, each major unit in the Kuomintang armies was to have a political commissar and a political section, charged with troop indoctrination and propaganda work among the civilian population. Chiang, contemptuous of these new-fangled notions as became a professional officer, frequently clashed with the urbane Chou En-lai. As a soldier he was scornful of civilians and saw no need for winning the masses to his side, and as commandant he was jealous of the young political director, who had usurped a share of his absolute authority.

When the Kuomintang armies marched out of Canton in July, 1926, Chou En-lai was political commissar of the crack First Army, which was directly under Chiang Kai-shek's command. The officer corps was composed almost entirely of Whampoa graduates, who were fanatically loyal to their ex-principal, Chiang Kai-shek. They were to be his most devoted supporters for the next twenty years. Dubbed "the Whampoa Clique," they still stand behind their stricken leader on the island refuge of Formosa. Only a few Whampoa men have thrown in with the Communists.

Chou En-lai was soon detached from the First Army. Chiang was delighted to see him go, and the Party had a better assignment for him in Shanghai. In that city, with the largest "proletarian" population in the Orient, Chou, under Ch'en Tu-hsiu's orders, organized terrorist bands among the workers. Besides these activist elements, the Reds trained militia units to march when the time came to take the city.

Ch'en Tu-hsiu and Chou En-lai performed a feat of organization fit to stand in revolutionary annals with Trotsky's accomplishment in forging a victorious army, without an officer caste, from the ragged and diseased remnants of the Russian Imperial Armies. The Shanghai rising came in late March, 1927, as Chiang's army approached the city. The remnants of the defending war-lord armies were disarmed and the workers took over the task of policing the city until Chiang arrived.

During the first days of April, 1927, the workers patrolled the city, brave in the dignity of their brassards and rifles—one to every fourth man. The regular troops were encamped outside the city, while Chiang conferred with the leaders of the Commune, and with bankers and gang leaders in the French Concession.

At four on the morning of April 12, gangsters dressed as workmen joined units of General Pai Tsung-hsi's Kwangsi army to attack the workers' strongholds.

The Kwangsi men did not like Shanghailanders. They were delighted to carry out Chiang's order to disarm the workers—and not bother being too gentle about it. By noon the Shanghai workingmen, who had expected a victory parade, were fleeing through the streets pursued by regulars firing rifles and sub-machineguns. The pickets defending the headquarters of the Federation of Shanghai Labor Unions were more resolute. Under their commander Ku Chen-chung and vice-commander Chou En-lai, they offered some resistance to the soldiers, but were finally themselves disarmed and slain.

Chou En-lai was taken prisoner. The manner of his escape was to become a minor mystery among the greater problems posed by Chiang's decision to turn on his allies at that particular moment. One story tells that the captain of the detail assigned to guard Chou was a former student, who permitted his teacher to escape. Another concerns General Pai Tsung-hsi, later to be the last Nationalist commander-in-chief on the mainland. Pai felt no particular love for Chiang Kai-shek, even at that early date, and was under obligation to Chou, who had saved his brother's life. He failed to recognize Chou En-lai when the Red leader was brought before him, and Chou was released. The story is probably not quite as apocryphal as it sounds, although the date and circumstances may be erroneous. If Chou does in truth owe his life to Pai Tsung-hsi's lapse of memory, it probably occurred later, when he was captured on the Long March.

Regardless of the manner of his release, it is certain that Chou En-lai was not long a prisoner. He next appeared in Nanchang as a member of the Revolutionary Committee which directed the rising in that city on August 1, 1927. Six days later he was in Kiukiang, some miles to the north, for the Emergency Meeting which removed Ch'en Tu-hsiu from the office of secretary-general and substituted Ch'ü Ch'iu-pai. Thence Chou went to Canton City for the Commune which held the seaport for a few days during December, 1927. That was orthodox Communism's last stand in China. Thereafter success was to come among the peasants, not in the cities, and Chou was out of it for a number of years. He continued to hold high office in the Party, but in reality there were two Communist Parties in China until 1931—both pledging their allegiance to the Comintern.

Chou, in exile in Hong Kong, chose the year 1928 for his pilgrimage. He was posted to Moscow as a member of the Chinese delegation to the Comintern, a body that swelled remarkably as the whipped Chinese Reds came home to lick their ideological wounds. In Moscow, Chou met Ch'en Shao-yü, better known under his alias Wang Ming, who was to lead an intra-Party revolt against Li Li-san, Chou's Paris schoolmate.

*　　　*　　　*

Li Li-san had come into effective control of the Party machinery after Ch'en Tu-hsiu's removal in August, 1927. Although he was not formally named to the top Party post, Li's doctrines prevailed from 1927 until he was reprimanded and exiled to Moscow in January, 1931. He was impatient of the moderate, peasant-based program of Mao Tse-tung, feeling that the time was ripe for general armed revolt in the cities, as well as in the countryside. Under his influence, the restive Red Army was to attack Changsha twice; the first time, in July, 1929, establishing a commune which endured for ten days with Li Li-san at its head, the second, a year later, meeting immediate defeat.

With the tacit support of Ch'ü Ch'iu-pai, secretary-general of the Party, Li scoffed at the conservatism of the rural faction under Mao Tse-tung and Chu Teh, demanding positive action to take advantage of the incipient collapse of world capitalism. China, he maintained, was particularly ripe for wide-scale revolt because her reactionary masters depended upon the support of foreign imperialistic capitalism to bolster their power. Since imperialism, the most dangerous enemy of the Chinese Communist Revolution, was weakened by economic crisis, a series of strong blows, Li concluded, could overturn imperialist capitalism in China.

The cautious Comintern, its self-confidence still weak from the wounds inflicted by the defeat in China and the struggle to unseat Trotsky, looked on Li's pronouncements with an unenthusiastic eye. After a time, however, the group in the Kremlin began to see in Li a threat to their own power, which was still not firmly established. Li, it seemed, was displaying symptoms of Trotskyism—dread disease. He was, in fact, pushing the Comintern faster than it wished to go. Having demonstrated to his own satisfaction that China was ripe for general revolt, Li went on to argue that a Communist victory in China would precipitate a world-wide crisis of capitalism. China, not Russia, he maintained, was the pivot of the world "liberation" movement.

"We have arrived [he wrote] at the moment for the total destruction of imperialism, with the destruction of the chief

209

international imperialists—England, the United States, and Japan—coming first. . . . The Chinese revolution must seize victory in this final battle, and in the same great battle the proletariat of the entire world can attain final victory. . . . The victory of our revolution must fix irrevocably the victory of the world-wide revolution."

Because he felt that the moment of decision was at hand, Li Li-san opposed the timorous policy of agrarian reform put forward by Mao Tse-tung with the Comintern's half-hearted backing. The Politburo, which had become the steering organ of the Chinese Communist Party after the purge of 1927, was captured by the Li Li-san faction. Secretary-general Hsiang Chung-fa was his man, as was the chairman of the Military Affairs Bureau. Liu Shao-ch'i in the Labor Bureau and Chou En-lai, returned from Moscow in 1929, would also go along with Li, though their support was tempered with consideration for the future, should Li prove unable to buck the farmer faction.

Chou En-lai was chairman of the Organization Bureau, a position second in formal importance only to the secretary-generalship. Li Li-san, a king-maker because he had aroused too much antagonism to be king himself, was content to head the Propaganda Bureau. This cabal held power for little more than a year, from November, 1929, when Ch'en Tu-hsiu was read out of the Party, until January, 1931, when they themselves were almost excommunicated.

Because the first attack on Changsha had been a success, albeit a limited one, Li wished to increase the scope of military action against the cities. On June 11, 1930, the Politburo passed a resolution sponsored by Li Li-san. Its title: "The New Revolutionary High Tide and the Question of Prior Victory in One Province or a Multi-Provincial Offensive." Its decision: An all-out offensive to snatch quick victory while the enemy was in a weakened state. Its first implementation: A second attack on Changsha in July, 1930. The result: Total failure.

A third group in the Party had already protested against Li Li-san's recklessness. They were the "Russian faction" led by twenty-four-year-old Wang Ming, who was backed by Mif, the Comintern's Shanghai representative, a past president of the Sun Yat-sen University in Moscow. After the defeat at Changsha, Chou En-lai scurried to Moscow to lay Li's case before the international body. Before Chou reached Moscow, the Comintern received a telegram from Mif in Shanghai, violently attacking Li's position.

Though the case was still undecided, Chou hurried back to China to be present at the Third Plenary Meeting of the Chinese Party's Central Committee, held at Mount Lu in Kiangsi Province in late September, 1930. With him came Ch'ü Ch'iu-pai, Moscow representative of the Party and former secretary-general, a man who spoke with double authority. Together they beat down the swords leveled at Li Li-san by Comrade Mif and Wang Ming, but they could not prevent the Central Committee's passing a resolution mildly critical of Li's tactics. The Comintern still had not acted, and Li continued in authority, though his prestige was tarnished.

On November 12, 1930, Shen Tse-min, a member of the Mif-Wang Ming "Russian faction," presented a resolution to the standing committee of the Central Committee, once more calling for the rejection of Li Li-san. On the sixteenth, the long-awaited telegram from the Comintern arrived. The Kremlin backed Mif and Wang Ming, pointing out the theoretical errors behind Li's position, and calling on the Chinese to concentrate upon training the Workers' and Peasants' Red Army in reinforced Soviet Areas. Although the Party was advised to continue to recruit cadres in non-Soviet areas, Li's insurrectionism was to be abandoned.

On November 25, 1930, the Chinese Politburo, meeting in Shanghai, came to heel. The policy ordered by the Comintern was formally adopted, and Li Li-san was castigated for his faulty analysis and for "opportunism"—a grim echo of the charges against Ch'en Tu-hsiu. Li withdrew from the

Politburo, but Chou En-lai and other Li supporters remained.

The controversy over Li Li-san had opened a chasm which could not be bridged by a resolution of the Politburo, powerful though that body was. To meet the emergency it was necessary to call the Central Committee into plenary session in Shanghai on January 1, 1931. At that session the first business was Li Li-san's presentation of a letter apologizing for his past errors. (The public confession is not a new technic.) He was stripped of his offices, but was rewarded for his belated cooperation with a face-saving appointment to the Chinese delegation in Moscow. Li was to remain in exile for sixteen years, returning to Manchuria with the Russian armies only in August, 1945. In Manchuria he was appointed political adviser to General Lin Piao, commanding the Manchurian Democratic Allied Armies, and is now vice-president of the General Federation of Labor. Li Li-san had merely been too hasty, for today even Mao Tse-tung is swinging the base of Red power to the cities and the "proletariat."

Li himself disposed of, the Party was cleared of his followers. Although Ch'ü Ch'iu-pai was severely reprimanded for temporizing with the Li faction, Chou En-lai was merely transferred to a new position, one that was to become at least as important as his previous post at the head of the Organization Bureau. With his strange talent for survival, he became chief of the Military Affairs Bureau, escaping the fate of his collaborators, whom Wang Ming, the new secretary-general, was sweeping from the Party. In March, 1931, a number of the diehards of the Li Li-san Line were read out of the Party, and on June 21, Hsiang Chung-fa, the previous secretary-general, was executed by Chiang Kai-shek and his followers arrested.

In the fall of 1931, Chou En-lai arrived in the Kiangsi Soviet Area to ally himself with the third major faction in the Party, the only one which could command substantial popular support and material resources. With him came Wang Ming to attend the First Congress of Soviet Representatives in Jui-chin, the Red capital. Although Chou and Wang were delegates to the Congress, neither man was elected to a responsible position in the Soviet Government, a slap in the face from the Congress which named Mao Tse-tung head of the Soviet Government, and Chu Teh chairman of the Soviet People's Military Affairs Committee. The power of the "Chinese faction" was firmly established, and Wang Ming would soon return to Moscow, although he was not to be removed from his post as Party chief in favor of Mao Tse-tung until a later meeting of the Central Committee.

The flexible Chou entered the service of the new masters of Chinese Communism. He was to be elevated to the vice-chairmanship of the Soviet Military Affairs Committee, and in time become vice-chairman of the new Politburo. There was little need for Chou's talents as a diplomat in the mountainous Soviet Area of southern Kiangsi Province, since all Red foreign relations, with the slight exception of surreptitious trading, were conducted with shot and shell. But Chou knew the Kuomintang armies better than any other Red leader, for he had helped train them. As adviser to General Chu Teh, he now helped train the Red armies to counter the political technics in which he had instructed the enemy a few years earlier.

After the successful conclusion of the Long March in the fall of 1935, Chou took on the functions of a foreign minister. The Communists had extended their fighting "foreign policy" by moving to the Northwest, where they were bound to clash with Japanese expansion in North China. As chief of the Foreign Office, Chou En-lai's first task was the political coordination of the thin-spread Red armies and guerrilla bands, which were operating all the way from the Tibetan border to Canton in the extreme Southwest.

His heavy chin veiled by a jet-black beard, Chou would ride a bristle-maned Mongolian pony out through the stone arches of Yenan. From the breast-pocket of his rude blouse peeped the caps of two fountain pens. They were his only badge of rank as he cantered through the yellow hills of Shensi and across the green plains of Kansu to gauge the military situation for himself. He was soon given an opportunity to assume more conventional diplomatic functions, but the change was wrought in a most unconventional manner.

*　　　*　　　*

Three cities in Shensi Province are most inappropriately named. The provincial capital, Sian, was once the capital of China and a model for city-planners throughout the Far East under the name Ch'ang-an, which means Long Peace, as Si-an means Western Peace. Two smaller cities, Paoan and Yenan, were successively the Red capital. The incongruity is consistent, for Pao-an means Guaranteed Peace, and Yen-an, Extended Peace.

But there was no peace in Shensi in the fall of 1936. On December 7, Chiang Kai-shek flew to Sian to assume personal direction of the campaign being waged against the Reds by young Marshal Chang Hsüeh-liang's Tung-pei (Manchurian) Army and Kuomintang General Yang Hu-ch'eng's Hsi-pei (Northwest) Army.

Japanese aggression, which had driven the Manchurians from their homeland five years earlier, was now threatening Suiyüan Province directly, and all of North China by extension. The Reds knew that the Nationalist troops were unhappy at being required to fight "Red bandits" when they wished to fight Japanese bandits. They launched a psychological counter-offensive aimed at destroying the Nationalist will to prosecute the anti-Communist campaign. "Chinese should not fight Chinese when the motherland is in danger!" was one of their most effective slogans in support of a United Front against Japanese aggression. The Comintern had approved the strategy.

Marshal Chang Hsüeh-liang, lately war-lord of Manchuria, was susceptible to Communist persuasion. His predatory

214

troops had been overwhelmed by a flush of unexpected patriotism after the flight from their Manchurian homes, and Chang himself had only in 1929 made peace in the war with Chiang Kai-shek which he had inherited from his father. Under pressure from his junior officers, Marshal Chang was receptive to Communist offers of friendship. He failed to press the attack on the Soviet Areas, demanding instead that Chiang allow him to move against Japanese forces in Suiyüan Province. Troops of the Kuomintang's own Northwest Army, under General Yang Hu-ch'eng, were also disgusted with fighting their own countrymen, and they too arrived at a tacit truce with the Reds, who were infecting them with radical ideas. From the Central Government's viewpoint, the situation had deteriorated alarmingly when Chiang Kai-shek himself dropped down at the Sian airport to put new life into the "bandit extermination campaign" in accordance with his slogan: "Unification [i.e., destruction of the Reds] before Resistance [to the Japanese]!" To Chang Hsüeh-liang's pleas for resistance to the Japanese, Chiang had but one reply: "First destroy the Reds!"

On the evening of December 12, the Central Government armies in Sian rose against their commander-in-chief, imprisoning his Blueshirt bodyguards while a company of Manchurians marched to the spa ten miles from the city, where Chiang himself was quartered. For five days, the captive Generalissimo wavered between despair and righteous indignation, convinced that his destiny was about to be thwarted by assassination. Sulking in his room, through the thin partition he heard the officers of his guard discussing his fate. They were agreed that he would be executed for his "crimes against the Chinese people," since the Communists would insist upon it. Then an emissary arrived with authority to stay the hands of the mutineers.

The angel of mercy wore a most unexpected guise, and was accredited by Chiang Kai-shek's own personal demon. On December 17, 1936, Chou En-lai landed at Sian in Marshal

Chang Hsüeh-liang's personal plane, which had been sent to Yenan to fetch him.

Chiang and his former political commissar had not met since the Northern Expedition. Just before the Kuomintang armies marched out from Canton in July, 1926, the two had exchanged pledges.

Chou declared: "I am a disciple of the Three Principles of the People!"

Chiang counter-pledged: "I am a disciple of Communism!"

But that pleasant interchange was only half-remembered when Chiang heard that Chou En-lai was coming to see him in his captivity. He lay seething in his room, one moment trembling with rage, the next shaking with self-pity. He was convinced that Chou sought his death.

The door opened to admit the man Chiang had not seen for ten years. Chou En-lai removed the cap from his close-cropped hair and the shadow fled from his olive face, with its high cheek-bones, precise, heavy eyebrows set wide apart, and straight, long mouth.

"Mr. Chairman," he said, "I have come to sign betrothal articles for the remarriage of the Kuomintang and the Communist Party."

Reassured by the knowledge that Chou did not desire his death, or felt it to be impolitic at the moment, Chiang Kai-shek listened non-committally to the Red proposals.

"Call off your army, and we'll put the Red Army under your command for the prosecution of the war with Japan. We'll give up our anti-Kuomintang activities and cooperate with your party to resist the Japanese. Moreover, we'll give up the expropriation of landlord holdings in the Soviet Areas and change the name of those areas to 'Socialist Experimental Regions.' In return, there will have to be a reorganization which will give us a voice in the Central Government. You've seen the recent open telegram of our Central Committee. That, in brief, is what will have to be agreed to."

216

Chiang could not agree without deep consideration, for it would have been too undignified. Nevertheless, he had no real choice but to meet Chou's demands. Agreement came only after Madame Chiang, her brother T. V. Soong, and their Australian adviser, W. H. Donald, had flown to Sian to back Chiang's hand, and only after long consultations with General Yang of the Northwest Army and Manchurian Marshal Chang Hsüeh-liang.

Once Chiang had recovered from his anger and his fear, he saw that the compromise was advantageous to himself as well as the Reds. Two groups in his own Kuomintang threatened his power. One, led by Chang Hsüeh-liang and the anti-Japanese clique in Nanking, could not stomach continuation of the profitless war with the Communists when Japan was threatening to take the country over. This attitude they held despite the fact that they had no particular use for the Reds. Other groups in the Central Government, notably War Minister Ho Ying-chin, wanted to get rid of Chiang in order to install themselves in power. They had revealed their rapacity when it seemed that Chiang would never return to Nanking. The Generalissimo knew that he had to get home to weed out the herd and do some fence-mending.

The Communists, on the other hand, desired resistance to Japan above all else. Their texts told them that imperialism was the most dangerous enemy of their revolution, and they knew that Japanese success would put a double obstacle in the road to Communism, for they would be forced to overcome foreign oppression as well as native reaction. They spared Chiang because they believed that only he could lead a coalition against the Japanese.

On December 25, Chou En-lai and Chang Hsüeh-liang gave Methodist Madame Chiang the Christmas present she had longed for. Marshal Chang announced that he would fly them back to Nanking in his own plane that very day, while General Chou returned to Yenan.

Chiang's return to Nanking was followed by a Chinese

217

juggling act so complex as to put to shame all the Japanese jugglers who have ever displayed their skill beneath the big top. The Generalissimo tendered resignations and took on new posts, reprimanded some subordinates and commended others—and raised a great dust cloud. When it settled, the situation seemed to be as it had been before, but the Nationalist government was prepared to fight alongside the Communists against Japan.

Poor Chang Hsüeh-liang was nominated whipping boy. He had resigned with apologies, been tried, convicted, and pardoned, but was informed at the end of the affair that he would be imprisoned. He has never been released, and at this moment occupies a cell on Formosa. His younger brother, Chang Hsüeh-ssu, has commanded Communist troops since 1943, and is now vice-commandant of the Reds' Naval Academy.

A lonely echo of the Sian Incident tinkled into public notice in 1947, when the Hangchow newspaper the *Flying Arrow* was suspended for a week, because it had asked in an editorial: "Could Chang Hsüeh-liang restore freedom?"

*   *   *

Through the winter, spring, and summer of 1937 the *Entente* was on the ways. It was launched in September. Chou En-lai was chief Communist builder, working alternately in Yenan and Nanking. On February 21, 1937, the Central Committee of the Kuomintang passed a resolution which approached the problem of reconciliation in the Nationalists' usual tail-end foremost fashion. Most of the resolution was devoted to a recounting of past Communist crimes. Then the Kuomintang, taking cognizance of the Communist Party's expressed desire to aid the National Government in the struggle against Japan, declared that the basis of any agreement must be Communist concession of four points. They were: (1) incorporation of all Red armies into the National forces; (2) unification of the Red areas with the rest of China under

218

the Central Government; (3) a halt to Communist propaganda and subversion; and (4) cessation of the class struggle.

The Communists accepted these conditions in a manifesto issued by the Central Committee on September 22, 1937. (Promulgation had been delayed by the outbreak of the "China Incident" in July.) Asserting their individuality by putting the same terms into different language, the Communists agreed to (1) strive for the enforcement of the Three Principles of the People, originally enunciated by Dr. Sun Yat-sen; (2) abandon attempts to overthrow the Central Government, and give up expropriation of property; (3) abolish the Soviet Government and enforce democracy; and (4) put the Red Army under the orders of the Central Government.

On September 23, 1937, the Nationalists issued a statement confirming the alliance. China, which had been at war with Japan since July 7, could finally present a united front to the enemy. But the untoward harmony did not long endure.

The Communists sent Chou En-lai to Nanking as their representative. To bolster the façade of the United Front, he was made a member of the Praesidium of the Extraordinary National Congress of the Kuomintang, which met in Hankow in March, 1938. He was subsequently appointed vice-minister of the Political Training Board under the National Military Affairs Committee, the body which virtually ruled China during the War. But he left that post in 1940, when it became apparent that effective cooperation between the two Chinese parties was more a pious wish than a reality. And the New Fourth Army Incident of January, 1941, demonstrated that Chou might soon be called upon to negotiate for separation, if not divorce, of the two whose remarriage he had arranged four years earlier.

From 1941 through 1944, the two sides alternately talked peace and made war upon each other, while Chou En-lai spent most of his time in Chungking, the war capital. It appeared to many neutral observers that the end of the war

219

against Japan would be followed by a full-scale civil war, and it was only by courtesy that they refrained from describing Nationalist-Communist relations during those years as small-scale civil war. Formal military resistance to the Japanese almost ceased as the Chinese contenders jockeyed for position against each other. Only guerrilla warfare continued in full force, as the Communists expanded the territory under their control.

On October 10, 1944, China's Independence Day, Chou En-lai issued a statement castigating the Kuomintang for the despotism, corruption, and non-cooperation which, he declared, made it impossible for the Chinese nation to offer effective resistance to Japanese aggression. He called for the convening of a truly representative National Assembly to lay the basis for *coalition government* by the Kuomintang, the Communists, and the splinter parties of the right and left. A half-year later, Mao Tse-tung was to confirm the Red catch-word for the next three years in his lectures *On Coalition Government*.

In the negotiations which followed upon this statement of his desires, Chou En-lai once more sat at the head of the Communist side of the conference table. Intermediary, justice of the peace, and midwife was white-mustached Major General Patrick J. Hurley, who fascinated the Communist leaders when they met him at the Yenan airport on November 7, 1944, by bursting into a Choctaw war-whoop, presumably to demonstrate his good intentions. The hard-headed Red bosses stood amazed at the ways of the mysterious Occident.

But General Hurley got from the Reds what he had come for—the draft of an agreement acceptable to them. He immediately flew back to Chungking to submit it to the Nationalists. In the light of events between November, 1944, and the present, the basic incompatibility of the two parties is obvious in the Red-approved Five Point Draft Agreement and the Kuomintang's three point counter-proposal.

At the moment matters looked brighter than they had at

220

any time since 1937. The American Chiefs of Staff envisioned a Pacific war lasting into the summer of 1946, and therefore felt it absolutely necessary that China be strengthened, lest her collapse necessitate vast additional expenditures of life, time, and money. President Roosevelt had, therefore, charged Hurley to take a hand in the difficulties between the Nationalists and the Communists. Once involved as supply sergeant, Dutch uncle, and judge, the United States was not to get out of the Chinese quarrel until the victorious Communists threw American diplomatic and consular representatives out of the country in 1950.

At that moment in 1944, American stock was high. Communist propagandists recalled "Lincoln, the liberator" rather than "McKinley, the imperialist," and the Kuomintang found it easy to get down advice chased with material aid—as long as it was not required to act on that advice. But the documents Hurley drew from the Communists and the Nationalists in November, 1944, offered grounds for annulment rather than reconciliation.

The Communists were prepared to agree to the following terms: (1) The two parties will cooperate militarily for Japanese defeat. (2) The government will be reformed and reorganized on a *coalition* basis. (3) The *coalition government* will follow the principles of Dr. Sun Yat-sen in order to promote progress, democracy, justice, and civil rights. (4) All anti-Japanese forces will carry out the orders of the organs of the *coalition government*. (5) The *coalition government* will recognize the Kuomintang, the Communist Party of China, and all anti-Japanese parties as legal political parties.

The Central Government, declaring the Communist draft-agreement unacceptable, offered its own: (1) The Chinese Communist armies will be incorporated into the national military establishment on a basis of equality with all other units with regard to pay, allowances, and supply, and the Communist Party will be recognized as a legal political party. (2) The Communist Party will agree to submit its armies to the control of the National Military Affairs Committee, which will include some high-ranking Communist officers. (3) The Communist Party subscribes to the desire of the National Government to put into effect the Three Principles of Dr. Sun, and provide for democracy and civil rights, subject to restrictions imposed by the necessity for security in the war against Japan.

No *coalition government*. Point, counterpoint, and discord. The Nationalists, wary of Communist ambition, would not grant the one concession which the Communists considered crucial.

On November 22, 1944, Chou En-lai carried the counter-proposal to Yenan, as he was to carry other proposals back and forth for the next three years, half messenger-boy and half diplomat, for the Party allowed him little discretion. The counter-proposal was not accepted.

Two years later, on January 10, 1947, Chou En-lai delivered a speech repeating the same requests, with the qualifying factor of effective resistance to the Japanese alone omitted. After the outbreak of civil war following Japan's surrender, a Political Consultative Council had been convened to discuss *coalition government*. Chou was a delegate to that Council, whose resolutions became the basis for a truce agreement signed in January, 1946. In a speech made in January, 1947, Chou castigated the Nationalists for their failure to implement those resolutions, which had provided for *coalition government*.

There was little prospect of reconciliation. Although peace talks continued intermittently, with General Chou playing a leading role, both sides looked upon negotiation as a continuum of war. Despite occasional local or general truces after January 10, 1947, Chou En-lai's speech of that date was a declaration of war, a proclamation that the Communists would not stop short of the total conquest of power. That aim was achieved in 1949.

Before discussing Chou's role in the establishment of the

222

Central Government of the People's Republic of China, there is a strong temptation to comment on the "sincerity" of the Communists' persistent cry for *coalition government*. Accepted at face value, it would seem to contradict the statement, often repeated here, that the Reds strode in a straight line toward their goal, the complete conquest of power. Yet it does seem that the Communists, demanding a *coalition government*, desired just that and nothing more—at the moment. But Communist notions of proper behavior in a *coalition government* were first made clear in the Popular Front governments of the 1930's, and have again been displayed in the present Central Government of China, which the Reds consider a true *coalition government*. The formation of a *coalition government*, with the Reds as partners, would merely have smoothed their road to absolute power.

*　　*　　*

With the attainment of the Communist Party's ends, the adroit mandarin Chou En-lai, member of the Politburo and the Secretariat of the Party, moved on to the top administrative post in the new China, Premier of the State Administrative Council (Cabinet). In his capacity of Foreign Minister, he no longer deals with the discredited Kuomintang, but with foreign nations. In that role he went to Moscow in January, 1950, to take part in the long dickering which brought forth the Treaty of Friendship and Alliance and the Economic Agreement between China and the Soviet Union. The one tied China into the world power-bloc of Communist nations; the other brought her into the *ruble* empire—financial, economic, and industrial—which the Soviet Union is building from the Elbe to the Pacific. As Foreign Minister, too, Chou fulminates against the United States in terms even more vehement than those he previously used to describe the Kuomintang.

But the agility Chou has displayed in his personal career may yet manifest itself in his conduct of Red China's foreign

223

relations. The Chinese will not knowingly lend themselves as the tail of anyone else's kite. Although Red China's involvement in Korea serves the interests of the U.S.S.R., the Chinese believe it is also in their interest to fight the U.N. troops.

Chou En-lai has been identified as the leader of the China First faction in the Party, in opposition to the group led by Liu Shao-ch'i, who owes primary allegiance to the masters of international Communism in the Kremlin. At present the interests of the two groups appear to coincide, and the Chinese Reds are convinced that the U.S.S.R. is their true friend. They may well preserve that aspect for some time to come. But the divergent interests of China and the Soviet Union must some day come into conflict, and Chou could not countenance a policy which weakened China in order to strengthen any other nation or group of nations. There is reason to believe that Mao Tse-tung would back Chou's hand against an imminent Red Russian threat, rather than knuckling under with Liu Shao-ch'i.

The possible fracture in the Party was pointed up by the composition of the delegation Red China sent to the United Nations in November, 1950. The titular chief, General Wu Hsiu-ch'üan was a member of the Russian-oriented faction. Number-two man, Ch'iao Kuan-hua, whose position in the Red hierarchy is higher than Wu's, and number-three, Miss Kung P'u-sheng belonged to Chou En-lai's China First faction. It appears that, in accordance with the usual Iron Curtain bloc procedure, Adviser Ch'iao had more authority than Ambassador Wu.

*   *   *

Before his trip to Moscow, Chou En-lai, like other Communist chiefs, came to a peak in his career when he addressed the People's Political Consultative Conference convened in Peiping in September, 1949. The Chous made it a family affair.

224

Madame Chou Teng Ying-ch'ao had grown stout, like the matriarch of an association of women's clubs. She was there in that capacity. Long a leader in Party-sponsored women's activities, and one of the few women members of the Central Committee—she is an alternate—Mme. Chou spoke as the delegate of the All-China Democratic Women's Federation. Her address was routine; she pledged the loyalty of China's women to the new government, and exhorted women to work and study in the service of the New Democracy, which had given them equality under the law and in fact.

Chou's speech was not routine, but one of the half-dozen which were significant rather than rhetorical. As chairman of the committee of the Preparatory Commission which drafted the Common Program, he presented it to the Consultative Conference for ratification. The Common Program, accepted without a dissenting vote, is in the nature of a manifesto expressing the designs and aspirations of the new Chinese regime. It does not have the force of law.

Speaking to the seven hundred hand-picked delegates seated on banks of semicircular benches before him, Chou discussed the controversial points in the Common Program. He treated them under eight headings.

The first was the *Unified Battle-line.* The Kuomintang, Chou declared, had betrayed the teachings of Sun Yat-sen by selling out to feudal and imperialist elements. But now the principles of Dr. Sun, as interpreted by Mao Tse-tung in his work *On the People's Democratic Dictatorship (sic),* would guide the Chinese nation. Eventually a representative assembly would be elected, but that was a long way off. In the interim, the workers, peasants, small bourgeoisie, intellectuals, and national capitalists would begin the job of remaking China into a New Democracy, all under the guidance of the working class, expressed through its organ, the Communist Party.

In the section called the *General Outlook,* Chou said that this New Democracy would become a true Communist nation only after an extended period of time. In the meantime, he made a sharp distinction between Chinese *People and Nationals*. The People, referred to in the name "People's Republic of China," were those classes which stood in the unified battle-line. A national was a second-class being, a Chinese who was not a member of the favored classes and had not contributed to the victory of the Communist revolution. Nationals are to be deprived of most civil and property rights until they reform, for the Reds are less generous in victory than they were in defeat.

The *System of Governmental Power* was to follow closely the model of the Soviet Union, adhering to the principle of "democratic centralism," with certain variations to provide for the different stages of development in which China and the Soviet Union find themselves. Complementary to the political system was the *Military System,* geared to the maintenance of a large professional army animated by "political training, which is its soul."

The *Economic Policy* looked to a transitional mixed economy, to be succeeded by state capitalism, and eventually by Socialism. The *Cultural Policy,* "discussed in passing" was aimed at encouraging "national, scientific, mass tendencies." The arts, themselves imbued with the spirit of the New Democracy, would have as their chief duty the inculcation of that spirit in the people. *Minority Peoples* would be guaranteed the right to local self-government, the right to bear arms, and freedom of religion and belief. In *Foreign Policy,* a free, independent China would line up with the Soviet Union "to promote world peace."

The full text of the Common Program of the People's Political Consultative Conference, covering ten printed pages, is well worth reproduction, though it must be omitted here. One characteristic provision "guarantees the freedom to report truthful news, and prohibits the use of public information to slander the people, or injure their interests and foment world conflict." The text of the Common Program itself is infinitely more comprehensive than Chou En-lai's introductory remarks, for it covers every aspect of human life.

The frustrated mandarin has moved an appreciable distance from the mild totalitarianism of Confucian China, which his fathers served, to a totalitarianism which he seems ready to enforce with all the devices of modern psychology and technology.

10. "WHEN WHIRLWINDS OF REBELLION SHAKE THE WORLD": MAO TSE-TUNG

For a week the city of Peiping had been waiting. It was March 25, 1949, in the second month of Communist control, and General Yeh Chien-ying, installed as chairman of the Military Control Commission, ruled the city through the old-line municipal civil servants. There had been street-dancing, torchlight parades, and a beginning to many reforms under Red rule, but Mao Tse-tung, chief of the triumphant Communists, still tarried in the back-country. The old imperial city had not yet seen the face of her latest master.

Now the street peddlers, the rickshaw-pullers, and the newspaper sellers were chewing a new rumor: "Mao Tse-tung is coming. Chairman Mao is finally coming to Peiping. His airplane has taken off from Shih-chia Chuang!" Day after day for a week, Mao's arrival had been promised by the rumor mongers, and he had not yet arrived in Peiping.

Today he was surely coming. At six-thirty in the evening, the first *extra* appeared: CHAIRMAN MAO HAS ARRIVED IN PEIPING! The newsboys were mobbed by customers who tore the flimsy single-sheets from their hands, smudging the damp, red ink of the four-inch-high headline characters. By seven-fifteen only the crowds around the newspaper buildings had gotten copies, for the newsboys could not fight their way through to distribute the *extra* to the rest of the city.

But the news ran faster than the feet of the newsboys. At seven-thirty, just inside the great Front Gate, two pedicab drivers were chatting nervously, perched on the bicycle-seats of their chain-driven velocipedes as they waited for fares.

"Now that Chairman Mao has arrived," said chauffeur Chang, "the common people of Peiping can stop worrying."

"Well," replied his mate, "there are certainly going to be some changes made, and I think it's a damn good thing. There are going to be plenty of changes made around old Peiping."

The night shift at the trolley-car repair shop took the news in like spirit, as the workmen strove to outdo one another in voicing their enthusiasm.

"It's wonderful news! Now we'll really begin turning the cars out to welcome our leader."

Some of the older workmen cried: "Our leader has arrived; the man we have waited for these many years has come!"

In the hushed, shady reading room of the library at Peking University, the news was more quietly received. The old porter, Kuo Fu, stopped his sweeping to talk with librarian Wang Hsi-ying.

"He used to work right in this room, at that desk over there, checking out newspapers and magazines."

"Yes, I remember. It was more than twenty years ago. It's twenty years since I saw him last. In his photographs he looks heavier, but there's not much change other than that."

"He was a fine lad," Kuo Fu answered. "Used to love to read. I remember how he'd watch the others laughing and talking, but wouldn't say a thing. Just used to sit upstairs and read for all he was worth."

The two climbed the stairs to find the chair in which Mao Tse-tung had sat to study when he was not earning his keep as a student assistant.

"There it is," said Kuo Fu, pointing with the handle of his broom.

229

"On that very chair he sat twenty years ago, reading all day long.

"Who could have known. . . ?"

*   *   *

So runs the account in the Chinese press. At the same time the various actors were voicing their reactions, the officers of the Student Self-Government Association were scheming to have Mao Tse-tung address them. As his schoolmates, albeit thirty years apart, they felt they had a claim to such an honor. And it would mean only a small additional effort for Mao, since he was sure to visit the campus where he had been drawn into Communism and had courted his wife. Even a living demigod might be allowed the pleasure of recalling his days of privation in these new days, when Fate herself seemed to have taken up the shafts of his chariot. But there was little likelihood that Mao would climb the stairs to the reading room to sit in his old place, like Henry Ford squeezing his skinny legs under his primary-school desk at Dearborn. The Chinese leader was not given to such exhibitions, since there was no need to demonstrate how high he had risen. He would not have been comfortable in his old chair, nor would the Chinese audience have been impressed, for they did not expect such histrionics from Mao Tse-tung.

If Mao had wished to point up the rags-to-riches cycle in his own life, he would have waited until Hunan Province was "liberated." Then he could have posed under the solitary tree in front of his father's house in the village of Shaoshan near Changsha. That farm was the beginning of his own story, and millions of farms like it gave him the tools with which he made his revolution. Unlike the bourgeois revolution of 1927, the Communist revolution was not won on the playing fields of Peking University and the Whampoa Academy, but in the millet fields of North China and the rice paddies of the South. The soldiers and aspirations of the People's Liberation Army were drawn from the farms of China, from two-acre plots of exhausted soil where only discontent flourished. It was not the pale intellectual Mao, who had sat reading in the library of Peking University, nor yet the unfledged agitator with his fiery speech and wooly ideas, but the farmer's son who had raised up the farmers of China to fling them at the wicked cities of the coast. The farmer's son now rode in triumph through Peiping.

The time spent at Peking University and as an introvert middle-school student were interludes in the life of the man. Determined in his youth to break away from the farm, he found success only when he returned to the farm. The decision was taken, only half-aware, in 1920, when he gave up a chance to study in France because he "knew too little of China itself." While Chou En-lai went to Paris to become one of the gilded young men of international Communism, Mao Tse-tung, in a frayed, white-cotton jacket and trousers, wandered among the peasants of his native Hunan Province. Chou won promotion first, for he was better known to the Comintern, but it was stubborn Mao Tse-tung, standing with his feet on the tired Chinese earth, who made Communism a living force among the impoverished peasants and sharecroppers of rural China.

The beginning of Chinese civilization is one with the beginning of practical agriculture. But China, unlike European nations, has remained predominantly agricultural, so that estimates of the number of Chinese earning their living on the land vary from eighty-five to ninety-five per cent. When the nation is in a state of unrest, as it has been since 1900, the farmer is hit first, but the remaining five to fifteen per cent of the population, which lives on his labor, soon suffers. Since there is little significant commercial or industrial activity in China, the banker, the general, and the professor all ride on the dusty shoulders of the dirt farmer. The same dependence prevails throughout Asia, with the exception of agriculturally incapable Japan.

*   *   *

Mao Tse-tung is today the paramount folk-hero of rural Red China. The man has become so much part of his mission that it is not merely difficult but flatly impossible to separate his public and private lives. To some farmers, whom he has given land and desire, he is "Chairman Mao, the Saving Star of the People"—the Earth Spirit *Salvator*.

The chief spiritual excitement in the life of the Chinese farmer derives from the tradition which binds him to his land. So strong is the bond that a Chinese intellectual will speak with deep emotion of his "homeplace" and the "ancestral acres," though he himself was born in Shanghai, and his grandfather left the sterile farm in disgust to make his fortune as a shopkeeper in Malaya. China's greatest folk-heroes are those who have contributed to the advance of agriculture, like Shen Nung, the mythical emperor called the Divine Farmer, who made the first plough, and the Great Yü, who perfected irrigation. Confucianism provided that the Emperor should open the spring season by ploughing a small field while dressed in Court costume and surrounded by his ministers in full regalia.

The seeds of fanaticism lie in this mystical relation with the earth, while constant awareness of utter dependence upon the land is a source of militant desperation. China's peasants are therefore easily roused to action in defense of their land or in the hope of acquiring more.

When Mao Tse-tung proclaimed, in the words of Sun Yat-sen, "The tiller shall own his fields!" the slogan won the immediate attention of the farming masses. When he began to distribute landlord holdings, he won their devotion. When he established a Soviet regime, which backed its expressions of concern with the fate of the common farmer by ruling with a minimum of corruption and a maximum of economy, the astonished peasants began to look at Mao with awe. When they saw him tending his own tobacco patch, they were even more astonished, but they were reassured too.

Mao Tse-tung created the peasant Soviets, with their primitive Communism which led journalists to report that the Chinese Reds were mere agrarian reformers. The busy Comintern was competent to dispatch emissaries and telegrams to China, but it was Mao who determined that the peasants must be the base of the Chinese revolution and forced the Comintern to sanction his tactics. Mao has shaped a new form of Communism in Asia, quite distinct from the Russian export model for Communism in Europe. Today, when the Kremlin is giving the greater share of its attention to Asian expansion, Mao Tse-tung stands on a plane with Joseph Stalin. Asia is becoming the key to Europe, and Mao holds the key to Asia.

*　　*　　*

This man Mao, who stands in the minds of many Orientals as the symbol of a resurgent agrarian Asia, came himself of a family of farmers. His father was comfortable enough to give him a good education, but the family was undistinguished, boasting only one degree-holder in all its branches. The crucial year in Mao Tse-tung's career, the year which provided the financial base of his entire life, passed in the 1880's, before his own birth in 1893.

Mao Shun-sheng owned a fifteen-*mou** farm at Shao-shan Village in the fertile Changsha valley. The Mao family had worked the land for generations, but Shun-sheng himself could not make a go of it, because the Taiping Rebellion had intensified the general economic disturbance which plagued China in the last half of the nineteenth century. Mao Shun-sheng quit the farm to join the army.

Banditry was a profitable business in China at the time, but soldiering might be even more profitable, for the bandit in uniform enjoyed legal sanction for his depredations. Mao Shun-sheng evidently found it so, for he returned to Shao-shan in little more than a year with cash enough to buy

---

* 6.6 *mou* roughly equal one acre.

seven additional *mou*. With the impetus this capital gave him, he continued moving forward, selling pigs and grain in the city and lending out his surplus cash at a good rate of interest. Soon his capital totaled 3,000 *yüan*. He had jumped from the poor peasant class into the group the Chinese call "middle farmers," and was soon to become a "rich farmer," although his holdings were never great enough to qualify him for inclusion in the landlord caste.

When Tse-tung was born in 1893 and his brother Tse-min a few years later, Mao Shun-sheng could give the boys the education he had missed. He wished to have them taught enough reading, writing, and ciphering to make them useful in the business. When the boys had finished the after-school chores, their father would continue their training. Tse-t'an, the baby, who was killed in the early 1930's, was too young, but Tse-tung and brother Tse-min, who died in a Nationalist prison in Sinkiang in 1941, used to sit in the moonlight beside the house while their father taught them the use of the abacus, the millennia-old calculating machine of the Orient. Mao Shun-sheng was an exacting teacher, for he believed that proficiency in handling the abacus would aid the boys in accumulating wealth, his own chief passion.

"My father," Mao Tse-tung later recalled, "insisted that we be able to use the abacus with both hands so that we might figure faster."

Young Tse-tung, resentful of his father's overbearing parsimony, early showed a complete disregard for money. He revenged himself by loosening the family purse-strings for every plausible beggar, acquiring an enduring reputation for open-handedness among the countryfolk of Hsiang-t'an County. Stories passed on by Hsiao San, his boyhood friend and biographer, reveal the intensity of Mao's resentment of his father, while lauding his largesse to the poor.

Once, young Mao, returning home with money paid for a pig he had delivered, gave the string of cash to a beggar on the road.

234

Another time he was sent to pay for a hog which his father had arranged to purchase ten days earlier. The market price had jumped, and the prospective seller refused Mao's money, saying, "The price has gone up, and besides I've fed the animal for ten days. I won't sell at the old price."

"Quite right," Tse-tung replied, "the price has gone up, and you have fed the animal for an extra ten days. You're right in not giving him to me at the old price."

Some years later, Mao Tse-tung returned from school in Changsha to find that his father had bought him a new overcoat, a major purchase for frugal Mao Shun-sheng. On the road back to school, he fell in with a youth who wore only a thin cotton-tunic against the winter cold. Mao gave him the new overcoat and went coatless all winter in Changsha to keep his undue generosity from his father's knowledge.

The compulsion endured long after the old man was dead. In 1934, Mao Tse-tung saw an old peasant woman shivering by the roadside as the fugitive Red Army marched through Kueichow Province. He removed his coat and threw it over her shoulders. Fortunately for Mao, this contempt for possessions, which would have ruined a businessman, has increased the capital of the leader of a peasant revolt.

Mao Tse-tung constantly spoke of his struggles with his father and his devotion to his mother, when he told Edgar Snow the story of his life. That section of *Red Star Over China,* translated under the title *The Autobiography of Mao Tse-tung,* was for some time the only long biography of Mao Tse-tung available in Chinese. Although Mao is touted as a supernal hero in China, there is now nearly as much biographical material available in English as there is in Chinese.

I shall, therefore, make no attempt to give a strict chronological account of his life, but shall limit this discussion to those points which seem necessary to an understanding of his political role.

*   *   *

Marxism, except as an intellectual exercise and non-functioning ethic, was not an essential factor in Mao Tse-tung's life during the days of his greatest achievement. While he was building the base of his power in the long years from 1927 to 1945, he lived the life of a bandit chieftain out of a traditional Chinese novel. Except for the iron-bound Party, substituted for clan loyalty, and the limited utilization of modern weapons, he might have been an insurgent smallholder of a thousand years ago, determined to snatch the Decree of Heaven from its unworthy possessor. Neither egalitarian demi-Socialism nor the *jacquerie* were alien to historical China, for the first had been an element of the policies of Wang Mang, the "Socialist Emperor" of the first century A.D., and the second was the chief resource of such peasant leaders as the historical Li Tze-ch'eng and the fictional heroes of the *Shui-hu Chuan*. That novel, which has been translated into English by Pearl Buck under the title *All Men Are Brothers,* was Mao Tse-tung's favorite reading in his early adolescence. Fervently admiring its heroes, he seems to have modeled himself on them, and may now look with satisfaction upon the result.

Mao would read old popular novels behind his copy of Confucius in the private school he attended from the time he was eight until he was thirteen. Discovery of the deceit would send the old teacher into a rage, for novels were abhorrent because they were not composed in the classical style. Worse yet, they exalted rebels against the established order. Mao Tse-tung first learned of revolution from these novels, which conveyed the powerful folk-tradition of rebellion against unjust rulers. He had already come upon a similar concept in respectable literature, where Mencius held that the ruler was responsible to the people. Though the Emperor held his power from Heaven, the Divine Right might be abrogated by the popular will.

Yet Mao is reported to have given up these novels when he saw, in a moment of revelation, that it was never the common people, but always the great man, the prince, who was

236

dominant. According to his biographer, Hsiao San, Mao turned from the novels to find more solid spiritual and intellectual nourishment in the revolutionary journals of Sun Yat-sen and Liang Ch'i-ch'ao—but he always returned to his first loves. In the latest edition of his account of Mao's early years and young manhood, Hsiao San set right the misunderstanding which grew out of his earlier story of Mao's revulsion from the popular novels. Mao Tse-tung, Hsiao San writes, does not desire that the faithful should abstain from reading the old novels, but wishes them to be approached in a spirit of critical analysis. There is in them, Mao holds, much which may benefit revolutionary cadres and the revolutionary masses.

Mao desires to retain the novels of his youth, while neutralizing those elements in them which are offensive to the devout Marxist. He still quotes extensively from the universally familar novels, and is capable of expounding a point of modern tactics by referring to the course adopted by a royal hero of 250 A.D.

Another attachment to Chinese tradition reveals itself in his own literary activities. He can still quote the classics or write an essay in the classical style. And he still relaxes by composing poems in the ultra-refined style developed by that manorial society he has given his life to destroy. But he is half-ashamed of this accomplishment, refusing to discuss his poetry, for has he not exhorted professional writers in these words: "All culture and all present-day literature and art belong to a certain class, to a certain party or to a certain political line. There is no such thing as art for art's sake, or literature and art which lie above class distinctions or above partisan interests. There is no such thing as literature and art running parallel to politics or being independent of politics. They are in reality non-existent. . . . Deviation from this principle inevitably leads to dualism and pluralism, and eventually to such views as Trotsky advocated: Marxist politics but bourgeois art."

The same man's own poetry, in form at least, is hardly

237

"revolutionary." In the verses which follow, the traditional classical style and the traditional popular style are met in an uneasy alliance. There is in them nothing of the post-1917 New Poetry. The "Ode of the Long March," written in a wholly "bourgeois" form, albeit "proletarian" tone, is a poem which would be unintelligible to most of Mao's followers:

> High heaven and the indifferent clouds!
> Watching the wild-geese spurt south,
> I swore we were not heroes
> Until the Great Wall rose before us.
>
> Twice ten-thousand *li*—the Long March;
> I count the miles on my fingers,
> As the west wind tears the Red Flag
> On the peak of Six-bowl Mountain.
>
> Standing here, a long rope in my hands,
> I ask: "When shall we snare the dragon?"

An aesthete dedicated to the destruction of the age-old Chinese aesthetic in favour of a political dogma, Mao ordered Peiping's makers of *objets d'art* to manufacture soap. A Chinese patriot, he has declared that there is no independent "middle road," that China must march with one of the two great world-power-states, and himself has chosen to follow the Soviet Union. A zealous puritan, whose only self-indulgence is chain-smoking, he has married four wives.

The paradoxes multiply. Some evolved in Mao's own personality; others were social in origin, like his many marriages. His first wife, chosen by his parents, was a wife in ceremony only, since he refused to live with her, and his second wife, Yang K'ai-hui, was killed by the Nationalists.

As for the wholly personal contradictions: Mao is an artist who has taken politics as his medium. Rather than create internal order in works of art, he has attempted to impose order on life itself. In the effort he has espoused an ideology which boasts that it orders all things human. Nevertheless, he has always been sensitive to the nature of his material in his attempt to shape Chinese society into a unity satisfying to his aesthetic sense. The peasantry have been his chisel, but he had first to hammer out the tool by raising the greatest *jacquerie* the world has ever seen.

From the moment of his formal entry into the Communist Party at its foundation in July, 1921, Mao has known his tool. An account of his life, published in the *Communist International* in 1935, was almost completely erroneous, but it did correctly state the "keynote" of Mao's life as his attachment to the peasants. After coming to Shanghai to participate in the formal establishment of the Party and report on the peasants of Hunan Province, Mao Tse-tung returned to Changsha as the chief of the Hunan Committee of the Communist Party. Since Hunan is predominantly agricultural, the "trade unions" he is reported to have organized were in fact peasant unions. With the true visionary's zeal, he concentrated upon the peasantry to the exclusion of other classes —and began to develop the *Maoist* heresy.

At subsequent Party meetings, Secretary-general Ch'en Tu-hsiu grew cool to the young upstart, for Mao, just twenty-nine in 1922, was defying the Comintern's clear edict. The Communists had been ordered to cooperate with the Kuomintang in the bourgeois national revolution before launching the Communist revolution. Moreover, the International insisted that the firm base of any Bolshevik revolution must be the urban proletariat assisted, perhaps, by the peasants. Mao, in recruiting peasants for independent Communist action, violated the Comintern's ukase on two counts. The classical revolutionist, who looked to the cities as the "centers of power," was contemptuous of strategy which assigned a primary revolutionary role to the peripheral peasants. The peasants, Moscow thought, were both feudal and bourgeois, and could, therefore, never serve as the prime mover of a revolution. Mao disagreed.

He had been a frequent contributer to the *Guide,* the Party organ edited by Ch'en Tu-hsiu. Ch'en was well disposed toward Mao, whom he had met while the younger man was a student at Peking University. But he was provoked by Mao's persistent refusal to subordinate his obsession with the peasants to the official attitude. In late 1923, he closed the pages of the *Guide* to Mao Tse-tung in a strong rebuke for deviationism. Mao was chastened by the reprimand, and he swung into line. Restored to the Party's good graces, he attended the First National Congress of the Kuomintang in Canton in the winter of 1924, and later served on the Executive Committees of the Shanghai Bureaus of both the Communist Party and the Kuomintang.

In the summer of 1926, coincident with the beginning of the Northern Expedition, Mao Tse-tung was allowed to return to his peasants. He was ordered to Hunan to head the Party's Peasant Bureau. In that capacity, he prepared a report, *On the Peasant Movement in Hunan,* which established him as the Red's chief agrarian authority, but offended the orthodox by the return to his old fixation. Mao wrote, in part: "The present upsurge of the peasant movement constitutes an extremely important problem, since in the near future it must bring about a movement among several hundred million peasants throughout the rest of China. . . . The peasants will break down all that stands in their way and will hasten along the road to emancipation. All revolutionary parties and all revolutionaries will be put to the test by these masses."

This report, though rejected by the 1927 Fifth Congress of the Communist Party, is today the first major work in the literature of *Maoism*—a term that is coming into use among the Chinese as the climax of the incantation: "Engels-Marxism, Lenino-Stalinism, *Maoism!*" I have before me not only the standard biographies of Mao and his own political and cultural commentaries, but a work titled *On Mao Tse-tung,* originally delivered as a series of lectures at North China University by Chang Ju-hsin, a major theoretical writer. As Soviet writers exalt Stalin, adulation pervades Chang's detailed appraisal of Mao's thought.

One section considers "Mao Tse-tung's *Weltanshauung,*"

240

a second "The Scientific Method of Mao Tse-tung," and others "Mao Tse-tung's Scientific Foresight," and "Mao Tse-tung's Behavior." The sub-titles to these sections, taken alone, do much to reveal the Chinese Communist attitude toward Mao's contribution to Marxism. Under "The Scientific Method of Mao Tse-tung" are discussed 'Mao Tse-tung's view on the integration of theory and reality' and the fact that 'Mao Tse-tung's revolutionary theories, derived from reality, are tested again and developed under the impact of reality.' Then, catching himself in mid-stride on the brink of heresy, the author notes that 'Mao Tse-tung's scientific method is opposed to scholasticism and experimentalism.'

Despite this near balk at the end, it is clear that the Chinese consider *Maoism* a further development of Marxist theory, characterized by its close attention to immediate reality and its ability to improvise in order to deal with emergencies. If a Chinese author were writing this passage, he would hurriedly add "all the while remaining true to the great central truths of scientific Marxism-Leninism." That, however, is the question. Until *Maoism* develops further in response to the "reality" of ruling the vast, incoherent landmass that is China, it is impossible to determine whether *Maoism* represents a substantive as well as a formal heresy of orthodox Lenino-Stalinism.

*   *   *

In 1927, Mao Tse-tung's first heretical doctrine, using the peasants instead of the proletariat, effected a split that cut him off from the Party until 1931. After organizing the Autumn Crop Rising in Hunan in the fall of 1927, he fled alone into the countryside, hunted by Kuomintang troops. The Party, or what remained of it in the spring and summer of 1927, had disapproved of his peasant agitation, and had ordered him to unfamiliar Szechwan. Evading the order, Mao stayed on to work among his fellow provincials.

241

He was captured by a company of militia, but escaped by feigning lameness and bribing the single soldier assigned to watch over his slow progress. Now he was a lone fugitive on the green plains, dressed in the castoff clothing of an old farmer who had taken pity on him.

Mao fell in with a band of fugitives in the neighborhood of Lien-hua on the Kiangsi border. Not even Communists, they were farmers who had risen to follow the red flag and now found themselves broken, dispirited, and almost leaderless. Their chief, a peasant who was somewhat less frightened than his men, asked Mao to address them.

The tall, awkward rebel rose to stand among the lesser rebels, who lay sprawling on the ground around him. He was gaunt and his gestures were angular. Though he was inclined to be fleshy, the months just past had shrunk the flesh from under his skin, which lay loose and unhealthy. Tossing his lank hair back, he began to speak, gesturing with his long hands, which seemed only faggots of bone.

"Comrades! We have evaded the enemy and he can only fire at random in our rear. And how can that harm us? We are all born of women. The enemy soldier has two legs, and each of us also has two legs. . . . When Comrade Ho Lung rose in revolt his entire arsenal was two kitchen knives! Today he is a general, a true soldier! We here have much more than two kitchen knives; we have nearly two battalions. Why should you fear that we will not succeed?"

Mao spoke with the practiced ardor learned in seven years as a professional agitator. And the tired rebels rose to his words. Their lives were forfeit if they were captured; all they wanted was a leader and a cause to give them another chance at life.

Those two battalions became the core of the force Mao led into the mountain called Chingkangshan in southern Kiangsi, where he was joined by Chu Teh and his regiment of insurgent soldiers. The two bands became the cadre of the Red Army, for a number of years called the "Chu-Mao Army" by friendly peasants and the enemy alike. While Chu Teh and Mao Tse-tung, cut off from the rest of China, built up the defensive strength of their own Kiangsi Soviet Area, the Party was suffering its own Reconstruction Days after the total defeat of 1927. Only after Li Li-san had been discredited did the formal leaders of the Party transfer their headquarters to the Kiangsi Soviet Area in the fall of 1931, and only in January, 1935, was Mao Tse-tung formally elected chief of the Party at Tsün-yi, Kueichow Province, during a halt on the Long March. Today there is no one to challenge Mao's power or position, for he is chairman of all ruling bodies of the Communist Party: the Central Committee, the Political Bureau, and the Secretariat.

Mao Tse-tung has been boss since 1936. A second disagreement with the Comintern would have found the Chinese Party squarely behind him. There has, fortunately for Mao, been no need to test his control. The Third International, which had already backed land reform, gave Mao ideological support in the war against Japan by passing the Popular Front resolutions in 1935, before his alliance with the Nationalists. Nor did the Comintern interfere after that date as Mao worked out his tactics with due regard to "the actual situation in China itself." In this freedom, Mao planned the *New Democracy,* given out under that title in 1940.

The New Democracy has already been established, according to Chou En-lai's statement of September, 1949. Its cardinal premise is an alliance of all "non-exploiting" classes against their exploiters. Farmers of all degrees, proletarian workers, artisans, professional men, intellectuals, and elements of the petty bourgeoisie, as well as national capitalists, are all part of the "unified battle-line" formed to establish control and begin rebuilding the nation. Cooperation with "progressive elements" in the Kuomintang was therefore possible in the past, and, under the same dispensation, non-Communist parties participate in the present government—in name at least. Excluded from the "unified battle-line" are

243

bureaucratic capitalists and those ultra-reactionaries in the Kuomintang, like the C C Clique, whose slogan is: "One flag, one race, one leader!"

The Ch'en brothers, leaders of the C C Clique, are fanatics, and Mao is a fanatic too. But so were Napoleon, Gauguin, and Moses. So indeed must any artistic genius be, except such transcendent geniuses as Shakespeare, Goethe, and da Vinci. Mao has the faults, as well as the virtues, of the lesser genre.

Through the pattern he seeks to impose on all Chinese runs a wide gray stripe of Puritanism, complemented on the one side by prudery and on the other by intolerance. Mao has not closed the theatres as Oliver Cromwell did, for he finds them too valuable a conduit of propaganda. But censorship is none the less censorship for providing what one must see, instead of what one may not see. Through newspapers, magazines, and a growing radio network to spread ideas, with mutual self-criticism sessions and study clubs to test the people's diligence in the prescribed lessons, Mao Tse-tung assures that there will be little time for idle amusement, on which the Reds frown. He has closed the dance-halls and the curio shops, discouraging "social" dancing under any circumstances in favor of the ritual *yang-kor,* and banning the manufacture of *objets d'art* in favor of soap-making. Soap-making is surely a laudable enterprise, but it seems to the Westerner that the Chinese might have both soap and decorative art. The Chinese Communist feels, with good reason perhaps, that he can not.

This bleak utilitarianism, justified in part by China's material poverty, is advanced with a zealotry which justifies the use of puritanical as a descriptive adjective. Mao Tse-tung first displayed his affinity for institutionalized morality in the fall of 1917. At the end of the summer vacation, nearly thirty upper-classmen of Changsha Normal School met to form a club. Mao Tse-tung, who had been a student at the Normal School since 1912, was the moving spirit in the organization, but contented himself with the title of assistant secretary.

Meeting at the home of Ts'ai Ho-shen, who was later killed by the Nationalists, the thirty drew up a statement of their goals and a code of by-laws. "Our Aim is to polish our conduct on the whetstone of mutual criticism and to pursue our studies most earnestly." Among the club's rules: "We will not gamble for money; we will not consort with prostitutes; and we will not fall into slothful idleness."

All noble sentiments, but Mao was twenty-four at the time, at an age when he might have taken those highly personal decisions without recording them among a group of his peers. Today the entire Chinese nation, grandfathers and striplings alike, is required to subscribe to similar pledges. Bourgeois levity, art which does not contribute to the revolution, and many of the graces of Chinese culture are being stamped out, half in the cause of necessity and half in the cause of austerity for austerity's own sake.

Mao Tse-tung is shaping Marxism *(Maoism)* into a quasi-religious creed to replace the spiritual values of traditional Chinese culture, which shattered under the impact of the West. The less concrete ideal of democratic evolution is incomprehensible to all but a few in China, a nation where economic insecurity retards the growth of abstract desires. But the Chinese mind none the less desires mystical inspiration.

Mao is filling that need. He has called a crusade against poverty, appealing to certain emotions which are universal, and to some which are peculiar to the Chinese. One of the latter is resentment of the intrusive West, which has upset China's civilization and humbled her people; Mao is arrayed against colonial imperialism. The universal human desire to feel noble, and the particular need of educated Chinese to feel that they are serving the masses, are roused and fed by the Reds' call for self-sacrifice in the interest of the people. The land hunger of the peasant, and his reluctance to see others fare better than himself, are allayed by land reform and a promise of equal distribution of China's scant wealth to all her people. Behind these drives, whose emotional content is not of the highest, is the joyous passion roused by the promise of a renaissance after the dark age of the past hundred years. Taken all in all, they portend a freely given and profound loyalty to the Red regime, if it can begin to do the things it has promised to do.

*   *   *

Mao Tse-tung has altered the course of Chinese history and changed the life of every Chinese. Now he is the undisputed ruler of the Chinese mainland as chairman of the People's Central Government Committee and the Revolutionary Military Affairs Committee, his position reinforced by his monopoly on the three top Party posts. Now, more than ever before, the fate of the individual Chinese, the Chinese nation, and the Far East as a vital sector of world politics, depend upon the character of the man called Mao Tse-tung. It is a most flexible character.

He has come a long way from the farmboy who was stirred by the tales of derring-do set forth in the old novels. He is not the same person who turned from traditional fiction to draw inspiration from the radical journalism of Liang Ch'i-ch'ao and the editors of the Sun Yat-sen faction. Nor is he really like the young man who was converted to Communism by Ch'en Tu-hsiu after reading the *Communist Manifesto,* the first Marxist tract translated into Chinese. One wonders whether he is the same man who labored among the peasants for twenty-five years to raise the greatest revolutionary army the Eastern world has ever seen. There are some indications that he is not.

The method employed here, pointing up the highlights of Mao's career and character within a short space, automatically creates the danger that the reader will be misled into thinking that Mao Tse-tung is a monolithic *homo politicus,* whose personal attitudes are sluggish in response to any but the most overt stimuli. This is emphatically not the case, for

Mao owes his advancement to a sensitivity which is hardly limited to political manifestations. Because he has led the life of a professional politician, however, most of the major adjustments he has made have been in response to political stimuli. But, as should have appeared by now, he has been most adaptable.

Today Mao Tse-tung, the man, faces a situation quite different from any he has ever before encountered. Political necessity still presses upon him in the shape of economic conditions and the international crisis, but within China there is no power that can say him nay. Just as he changed from the professional intellectual and agitator to become the peasant leader, and again into the chief of half a nation at war, he is today assuming the costume and the bearing of the absolute master of China. Photographs taken of Mao within the past fifteen years seem to have caught the progress of the transition, since he has always presented to the camera the face which he wished the world to see.

The earliest shows a tall man clad in an unpressed tunic like an American Army fatigue uniform; the right breast-pocket is unbuttoned and the collar points unrestrained. Above the rude garment is a face that is both sensual and intellectual. In imitation of the physiognomists, who used to delight in demonstrating the dissimilarity of the right and left halves of the same face, splitting Mao's face, horizontally instead of vertically, displays the sensualist and the intellectual. The lower half is plump, with a rounded chin and full, feminine lips topped by a slightly bulbous nose. The upper half is dominated by the high-domed forehead and the long hair, parted in the center to hang carelessly in tufts over his ears. It is the face of a self-confident man, self-confident because he has succeeded in disciplining himself to ignore material non-essentials in favor of the spirit.

The next portrait is more ordinary. The same face, grown plumper and glowing with good living, rises from the collar of a well-pressed jacket of good woolen fabric. The full-bodied man within it is quite obviously well satisfied with himself and his world. Mao's hair is covered by a spotless sunhelmet in this picture, which was taken in 1949 at the moment of triumph.

The last two photographs are the most recent. The first, taken in Moscow in December, 1949, shows Mao standing behind a long banquet table among the Russian leaders. He wears the stern mien of a brooding god surrounded by lesser gods. Even Stalin, with his amiable air of *petit bourgeois* self-assertion, is unimpressive beside Mao.

The most recent of the four was snapped when Mao received a delegation of Chinese Stakhanovites, male and female, who stand around him grinning nervously. Mao Tsetung, a head taller than the tallest of them, stands stiff and straight, staring the camera down. He is thinner than he was a year ago, but his unadorned uniform is better tailored. He does not smile—he rarely smiles for the camera—and his face is set, and rigid with a sense of mission. No longer merely self-confident, he is completely aware that he is the Great Man.

11. FIERCER THAN A TIGER

Confucius was driving past T'ai Shan, the sacred mountain, when he saw a matron wailing beside a new-made grave. Stopping his chariot, he spoke to her: "From the anguish in your voice, your sorrow must be heavy."

"That is so," she replied. "Some time ago my brother was killed by a tiger—and later my husband. Now my son has been slain by the same tiger."

The Master asked: "Why do you not live elsewhere?"

"Here," she answered, "there is no oppressive government."

The Master turned to his disciples, saying, "Now mark this well. An oppressive government is fiercer than a tiger."

Nearly every Chinese has either read that story or heard it from the lips of the old men. His horror of an oppressive government extends to an officious government. Through the centuries, the Imperial Government reigned over China, but it did not rule the rural counties. Today, the hand of the Central People's Government is reaching into every household to control the intimate details of everyday life and thought. But the people's resentment at this interference with the bases of Chinese social life is tempered by the gift of land the same hand brings them.

Resentment springs up again when heavy taxation for industrialization takes back the wealth. The intensity of that resentment is of vital significance. Despite the commentators' emphasis upon the obtrusive intellectual, the farmer remains

249

the basic unit of Chinese society. His attitudes will determine the future of the Red dynasty, as they have the fate of all preceding dynasties.

Intellectuals—the Chinese term means simply "literate elements"—are not finding the adjustment to Communism difficult. There are more rice Communists in China today than there ever were rice Christians. Ambition does not discriminate.

ˋ Communist practices dovetail with several aspects of traditional Chinese civilization. Thought control through restriction of reading to prescribed texts is a feature of both. The monolithic state reared on a state ideology is common to both, and so is the subordination of the individual to a larger social unit. But a major discrepancy appears in the character of the group to which the individual must subject his own will. For the Communists it is the state; for the Confucians it was the family. ˋ

Though classical Chinese culture, the ground floor of the Confucian state, has been gutted in the years since 1911, the foundation is barely cracked. Loyalty to the family has continued to be the governing emotion of the Chinese peasant masses. Since the Communists cannot tolerate a dual allegiance, they are attacking this family loyalty. Among intellectuals they may succeed quite easily; with the farming masses the task will be extraordinarily difficult, if not impossible.

Communism in China will, in the long run, either adjust its doctrines to the limited Communism of the Chinese family system or perish. If an adjustment does take place, *Maoism* will bear only the slightest resemblances to orthodox Stalinism.

Foreign adventures may delay the day of reckoning for the Reds. But it must come.

However, both the Westernized merchant in frenetic Shanghai, who is being stripped of his possessions, and the Szechwan farmer, who has been shown a vision of hope, are intensely realistic. The merchant and the farmer, the student and the soldier, are all aware that they will have to live with

250

the Red rulers of China for a long time to come. Despite unrest and dissatisfaction, expressed in small-scale guerrilla resistance, the Chinese know that only time itself can alter the character of the Peking government.

The Western world too must realize that the revolution, which Mao Tse-tung's politicians, generals, and theoreticians have made, cannot be wiped out by a refusal to recognize its existence, nor by minimizing the grievances on which it rode to power.

The United States can neither "write China off," nor sponsor a Hundred Days for Chiang Kai-shek. The United States must examine its position with regard to the Chinese Communists quite coolly, in the spirit of what used to be called "enlightened self-interest" in simpler times than these.
The fate of the Eastern world—perhaps the fate of the Western world as well—depends on the relations between China and the United States on the one hand, and China and the Soviet Union on the other. At present, relations between China and the United States have grown as bad as they can be short of full-scale war. The Korean war and the Formosa blockade are the latest manifestations of tension which has been growing since 1945. Relations between the Soviet Union and China appear as amicable as they can become short of political unification.

*　　　*　　　*

There is in the making, in Peking, in Moscow, and in the newly seeded wastes of Central Asia, an alliance which could conceivably carry out the threat of its leaders to destroy both Western civilization and Asian civilization and put in their places brutal oppression masquerading as egalitarianism. The masters of Communist Russia and the leaders of Communist China, acting in concert, might well be able to impose their dreary tyranny upon the entire world.

Like any alliance, the union between China and Russia is hardly perfect. Nor can it ever be, for the past and the pre-

251

sent have created too many areas of discord between the partners. But a common fear and a common greed bind them tighter than a shared loyalty could. The subject of the fear and the object of the greed are one, the United States of America, clutching her factories to her, behind her ocean moats.

The Russian rulers half believe, but the Chinese Reds are wholly convinced that America is stretching her long arm across the oceans to steal their wealth. The Asian Communist sees America feeding her factories with stolen raw materials to produce still more luxuries for her pampered darlings, the "ruling circles" of Communist rhetoric.

The Chinese fears that America will be driven by the avarice he attributes to her to steal his independence as well as his goods. His own greed, in its turn, is aroused by the prospect of seizing the vast wealth of America's industries and the power that goes with them.

As long as Russian lies and American mistakes continue to blind the Chinese to the truth, so long will the threat of a massive, inert Asiatic despotism lie over the spirits of mankind. As long as the fabrications of the Kremlin are not effectively refuted by American action, so long will the Chinese Red continue to ignore the robber in his strongroom for the one he fancies is over the horizon. He will continue to rejoice when the U. S. S. R. magnanimously returns a portion of its Manchurian loot, as he did on January 21, 1951. Until he can be shown that America covets neither his goods nor his sovereignty, he will refuse to recognize that the Soviet Union has stolen more of China's wealth in the five years since the end of World War II than has been pocketed by Americans since the days of the Canton tea and opium trade.

*   *   *

The United States appears to have lost the political initiative in China, and perhaps in Southeast Asia, where Sino-Communization is an immediate threat.

252

But, in reality, American policy is still the dominant force, even in the relations between China and the Soviet Union. Fear of American power and greed for American wealth hold the Soviet Union and Red China together. American hostility to the Chinese Reds and American support of Chiang Kai-shek's lost cause were at least as important in bringing the two together as was the pull of the somewhat frayed ideological ties between Moscow and Mao Tse-tung.

The tenuous ties between China and Russia are subject to considerable strain. The more successful Mao is in spreading his Sinified brand of *Maoist* Communism, the more the Soviet Union will fear China as a military and ideological rival. Stalin cast Tito out of the Cominform on much slighter provocation than he will face in the mere existence of a spreading *Maoist* revolution in Asia. Just as Mao made his own revolution in China, so any revolution he sponsors in agrarian Asia will be his own.

The Russians, aware of this threat to their supremacy, are attempting to keep Mao in subservience by isolating him from the rest of the world. They have encouraged his defiance of the United Nations in the knowledge that it would effectively keep Red China out of the international body. And they are pleased to have Peking depend on their news-gathering services for knowledge of the world.

The rapidity of his triumph has left both the world and Mao Tse-tung gasping. A man and a party which had defied authority throughout their political lives, are confronted with the task of governing all China and conducting her complex international relations. In the past they ruled their own territories as a revolutionary base; today the enemy is still greed, ignorance, and poverty, but he is no longer conveniently embodied in the Kuomintang. Accustomed to dealing with a specific enemy, the Chinese Reds have therefore set America in the Kuomintang's place, evidently unwilling to recognize that railing against the United States will neither help them build factories, nor fill the rice-bowls of hungry Chinese.

253

A year ago, Mao spoke hopefully of demobilizing some of the five million men then under arms in Red China. Today he is conducting a full-dress recruiting campaign and has begun to build a Sixth Field Army under General Yeh Chien-ying to add to the five already in being. Mao has found the Korean crisis a convenient pretext for postponing the problems of demobilization—which he must eventually face. The demobilization of even four million soldiers will cause another major dislocation in the Chinese economy, already broken by fifteen years of war, interspersed with famines and floods. Moreover, the Chinese Reds are hampered by a shortage of trained personnel, both technical and political.

Mao Tse-tung, in short, needs material assistance, which only the United States can provide. After two months of negotiation in Moscow at the beginning of 1950, he returned to Peking with a short-term loan of $300,000,000—at six per cent. He went to Moscow for aid because he could go nowhere else.

*   *   *

In the two years that have passed since they achieved real power with the taking of Nanking, the Chinese Communists have shown themselves to be bold rulers. They have been bold in distributing the land, in suppressing and combining private concerns, and in destroying their enemies. (Newspaper correspondents have been shot as "cultural traitors" because they continued to send dispatches to Nationalist papers on Formosa after the city of Canton had fallen to the Reds.) Bold indeed was the Chinese march into Korea, and bold their invasion of Tibet, their intervention in Indo-China, and their threat to Burma and northern India.

That very boldness may undo them when it strikes the bed-rock of integrity in Chinese society and the Chinese individual. The impotence of external forces to affect the resolution of that conflict has already been demonstrated. The great backlog of Chinese culture, history, and society, alone,

254

will force the growth of Chinese Communism along lines quite different from those imposed upon Soviet Communism by the Russian tradition.

Regardless of the manner in which history has altered their aims, it would be foolish to deny that the Chinese Communists are part of a vigorous protest against the barren misery of life in so much of the world.

Supreme Court Justice William O. Douglas defined the fundamental character of the Asian revolution better than anyone else has done, when he said in February, 1951:

"The world is different than we in America have thought. The plain fact is that the world is in a revolution that cannot be bought off with dollars. There are rumblings in every village from the Mediterranean to the Pacific.

"We think of that force as Communism, but it is not. The Communists only exploit the situation."

BIBLIOGRAPHY

There follows a partial list of the works consulted in the preparation of this book. Perhaps most valuable was a close reading of the Chinese newspapers, particularly the Hong Kong *Ta Kung Pao,* and particularly for the years from 1948 to 1950.

I should like to thank the many friends, both Chinese and Occidental, who have allowed me to make use of their specialized knowledge and personal contacts with the Communist leaders. To the staff of Columbia University's East Asiatic Library my gratitude for their patience and resourcefulness.

I must particularly acknowledge my debt to Richard C. Howard for giving me so much of his time and counsel, and for his assistance in finding material and in typing. Professor Chi-Chen Wang was kind enough to read the manuscript and offer many suggestions for improvements in style and emphasis. But the errors I have persisted in are my own. By no means the least valuable assistance was my sister Joanne P. Elegant's typing and retyping.

I should also like to thank *The Reporter* for permission to use the material on Kuo Mo-jo, much of which originally appeared as an article in that magazine.

Translations from Chinese are generally my own unless otherwise indicated.

GENERAL

Chung-kuo Hsin Min-chu Yün-tung chung ti Tang-p'ai (Parties in China's New Democratic Movement), Hong Kong, 1949

Chung-kuo Jen-min Kung-ho-kuo K'ai-kuo Wen-hsien (Documents on the Establishment of the Chinese People's Republic), Hong Kong, 1950 (The complete proceedings of the People's Political Consultative Conference of October 1949)

Chung-kuo Kung-ch'an-tang ti Chung-yao Jen-wu (Important Figures in the Communist Party of China), Peiping, 1949

K'ang-chien Kuo-ts'e hsia chih Chung-kuo Kung-ch'an-tang (The Chinese Communist Party in the National Policy of Resistance and Reconstruction), Kweilin, 1941

United States Relations With China, compiled by the United States Department of State, Washington, D. C., 1949

Yi-chiu-wu-ling Jen-min Nien-chien (1950 People's Yearbook), compiled by the Hong Kong *Ta Kung Pao*

Morse, Hosea Ballou: *The International Relations of the Chinese Empire,* New York, 1910-18

"Asian Horizon", Vol. II, No. 2, Summer 1949

BIBLIOGRAPHY

CHAPTER 1

"Asian Horizon", Vol. II, No. 3, Autumn-Winter 1949
"China Institute Bulletin", V. III, No. 1 (Translation of Ch'en Tu-hsiu's program for Literary Revolution)

CHAPTER 2

Chukoku Kyosanto Ichikyusango Nen Shi (History of the Communist Party of China in 1935), Foreign Office of Japan, Tokyo, 1936
Ch'ü Ch'iu-pai: *Chieh-t'ou Chi* (The Street Corner), Shanghai, 1940 *Chukoku Dai Kakumei Shi* (The Great Chinese Revolution), Tokyo, 1929
Hsün-kuo Lieh-shih Ch'ü Ch'iu-pai; Ch'ü Ch'iu-pai T'ung-chih Hsi-sheng Chou-nien Chi-nien (The Martyr for the Nation, Ch'ü Ch'iu-pai; the Anniversary of the Sacrifice of Comrade Ch'ü Ch'iu-pai), Moscow (?), 1936
How, Julie Lien-ying: *The Development of Ch'en Tu-hsiu's Thought, 1915-1938,* manuscript, 1948
(Translations of Ch'en's writings are from this source.)
Hua Ying-shun (ed.): *Chung-kuo Kung-ch'an-tang Lieh-shih Chuan* (Biographies of Martyrs of the Chinese Communist Party), Hong Kong, 1949
Okubo Koichi, Lt. Col.: *Sekishoku Shina* (Red China), Tokyo, 1935
Isaacs, Harold R.: *The Tragedy of the Chinese Revolution,* London, 1938
Roy, Manabendra N.: *Revolution und Konterrevolution in China,* Zurich, 1932
Shina ni okeru Kyosan Undo (The Communist Movement in China), Tokyo, 1934
Teng Hsi-hwa: *Chinese Testament,* New York, 1934
Wang Ching-Wei & others: *The Chinese National Revolution; Essays and Documents,* Peiping, 1931

CHAPTERS 3 & 4

Chang Kung-ch'i (ed.): *Ti-pa Lu-chün K'ang-jih Hsing-chün* (The Role of the Eighth Route Army in the War Against Japan), Shanghai, 1938
Ch'ang-cheng Ku-shih (Tales of the Long March), Hong Kong, 1949
Chu Kyo Gairon (A Survey of the Chinese Communists), The Foreign Office of Japan, Toyko, 1949
Chu Teh: *K'ang-jih Yu-chi Chan-cheng (Anti-Japanese Guerrilla War),* Hankow, 1938
Lun Chieh-fang Ch'ü Chan-ch'ang (On the Battle Fields in the Liberated Area), Hong Kong, 1947
Chu Teh et al.: *K'ang-chan Hui-yi Lu* (Memories of the Resistance), Shanghai, 1938
Wo-men Dzen-yang Ta-t'ui Ti-jen (How We Are Driving the Enemy Back), (articles by Lin Piao, Liu Po-ch'eng, Hsiang Ying, and others), Hankow, 1938
Forman, Harrison: *Report from Red China,* New York, 1945
K'ang Ch'en: *Sui-chün Hsi-cheng Chi* (With the Army on the Western Campaign), Hankow, 1938

Hsi-Pei Yu-chi Chan (The Northwest Guerrilla War), Chungking, 1939
Pei Chan-ch'ang shang ti Yu-chi-tui Pao-kao (A Report on Guerrilla Troops in the Northern Battle Areas), Hankow, 1938
Payne, Robert: *Journey to Red China*, London, 1947
Taylor, George E.: *The Struggle for North China*, New York, 1941
P'eng Teh-huai: *San-nien Lai* (*The Past Three Years*), undated,
T'ien Han, Kuo Mo-jo et al.: *Ch'ien-hsien K'ang-ti Chiang-ling Fang-wen Chi* (A Record of Journeys to the Front Lines), Shanghai, 1939

CHAPTER 5

Carey, Catherine: *Biographical Studies of the Chinese Politburo*, manuscript, 1950
"China Digest", October 19, 1949
"China Weekly Review", June 4, 1949
House Document, No. 707, Supplement III, Country Studies—*Communism in China*, Government Printing Office, Washington, D. C., 1948
   Supplement IV, *Five-Hundred Leading Communists in the Eastern Hemisphere*, Government Printing Office, Washington, D. C., 1949
Shu Ch'ing: *"Jen-min Chiao-yü-chia: Hsü T'e-li"* (The People's Educator: Hsü T'e-li), 4 articles in the Hong Kong *Ta Kung Pao*, April 17-20, 1949

CHAPTER 6

L. Lusun: *Ting Ling Tsai Hsi-pei* (Ting Ling in the Northwest), Canton, c. 1938
Shen Ts'ung-wen: *Chi Ting Ling* (Remembering Ting Ling), 2 vols., Shanghai, 1939
Ting Ling: *Ting Ling Tai-piao Tso Hsün* (Selected Representative Writings of Ting Ling), Shanghai, 1937

CHAPTER 7

Liu Shao-ch'i: *Chung-kuo Kung-ch'an-tang Tang-chang chi Kuan-yü Hsiu-kai Tang-chang ti Pao-kao* (The Party Constitution of the Communist Party of China and A Report on the Revision of the Party Constitution), 1949
   Lun Kuo-chi-chu-yi yü Min-tsu-chu-yi (On Internationalism and Nationalism), Hong Kong, 1949
   Lun Kung-ch'an-tang-yüan ti Hsiu-yang (On the Eduucation of a Communist Party Member), Hong Kong, 1949
   Lun Tang (On the Party), Suchow, 1949

CHAPTER 8

Kuo Mo-jo: *Chin Hsi; P'u-chien* (Now and Then; The Rush Sword), Shanghai, 1946
   Ch'uang-tsao Shih Nien (Ten Years of Creation), Shanghai, 1933
   Fan-cheng Ch'ien-hou (Anyway, Forward and Backward), Shanghai, 1938
   Ko-ming Ch'ün-ch'iu (Annals of Revolution), Shanghai, 1946
   San Yeh Chi (Trefoil Collection), Shanghai, 1920

Wen-yi Lun-chi (Collected Writings on Literature) , Shanghai, 1930
Wen-yi Lun-chi: *Hsü-chi* (Collected Writings on Literature: A Continuation) , Shanghai, 1931
Li Ho-lin: *Chin Erh-shih Nien Chung-kuo Wen-yi Ssu-ch'ao Lun* (Currents in Chinese Literary Thought for the Past Twenty Years) . Shanghai, 1947 (first published 1939)
Li Lin (ed.) : *Kuo Mo-jo P'ing-chuan* (Symposium on Kuo Mo-jo) , Shanghai, 1936
Wang Che-fu: *Chung-kuo Hsin Wen-hsüeh Yün-tung Shih* (A History of the Chinese New Literature Movement) , Peiping, 1933

CHAPTER 9

Ajia Mondai (The Asian Problem) , Second Supplement: "Shu On-rai no Shiruretto" (A Silhouette of Chou En-lai) , by Nakayasu Yosaku, Tokyo, 1941
Chukoku Kyosanto Ichikyusanshi Nen (The Chinese Communist Party, 1934) , The Foreign Office of Japan, Tokyo, 1935
Ch'en Shao-yü (Wang Ming) : *Liang t'iao Chan-hsien* (Two Battle Lines) , 1931
Kuang-chou Shih-pien yü Shanghai Hui-yi (The Canton Incident and the Shanghai Conference) , c. 1932
Sheng-Cheng: *A Son of China* (translated from the French by Marvin McCord Lowes) , New York, 1930
Shina Kyosanto Shi (A History of the Chinese Communist Party) , The Foreign Office of Japan, Tokyo, 1933

CHAPTER 10

Chang Ju-hsin: *Mao Tse-tung Lun* (On Mao Tse-tung) , Hong Kong, 1949
"The Communist International", (Special Chinese Number) , Feb. 1936, New York
Hsiao San: *Mao Tse-tung T'ung-chih ti Ch'ing-shao-nien Shih-tai* (The Youth and Childhood of Mao Tse-tung) , Shanghai, 1949
Hsü T'iao-hsin (ed.) : *Hsin Chung-kuo ti Tan-sheng,* (The Birth of New China) , San Francisco, 1949
Mao Tse-tung: *Ching-chi Wen-t'i yü Ts'ai-cheng Wen-t'i* (The Economic Problem and the Financial Problem) , Hong Kong, 1949
Chung-kuo Ko-ming Chan-cheng ti Chan-lüeh Wen-t'i (The Question of Strategy in the Chinese Revolutionary War) , Hong Kong, 1949
Hsin Min-chu-chu-yi Lun (The New Democracy) , Hong Kong, 1948
Chung-kuo Ko-ming yü Chung-kuo Kung-ch'an-tang (The Chinese Revolution and the Chinese Communist Party) , Hong Kong, 1949
Mu-ch'ien Hsing-shih ho Wo-men ti Jen-wu (The Present Situation and Our Task) , Suchow, 1949
Wen-yi Wen-t'i (The Question of the Arts) , Yenan, 1943
Payne, Robert: *Mao Tse-tung: Ruler of Red China,* New York, 1950
Snow, Edgar: *Red Star Over China* (revised edition) , New York, 1939

INDEX

260